HF2

W9-AEO-142

Managing
Executive Stress

MANAGING EXECUTIVE STRESS

A SYSTEMS APPROACH

JAMES W. GREENWOOD, III
and
JAMES W. GREENWOOD, Jr.

A Wiley-Interscience Publication / JOHN WILEY & SONS
NEW YORK · CHICHESTER · BRISBANE · TORONTO

Library of Congress Cataloging in Publication Data:

Greenwood, James W   1932–
    Managing executive stress.

    "A Wiley-Interscience publication."
    Bibliography: p.
    Includes index.
    1.   Stress (Psychology)   2.   Executives—
Psychology.   I.   Greenwood, James W., 1912–
joint author.   II.   Title.
BF575.S75G68   158.7   79-4100
ISBN 0-471-04084-3

Printed in the United States of America

10 9 8 7 6 5 4 3 2 1

To the spouses and families
of all overstressed executives everywhere

Foreword

Around 1925, Walter Cannon suggested that man responds to stressful events with a physical and psychological set that prepares him for either fight or flight. Next, Hans Selye in the 1930s developed a somewhat more specific concept of human reactions to stressors, which he called the general adaptation syndrome. In the early 1940s Harold Wolff and Stewart Wolf at Cornell University methodically studied the response of the human stomach to an extraordinary range of emotions precipitated by a variety of stressful events in everyday life. These four men laid the medical and biological foundations for understanding "stress."

In the last 30 years medical and psychological research on stress has burgeoned, moving into every aspect of life's conditions and events. Yet, with the conclusion of each study, new research is suggested and even more new avenues of exploration are opened. New research methods allow increasingly sophisticated understanding of the details of human behavior and new methods of coping with the world around us.

This book represents a contemporary picture of much of the current knowledge we have about stress, and it is written in terms understandable to the lay reader. It is a systematic translation for the intelligent manager of the reasonably complex state of the art in the late 1970s. It accurately presents many of the current issues and concerns about stress in general and occupational stress in particular.

The book goes further and samples techniques that some have found effective in coping more successfully with the stressful events of life. In doing so, the Greenwoods approach the subject, not as clinicians, but as students of the literature as they find it—as nicely organized students who set about their study with academic integrity and with thoroughgoing research that covers the ground with sufficient comprehension to satisfy the more exacting scientist.

An occasional reader from the medical community may criticize one or another section of the text as being nonselective—as giving equal weight to well-established theory and practice and to some of the newer and less well-accepted methods of stress research or management. But each student of stress applies his or her own frame of reference, research, and experience in asserting a particular viewpoint or assessing another's work.

The Greenwoods come from the perspective of businessmen and students, managers with a very real concern for the impact of work on workers and with a very strong desire to contribute to the betterment of the working life—particularly to that of the manager. This volume clearly reflects that humane concern. *Managing Executive Stress* uses systems theory as a unifying framework. The systems approach with which I am comfortable tends to classify stressors and stress reaction according to the components of a more medically oriented model that, for lack of a less complex term, we might call the biopsychosocial system. Biologically, we adjust to stressors to survive both as individuals and as members of the human race. Psychologically, people also cope in order to develop and maintain self-identity and self-esteem. Socially, we learn how to tolerate the stressors in the context of society and to accept delay of gratification. In a rapidly changing industrial society, the individual must constantly deal with new situations, new temptations, and new stressors both at work and off the job. He or she must increasingly adapt to new technologies, a changing social order, and to conditions increasingly associated with stress reactions.

This well-organized volume is an intellectual aid to the understanding required to do so. It should be particularly helpful to one who is approaching thoughtful consideration of these complex issues for the first time and who seeks an introduction to the application of a massive literature to the work life of the manager.

ALAN McLEAN, M.D.

Preface

In this volume, we view human stress as one of the major factors in the management of systems. For this reason, we address our argument primarily to managers and executives, and to those who aspire to become managers or executives. In effect, however, everyone is a manager, even if only of one's own self-system.

The literature on human stress, already copious, is ever more rapidly increasing in volume. In part, this may be due to the almost universal appeal of the subject to researchers in almost all of the biological and behavioral sciences. Not only does the annual production of scientific literature continue to increase in volume, but also the range of special studies is broadening, now involving such disciplines as biology, endocrinology, medicine, nutrition, physiology, psychiatry, psychology, psychosomatic medicine, and occupational health, to list only a few. The popular literature on the subject is expanding even more rapidly, with *how-to-cope* manuals for almost everyone.

The sheer volume of this reading material alone poses a problem of information overload for executives who desire to keep up with current developments that affect their jobs. The variety of disciplines involved and the conflicting advice on coping mechanisms and proposed cures for stress merely add an element of confusion to this problem. At the risk of anthropomorphizing, we might suggest, not unjustly, that the literature on human stress in general and executive stress in particular is exhibiting somewhat the same type of behavior as the hero of one of Stephen Leacock's *Nonsense Novels,* who rushed out the door and "rode madly off in all directions." What sparked the sudden explosion is not entirely clear, but, following Selye's seminal work, first reported in 1950, the amount of stress-related research has mushroomed to a degree exceeding the capacity of any one individual to comprehend, and the volume of literature exceeds, by several orders of magnitude, the amount of serious research. As might be expected of any field of scientific research of such recent origin, the literature is characterized by considerable disagreement, many overlaps, and numerous lacunae.

Executives would be hard put to find their way through the maze. This offering may facilitate their task.

Considering the plentiful advice already published on human stress, there would appear to be little reason for yet another volume on the subject—unless the writers have some new ideas to offer. We believe we can satisfy this requirement for novelty with a new viewpoint, a new perspective on the phenomenon. We view stress not simply as a personal problem but as an executive challenge. Because of its systemic nature, which we shall demonstrate in the ensuing chapters, we believe that one may successfully deal with human stress only by a systemic approach.

Few, if any, of the scientific studies, are so broadly based. The traditional scientific approach to any subject is highly analytical. The studies on stress are no exception. This is neither a complaint nor a criticism—simply a statement of fact, since most of our scientific progress is made and reported in this manner. In the systems view, however, we recognize that, while scientists may specialize in their studies of a problem, the problems are rarely, if ever, specialized in nature. Occasionally, therefore, as Selye himself suggested, there is need for a more comprehensive view, an integration of the available information for practical application and as a basis for further research. In that spirit, we attempt in this volume to present an integrated view of the facts concerning stress that an executive needs for effective management.

As we shall try to make clear, stress is not necessarily an evil; rather, it is actually essential to life. Without stress, there is no life. Conversely, the only cure for stress is death. Despite the plethora of coping mechanisms and proposed "cures" for stress to be found in the popular literature, the fact remains that one can escape the vicissitudes of stress only by dying.

Since such a drastic measure is likely to have little appeal for most of our readers, we recommend proceeding with more modest warrant. Further, since there are significant advantages to be gained from the constructive use of the positive values of stress, we propose a course of action that will provide for realizing such benefits with minimum detriment. We view the phenomenon of stress as an opportunity as well as a problem. For the members of any organization stress may be either functional or dysfunctional. Capitalizing on the opportunities afforded by the occurrence of stress may lead to achievement and excitement. Viewed solely as a problem, stress may be harmful to the individual and the organization, representing merely an adversary to be overcome in order to maintain the status quo. Viewed as an opportunity, stress may provide a desired stimulus to growth and progress. The executive may choose the elementary homeostatic reaction to stress, or a goal-oriented, creative, adaptive response—as we hope to demonstrate, the perspective is vital.

Our aim is to develop a systemic synthesis of the currently available information on human stress so as to indicate to executives the opportunities open to them, as persons and as managers, for more effectively dealing with this highly significant and extremely expensive phenomenon of modern business life. To take full advantage of such opportunity, executives will need an adequate understanding of the human stress response, as well as a sound approach to its management. This requires full recognition that the human being is an open, organismic system operating in, and interacting with, an environment comprising a complex multiplicity of other systems. Neither the traditional psychological model of the human being as a stimulus–response mechanism, nor the traditional two-variable, linear, causal, interaction explanation of events, is any longer adequate as a basis for action. Further, continuing efforts to apply the traditional analytical methodology of the physical sciences will not provide the necessary understanding of human behavior, nor of the stress response. Our unit of analysis must be, not merely the whole human, but the whole human operating in and interacting with the systems in the human environment.

In the systems approach, we view the human as a highly complex system comprising a nested hierarchy of highly complex subsystems, and, at the same time, as a subsystem within a hierarchy of highly complex environmental systems. Further, we view the human not as a simple stimulus–response, reactive robot, but as a self-reflexive, open, organismic, cybernetic system capable of primary action, and of exercising some degree of initiative and creativity. Moreover, we believe absolutely essential the recognition of the role of humanistic values in the management or direction of human behavior.

The systems approach also requires that we recognize pathological behavior—physiological or psychological, individual or organizational—as a systemic dysfunction, not merely the result of a simple, linear, causal chain. Thus, stress, wherever it occurs in an organization, at whatever level, is both a problem and an opportunity for the executive. Further, since stress tends to induce further stress, not only in the overstressed individual, but in all with whom that individual interacts, it tends to become self-propagating—not only within a given organization, but throughout society.

The resulting cost—to individuals, organizations, and society as a whole—is, as we will demonstrate, not only enormous, but potentially ruinous. Simple coping mechanisms and factitious cures will not provide adequate solutions. A systems approach to understanding and managing stress offers the only viable alternative. The survival of mankind as a species may well depend on the successful management of stress.

JAMES W. GREENWOOD, III
JAMES W. GREENWOOD, JR.

Marietta, Georgia
Clearwater, Florida
January 1979

Acknowledgments

We are indebted to Dr. Hans Selye, whose original model of the stress response forms the foundation of our work, and whose subsequent observations, both physiological and philosophical, provided one of the bases for our analysis of executive stress and our recommendations for managing it. We are indebted to Dr. William T. Powers, whose model of human behavior provides the framework for our discussion of the psychological causes of stress. We are especially beholden to Dr. Powers for his critical review of, and comments on, Chapter 5, and for his efforts to facilitate our understanding of his model and its implications for our work.

We are also indebted to Dr. Alan A. McLean for his encouragement and help from the very beginning of the research on this volume. We have adapted his model of stressful situations for our purposes in Chapter 7 and in subsequent chapters.

None of the aforementioned authors should be held responsible for the uses we have made of their models, nor for our manner of presenting their ideas.

Also, thanks go to Professor John E. Flaherty of Pace University for his encouragement in the research and publication of this work. Gerald Papke, our editor at Wiley-Interscience, also deserves a note of thanks for his velvet touch while keeping our noses to the grindstone.

We would also like to thank the IBM Corporation and the many managers who have supported this work. Among the managers we should like to mention are Don Davis and Don Skriba for their special support.

We wish to thank the Western Electric Company for permission to use the Venn diagram illustration of Dr. McLean's model, first published in *Man and Work in Society* (Eugene Louis Cass and Frederick G. Zimmer, eds., Western Electric Company, 1975).

Finally, we would like to thank JoAnne A. Greenwood, who typed the manuscript and the many revisions; in addition, JoAnne executed a thousand other chores that brought this volume into being.

J.W.G., III
J.W.G., Jr.

Contents

PART IV
THE MANAGEMENT OF STRESS

Chapter 1
Introduction

Stress is part of the very fabric of life; it is just as essential as eating or breathing. Yet of all the processes of human life, stress is probably the least understood, the most misunderstood. In recent years, the problem of executive stress, in particular, has received an inordinate amount of attention in the literature of management and management psychology. Despite this attention, executive stress continues to take its toll of human health, human life, and human enterprise—by aborting careers, shortening lives, impairing mental and physical health, diminishing the effectiveness of executives and their subordinates alike, and generally undermining the organizations in which they both work. The costs of these adverse effects—to the individual, to the organizations, and to society in general—are incalculable.

Our failure to arrest the progress of this social disease is certainly not due to lack of proposals for its cure. Almost every few months a new cure or coping mechanism blazes across the pages of professional journals or the popular press, only to fade as soon as a new idea comes on the scene. The proposals vary widely in nature, involving in turn almost every one of the scientific disciplines as well as some of the more esoteric philosophies. They range from autogenic training and biofeedback to yoga and Zen, with health food diets, meditation, and megavitamin therapy in between. Nor should we be too quick to denigrate any one of these proposals, because, although none is in itself a panacea, each may have some potential usefulness to some individuals, at some time, when properly administered. But therein lies the mystery. Proper application of any cure or coping mechanism requires, in addition to an appreciation of its potential effects and value, some knowledge and understanding of the system to which it is being applied.

The aim of this book is to provide, in layman's language, a systematic explanation of the nature and role of stress in human life as a basis for its proper management. To accomplish this purpose, we view the human body as a dynamic system in continuous interaction with its environment, consisting of an infinite number of other systems of widely varying complexity. We believe that only by firmly grasping the fundamentally systemic nature of stress may executives—or any other individual—learn to manage their own stress levels and properly evaluate the worth to them of any particular proposed cure or coping mechanism.

In our analysis, we shall see that stress is like Janus, the Roman god who had two faces looking in opposite directions. Stress is both therapeutic and debilitating; it has beneficial as well as adverse effects. Part of our task will be to delineate these effects and trace their several causes. To the extent that we succeed in this respect, we (hopefully) shall guide our readers toward those courses of action which will enable them to maximize the benefits and minimize the adverse effects of stress—on themselves, their organizations, and society.

We shall see that some degree of stress is essential to life; any organic system without stress is dead and disintegrating. When, however, stress becomes excessive or uncontrolled, it can cause or contribute to, mental or physical illness and even the premature death of the overstressed individual. Much, if not most, of the literature on executive stress deals with these aspects, its deleterious effects on the individual. Little consideration has been given to its beneficial or therapeutic effects. Nor has much consideration been given to its effects on the organization or enterprise in which the overstressed individual operates. But when the individual stress levels become too high, they tend to interfere with operating effectiveness, with the contribution of executives to their organization. At that point, individual stress becomes a problem for the organization. Furthermore, the fact is that the effects of stress tend to ramify; one overstressed individual in an organization tends to produce stressful effects on other interacting individuals. We shall, in subsequent chapters, invite particular attention to these neglected aspects of stress—the beneficial and therapeutic effects on individuals as well as the ramifying effects on the organizations of which they are part. We shall present stress in its true light as an organizational as well as a medical problem.

The problem, however, as we shall see, is not to limit or eliminate stress, for if stress levels are too low, executives find no challenge in their work or their lives. They may then start to seek or develop higher levels of stress so as to improve their own performance and satisfy their own egos. Failing to find the desired challenge they may develop stress from the imposed inactivity. Either way, they may, in the process, and through conflict and competition, elevate the stress levels of their associates beyond their levels of tolerance. The problem, then, is managing or controlling stress so as to keep it within certain limits, with a minimum sufficient to stimulate the executive to optimum performance, productivity, and personal satisfaction, and with a maximum below the level at which it will produce adverse effects on the individual or others with whom he or she associates.

We do not propose any pat solutions to such a problem. Rather, we aim to provide a framework for the analysis of the causes of stress and for the design of a system of managing it. There is no standard level of stress which is optimal for everyone. In fact, there is no objective way of measuring stress levels. Individuals must determine for themselves their own optimum level of stress and, given the appropriate information and adequate degree of intelligence, they are in the best position to decide when they are exceeding that level. We aim to provide, or direct our readers to reliable sources of, that information, and to suggest effective ways of applying it.

To accomplish these aims, we must first establish some basic concepts. This we do in Part I, where we first discuss some of the fundamentals of systems thinking in chapter 2. Our discussion of systems thinking is heavily oriented toward general systems theory and is entirely nonmathematical. We have tried to present the basic elements of systems theory in layman's language. This presentation provides the conceptual framework for our whole discussion of executive stress. In chapter 3, we provide a similar treatment of the stress response. With a minimum of medical and clinical detail, we describe the essential nature of the stress response in the human being. While recognizing the infinite complexity of that phenomenon, we try to focus on those aspects which are of the most significance for a layman's understanding. These two chapters, together, provide an essential basis for a proper understanding and appreciation of the more detailed discussion of executive stress which follows—chapter 2 providing the conceptual framework for our analysis, chapter 3 providing the substantive information about the nature of stress.

In Part II, we treat the infinite variety of the potential causes of stress—physiological, psychological, and environmental. In the latter category we include the organizational causes of stress, among which even so apparently innocuous a stimulus as the "principles of management" will be found to serve as a cause of stress. Individuals who desire to manage or control their own stress levels need to be able to identify the sources of their stress. The discussion in Part II should aid them in discovering those sources, which, although infinite in variety, are, in the end, as the reader will learn, essentially unitary.

In Part III, we identify some of the more significant effects and costs of stress—for the individual, for organizations, and for society as a whole. While the economic costs, as we shall demonstrate, run into the billions of dollars, they are probably the least significant aspects of the toll exacted by this ubiquitous disease.

Finally, in Part IV, we first present in chapter 11, a brief review and appraisal of the wide variety of coping mechanisms which have been offered over the years as means of alleviating the adverse effects of stress. Chapter 12 presents some more generalized measures for dealing with undue stress. Then, recognizing the inadequacy of any one, or any combination, of these means of control, we expound in chapter 13, some ideas for a more balanced, a more rational approach—a systems approach to the management of stress.

PART I
SOME BASICS

Because we propose to take a "systems approach" to our analysis of stress, and because we propose to recommend that the reader take a "systems approach" to the management of his or her stress levels, it is essential that we try to make clear what we mean by the term "systems approach." We make this effort in chapter 2, which follows. Stripped of their mumbo-jumbo and absent the frequently accompanying, but often confusing, mathematics, the concepts of systems thinking turn out to be remarkably simple in their fundamental character. We emphasize this fundamentally simple nature of systems thinking by reducing it to its basic essentials. We believe these concepts will provide a useful framework both for our analysis of stress and for a practical approach to its successful management.

Since Selye's first paper on stress in 1936, the subject has received a great deal of attention in both the scientific literature and, more recently, the popular press. Most of the scientific discussions are highly technical and very detailed, dealing, in most instances, with clinical experiments of a highly specific nature, and with little indication of the implications for human beings. Chapter 3, which follows, summarizes, in layman's language, the currently available results of the scientific research on the subject. It provides the basis for our more detailed discussion of causes, costs, and coping mechanisms.

Chapter 2
Systems Concepts

2.0 The utilization of a systems framework for our description of the phenomena of executive stress and our exposition of causes, costs, and coping mechanisms entails the use of certain highly significant terms and concepts which may require some degree of elucidation before we proceed further. In this chapter, we discuss these half dozen terms and illustrate the sense in which we use them in subsequent chapters. We believe the reader's patience in considering these fundamentals will facilitate mutual understanding of our further argument in Parts II through IV.

Because of the importance of point of view in the formation of concepts and in our perceptions of reality, the first topic we discuss here is the *role of perspective*. As we shall see, our perspective determines whether we perceive a given system and how we interpret its structure and operation. This leads us to a consideration of the *concept of system*. Most, if not all, of the systems we shall be dealing with are dynamic in nature, they are engaged in a continuing interaction with their environment. Interaction involves change, which leads us to a consideration of the *constancy of change* and the reasons therefore—*cause and effect*. However, not all the systems we examine are amenable to such detailed analysis, they conceal some of the internal changes which they undergo. We call such systems *black boxes,* another concept we need to explore. Sometimes when a system is not amenable to direct analysis, for one reason or another, we can simulate its operation by the use of a *model,* our final concept for consideration in this chapter.

THE ROLE OF PERSPECTIVE

2.1 We each have our own view of the world in which we live. That view is a product of our own particular perceptions as conditioned by our genetic heritage and our life experience—our education, training, cultural development, motivations, drives, moods, etc. Thus, our perceptions are conditioned by our concepts and our concepts are conditioned by our perceptions in a continuing feedback cycle. We shall elaborate on the mechanics of this process in chapter 5 (see: 5.2, and 5.6). Further complicating the processes of perception and understanding is the role of language. The Whorfian hypothesis suggests that all higher levels of thinking are dependent on language, and the structure of the language one habitually uses significantly influences one's understanding of his environment. (Whorf, 1956.) The general semanticists (Korzybski and his followers) added a great deal of evidence in support of the view that human understanding and human behavior are strongly influenced by the structure of language and by linguistic habits. (Korzybski, 1941; 1948.)

Given the infinite variety of events in the world and the infinite variety of individual abilities, attributes, and experiences of those events, it is obvious that no two individuals are ever likely to have precisely the same perception of any event or precisely the same concept of any object or event. In other words, no two individuals share the same view of reality.*

Despite this fact, most of us do manage to operate with at least a moderate degree of effectiveness and we manage to secure a fair degree of mutual understanding with those with whom we deal. The reason we operate with any degree of success at all in these respects is that most of our dealings are at a macrolevel of resolution. This term may require a few words of explanation.

A wide variety of scientific disciplines deal with the analysis of matter. The astronomer is concerned with the structure and movement of galaxies, stars, planets, and other celestial bodies in outer space. The geologist is concerned with the composition and structure of our own planet, the earth. The chemist deals with smaller portions of the substances of which the earth is composed and is concerned with the composition, structure, and properties of these substances and with their constituents, the various elements and their compounds. The nuclear physicist deals with these same elements, but he probes deeper into the inner structure of individual atoms, seeking to determine the composition, structure, and properties of the subatomic particles. Each of these scientists is dealing with the same basic substances, but at a different level of resolution, the nuclear physicist at a microlevel, the astronomer at a macrolevel, the others at various levels in between.

A corporate organization may provide a more familiar example for

*The writers explore this topic of the manager's perspective in more detail in chapter 2, of *Systems Thinking for Managers,* forthcoming.

our readers. Assume you are a wealthy entrepreneur casting about for a new investment. You may want to analyze any prospects at several levels of resolution. Probably first you will inquire about the general nature of the business: manufacturing, insurance, transportation, etc. Next you will examine the balance sheet and profit and loss statements. Later you may probe more deeply into the organizational structure and the performance of individual divisions, departments, and units. Eventually, you will have to deal with individual persons— officers and employees, directors, customers or clients, etc.—and with individual instances of their behavior. Your analysis proceeds from the macrolevel to the microlevel.

Thus, at the macrolevel of resolution we deal with large objects and large clusters of events. At the microlevel, we deal with individual events at the lowest discernible level. What we are suggesting here is that human beings will find agreement easier to achieve at a macrolevel of resolution than at a microlevel of resolution. This is simply because the lower the level of resolution of any given perception the less likely is the possibility of any other person sharing that perception. At the ultimate, any given stream of photons can strike the retina of only one person; that person alone is capable of that particular perception. At higher levels of resolution, the events in any given cluster may be sufficiently similar to allow for perceptual agreement among several observers. For example, two or more observers at the scene of an automobile accident may well agree that there was a collision, but still have widely varying views about the time of the collision,the descriptions of the cars involved, the speed and directions of the cars, etc.

If we clearly understand the role of perspective, we find little cause for wonder in this failure to agree on details. The real cause for wonder is the fact that we succeed in securing agreement at any level of resolution.

In summary, the impossibility of any two individuals receiving precisely the same sensory stimulus is a scientifically demonstrable fact simply because at the microlevel any given event can happen to only one person. Granted that at that level it is possible for very similar events to happen to two or more persons, that is, they may receive very similar sensory stimuli, the internal processing of those stimuli will be entirely different. Perception involves more than the receipt of sensory stimuli; the stimuli are conditioned by genetic heritage, cultural development education, and all the rest of life experience (see 5.11). Since none of these factors are precisely the same in any two individuals, no two individuals will have precisely the same perception even of very similar events. The same factors condition our concept formation and our concepts and perceptions condition each other in a continuing feedback cycle. With so many factors operating to produce differences, the miracle is the occurrence of agreement, but when agreement does occur, it occurs only at the higher levels of resolution.

Thus, even at the higher levels of resolution any particular set of events may be seen as interrelated by one individual and as unrelated by another individual. This fact affects both our perception of *systems* and our concept of *system*.

THE CONCEPT OF SYSTEM

2.2 The concept of *system* is at once both simple and complex. The term system has no single, universally accepted meaning, instead it has many different meanings, depending on the use to which it is being put and on the user. For example, George Klir lists twenty-four definitions of the term *system*. (Klir, 1969, pp. 283–285.) Despite this great variety, there are some common threads in these meanings. There are some fundamental ideas which occur in all of the various uses of the term. With these fundamental ideas a simple definition can be established which will serve our purposes as a basis for further discussion.

THE UBIQUITY OF SYSTEMS

2.3 We live in a universe of systems. We see and recognize systems all about us every day of our lives. Although we might have some difficulty in framing a satisfactory definition of the term, none of us has any difficulty in recognizing a system when we see one. We use water systems, telephone systems, transportation systems, continually. In addition to these systems of physical entities, we also use a variety of conceptual systems—systems which exist in our minds—for example, a number system for counting, a language system for communicating, a great variety of classification systems for filing papers and books and for arranging other objects. We speak of certain methods of working as "systems," for example, the touch system of typing. We refer to the education system, a banking system, a manufacturing system, etc. Even the race-track tout has a "system." Thus, in common usage the term system applies to a wide range of phenomena—physical and conceptual, concrete and abstract, pragmatic and theoretical.

The use of the term system is equally widespread in scientific endeavors—and equally varied. The astrophysicist refers to a gravitational system—a group of physical bodies interacting under the influence of related electromagnetic forces. The biologist studies organic systems—cells, plants, animals, animal societies. The anthropologist studies cultural systems; the sociologist, social systems; the economist, economic systems. The political scientist deals with systems of government. The engineer applies the term to a group of objects organized by humans to serve a specific purpose—for example, an electrical switching system, a highway system, a sewer system, an electronic computer, an ignition system. The geographer speaks of a river system or a mountain system; the geologist applies the term to particular types of rock formations in the earth's crust.

The philosopher applies the term system to an organized set of doctrines, ideas, or principles intended to explain some aspect of nature or of human behavior—for example, a theological system, a system of natural law, a political system.

Artists, too, have systems—musical notation, styles of painting, sculpture, architecture.

From this partial inventory of applications of the term system, we see that the notion of system pervades our very existence and all of our daily activities. We also see that the term is used on several different levels; on a formal level we use it in the traditional sense to identify or describe familiar entities comprising several components working together; on an informal level we use it more loosely to apply to many types of methods, patterns, or orderly arrangements; on a technical level we use it with varying degrees of rigor and specificity in practically all of the scientific disciplines.

TOWARD A DEFINITION

2.4 Despite this great diversity in the use of the word system, we can by inspection identify some common threads of meaning running through these many applications. These common threads of meaning constitute the basic notion of system.

The Basic Notion

2.5 Implicit in all uses of the word system are three fundamental ideas. First, a system consists of parts or components—there must be more than one member of the set of elements comprising the system. Secondly, these parts interact or interrelate in some way; there must be some kind, and some positive degree of, interdependence. Thirdly, through this interdependence the otherwise separate parts acquire a degree of wholeness or unity; it is possible to perceive, or at least conceive of, a pattern or orderly arrangement of the parts which has an existence of its own and some continuity, however brief, in time. These three, essential characteristics, then, constitute the basic notion of system; separate parts, interaction or interdependece, and wholeness. Systems, of course, may have other characteristics or properties in addition to these three.

A Working Definition

2.6 From the above mentioned three essential characteristics we formulate the following definition:

A system is any set of elements which interrelate in some way to form a unified whole.

The set must consist of two or more elements. The elements may be any objects or events in the universe—physical or conceptual, concrete or abstract. The unifying force, that which makes the otherwise independent entities into a system, is the interaction or interdependence of the elements the way in which they interrelate. The system functions as a whole because of the interdependence of the parts. Finally, the system is, or may be viewed as, an entity in itself.

IMPLICATIONS OF THE DEFINITION

2.7 Even this highly simplified definition of the term *system*, however, has certain implications which should be explored before proceeding with more complicated matters. From the preceding discussion, a reasonable person might well inquire whether systems really exist in nature or are merely figments of one's imagination. This is a legitimate question about the reality of systems. Further, the reader may have noticed that different observers looking at the same entities may see different systems—looking at society as a whole, the economist sees an economic system, the sociologist a cultural system, the political scientist, a governmental system.

Three concepts must be considered: 1) the relationship of the concept of system to the viewpoint of the observer, 2) the relationship of system and purpose, and 3) some implications of the idea of wholeness, which we discuss under system organization, below.

The Reality of Systems

2.8 Some writers raise a question about the reality of systems; do systems really exist in the physical world or are they merely constructs which exist only in the minds of men. This question raises many metaphysical issues which need not detain us here. There is, however, at least one issue of concern which deserves further discussion at this point. The issue has to do with the necessity for an individual establishing and maintaining the proper perspective in dealing with systems and, more importantly, recognizing the nature of that perspective so as to avoid self-deception. It is worthwhile expatiating a little on this point—perhaps an example will facilitate understanding.

Long ago, biologists classified the animal kingdom into a number of categories—divisions, classes, orders, families, genera, species. No one, however, ever took the trouble to explain this classification system to the animals. Somewhat to the chagrin of the biologists, nature now and then turns up an organism never before observed by scientists which does not quite fit into any one of the established categories. The point of this story is simply that the biological scheme of classification is a *system* which originated in the mind of man and was imposed on nature. The system was abstract, conceptual; the elements of the system were physical, concrete.

Another way of stating the matter is in terms of theoretical and empirical systems. A theoretical system is a coherent body of ideas, assumptions, and logical propositions—with or without empirical referents. An empirical system is a group of physical objects that can be observed, described, and analyzed by means of a theoretical system. Note, however, that the use of the term system in referring to the empirical world rarely embraces the concrete totality of the objects and their interrelationships. Rather, we select some particular aspects of the totality for consideration as a system. In other words, we abstract the system.

System and Purpose

2.9 From the above, we may see that the concept of system is related to purpose and viewpoint. Under certain circumstances, it may suit the purpose of an individual to view a certain group of interacting components as a system, even though others involved in that system may not share his view. For example, individuals in an organization may be so engrossed in their daily duties that they are unaware of the fact that the manager sees each of them as involved components in a number of systems, including the personnel system, the financial system, the manufacturing system, the distribution system, the communication system, etc.

Further, the manager's view varies with his or her purpose. For example, if one is concerned about the effectiveness or efficiency of a certain function (marketing, production, distribution) one may choose to view the particular function as a system. At another time, some of the same components might be viewed as parts of other systems, for example, organizational units, hierarchical levels, communication networks. In another instance, the manager may look upon a specific prócess as a system with certain identifiable inputs and outputs. Again, one may use the concept of system as an analogy; starting with a particular activity one may seek to identify it with a mechanism, organism, circuit, or other type of physical system for purposes of analysis, explanation, illustration, or other. One might also utilize the concept of system merely as a problem-solving aid, developing an analytical model in one of a variety of forms (mathematical, verbal, physical, etc.)

This flexibility of the concept of system increases its power as an intellectual tool. Individuals are free to abstract from the physical reality the particular elements or properties in which they are most interested at the moment, and to mentally manipulate those elements or properties as necessary to solve a particular problem or serve another purpose. Thus, their definition of a specific system will vary according to the particular aspects of it that they have selected or abstracted for attention.

Similarly, the degree of precision to be applied in defining a system or predicting the results of its operation will vary according to the purpose of the observer. Most social systems—including business organizations—will have relatively imprecise boundaries, as we shall see below.

SYSTEMS ORGANIZATION

2.10 Through their interdependence, the otherwise separate elements of a system acquire a degree of wholeness or unity. Thus, it is not merely the properties of the individual components which determine the nature of the whole, but the way in which these components interrelate. Any interaction between any two given components necessarily involves some degree of constraint; that is, there is some degree of correlation of the activities of the two individual components. Further, the relationship between any two components is necessarily conditioned by their individual and joint relationships with the other components of the system. This reciprocal constraint among the components constitutes the *organization* of the system. From this we see that the components assume properties or modes of behavior which they owe specifically to the fact that they are parts of an organized whole.

Wholeness

2.11 This whole or unity is seen, also, to be something more than, or at least different from, the mere sum of the individual elements—not in any mathematical or metaphysical sense, but in the very important and practical sense that one cannot necessarily derive a knowledge of the nature and properties of the whole from the mere aggregation of the natures and properties of all the individual elements. (Compare the unassembled parts of a bicycle with the organized, assembled whole.) Further, the behavior of the system (that is, the whole) depends, not only on its components and their interactions, but also on the interactions of the whole with other systems in its environment. Thus, the system has an individuality of its own which is not solely dependent on the qualities and interactions of its components, but which can be determined only by examining its behavior as a whole.

Just as the interactions of the components provide some degree of constraint on their activity, so do the interactions of the whole with other systems provide some degree of mutual constraint. This constraint on the whole, likewise affects the behavior of its components and their interrelationships. This fact reinforces the idea stated above that components assume properties or modes of behavior which they owe specifically to the circumstance of being parts of an organized whole.

Subsystems

2.12 The working definition is quite explicit in terms of composition of system, it says: "any set of elements . . ." Each system is made up of elements; each element, however, may also be a system in its own right, that is, a subsystem. Each subsystem, in turn, may have its own subsystems; sub-subsystems of the first mentioned system. This observation may be generalized in the form of a proposition which has strong empirical evidence.

Proposition: Every system is a subsystem of a higher level system.

For example, in this study the executive is the system under primary consideration, and his or her body is made up of subsystems: the respiratory system, the digestive system, the skeletal system, etc. Each of these systems is made up of subsystems, that is, organs. Organs are made up of tissues. Tissues are made up of cells. Cells are made up of organelles. Organelles are made up of molecules. Molecules are made up of atoms. Atoms are made up of subatomic particles. At this point, science begins to lose its ability for further resolution, but we may expect to find the next level to be likewise composed of subsystems (quarks?), if and when we can improve our analytical ability sufficiently to enable us to observe these lower levels.

If we once again start with the executive, we see he or she is a member (subsystem) of an organization, a family, a church, a community, etc. Each of these are subsystems of higher systems. Communities form states, states form nations, etc. Finally, we embrace all of mankind on earth (not a well integrated system) and at this point, we lose our ability to specify higher order systems except on a speculative basis, that is, we can only speculate on whether there is a higher level system, including mankind (or related beings) on other planets, and still higher levels in other universes, etc.

Resolution Level

2.13 When an observer selects a system for study from the universe, he or she simultaneously selects a resolution level. The importance of resolution level lies with human observers. When a human observer studies a system at a particular resolution level he or she cannot simultaneously observe the subsystem or supersystem. For example, a physician who has taken a blood sample from a patient can look at the blood on a slide in the microscope or watch the patient, but not both simultaneously. The physician who looks in the microscope does not know what the patient is doing—he may be fainting. Attention can be switched back and forth between resolution levels, but at the expense of possible loss of information.

SYSTEM, ENVIRONMENT, AND BOUNDARY

2.14 Every system is embedded in an environment. Without an environment, there can be no system, because the term system implies a distinction between one set of elements (the system) and all other elements (the environment.) Figure 2.1 shows such a relationship between environment and system. As may be seen from this diagram the element that separates the system from the environment is the boundary.

The boundary need not be a physical entity separating the system from the environment, although in particular cases this may be so. In some instances, however, the boundary may be simply a region or fuzzy area separating the two. Whatever is inside the boundary is part of the system, whatever is outside is part of the environment.

The boundaries of most systems are fuzzy, so that in many instances it is necessary to observe closely to determine whether a given element is in the system or in the environment. Even then problems present themselves; for example, if the boundary of the human body is determined to be the skin, then one has difficulty classifying hair, which is both inside and outside the boundary. This is frequently referred to as a boundary condition. The import of boundary conditions may be seen by watching how different observers classify an element as part of the environment or as part of the system. The closer such an element is to the boundary, the more likely there is to be disagreement as to where it lies. Although it should be noted that the more closely interrelated the elements of a system, the easier it is to determine whether a given element is in the system.

Generally speaking, the boundary is thought of as part of the system. As a part of the system, the boundary is generally functional.

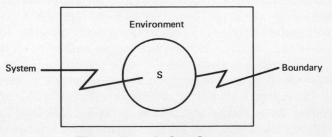

Figure 2.1   A closed system.

OPEN VERSUS CLOSED SYSTEMS

2.15 A glance at Figure 2.1 reveals that there is no interaction between the system and the environment in this model. However, in Figure 2.2 arrows are crossing the boundary, from the environment into the system and from the system into the environment. These arrows represent inputs and outputs of the system. These are the interactions between system and environment.

The differences between Figures 2.1 and 2.2 are the absence or presence of input and output. The system in Figure 2.1 is classified as a closed system because it exchanges no inputs or outputs with the environment. The system in Figure 2.2 is an open system because it does exchange inputs and outputs with its environment.

The closed system is merely an idealized concept. It is an approximation or a pretension that allows an observer to concentrate attention on the system. Closed systems exist only in the minds of observers studying systems.

Consider for a moment, the opposing proposition: "Closed systems exist." If a system is really closed, it will give no output (by definition) and, therefore, an observer will receive no sign of its existence. This point is important only because it is so easy for an observer to get trapped into "believing" that an approximation is actually a closed system.

A third classification of systems will show that the above argument is non-trivial. This third type of system is the relatively closed system. It is a classification of system that allows the observer to pretend that only certain inputs are important, and all others are not. For example, a watch is an open system. It is wound once a day, and the energy input is stored in the mainspring. After winding the watch in the morning the owner does not have to think about its energy requirements until the following morning—for the rest of the day one can treat it as if it were input closed. Watch manufacturers have capitalized on this idea by selling electric watches, but since the electric watch requires an energy cell replacement every one to two years, it is easy to see that only the storage capacity has changed—the watch is relatively less open, but still open nonetheless.

The concept of a relatively closed system allows the observer of a system to concentrate attention on system behavior and on inputs affecting the system during the period of study. One can ignore the infinite variety of inputs that are bombarding the system, which appear to have minimum effect on the system under study or on the

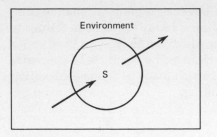

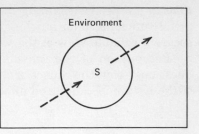

Figure 2.2   An open system.

Figure 2.3   A relatively closed system.

system outputs of particular interest. The observer could be wrong, the system might be closed off to supposedly unimportant inputs, which really are important, for purposes of the study. This is the history of science, those who close the system to important inputs generally have no success. The key to explanation in science is finding the appropriate inputs that allow for predictions of future behavior. The burden of Occam's razor is not to treat with superfluous inputs.

One way of representing the relatively closed system is shown in Figure 2.3, the dashed lines represent inputs and outputs that have been selected by the observer for study.

THE CONSTANCY OF CHANGE

2.16 The fact that there are no closed systems (or, at least, that we are not and cannot be aware of such systems) suggests that we live in a world of open systems. Every system we can observe is subject to a continuing flow of inputs and outputs—in a word, change. We live in a world of constant change. Every perception is an event; we perceive only events, not objects. In the very process of perception there is change in the world around us. This constancy of change applies equally to each of us, as well as to the organisms and objects in our environment. Every object, every organism is constantly changing.

We get into difficulty when we neglect to take into consideration this constancy of change, when we attribute to persons and systems an unwarranted degree of stability. True enough, we depend on a certain degree of stability in the environment and in our relationships with others, without which we might all go mad in a world of totally unpredictable events. Still, we confuse relative stability with static conditions at our peril. Assuming that any object or organism remains completely unchanged for any length of time is likely to result in failure to secure a reliable view of the world in which we live.

Recognition of the constancy of change, however, tends to raise questions about the causes of change, which leads us to a consideration of the nature of cause and effect thinking.

CAUSE AND EFFECT THINKING

2.17 In normal, everyday life we tend to think in linear terms, with each event having a single cause. This type of thinking, which we characterize as single cause and effect thinking, is usually adequate for meeting most of our daily problems; it usually provides an adequate basis for action. Even in the older scientific approach there was a tendency to focus on a single cause for each effect. A scientist who found multiple influences at work would try to control (to maintain constant) all but one influence at a time in an effort to isolate the cause. Only recently have scientists begun to realize the insufficiency of this approach and to recognize the importance of systems effects, especially in dealing with organic systems. This tendency towards systems thinking has been significantly influenced by the development of general systems theory and the new science of cybernetics, as well as information theory.

As a result, we have discovered that in some instances our efforts to isolate the effects of individual elements have served to eliminate from consideration what may be very significant effects of a system as a whole. We have discovered that many systems, particularly organic systems, exhibit types of behavior which cannot be attributed to any one or more of the constituent elements, but only to the system as a whole. The interrelationships of the constituent elements provide holistic effects which would never occur absent the organization of the elements into a system.

Scientists have also discovered the principle of equifinality, the tendency of an open system to reach a given characteristic state from any of a variety of initial states and in any of a variety of ways. The correlative principle of multifinality applies to the tendency of an open system to reach any of a variety of given characteristic states from a given initial state. These two principles clearly indicate the inadequacy of linear thinking with its emphasis on single cause and effect.

The science of cybernetics, enhanced by notable advances in computer science and the development of information theory, has made clear the role of feedback in the behavior of open systems. The ability of organic systems and certain appropriately designed inorganic systems to monitor their own behavior and to return as input some information on system performance has greatly expanded our understanding of cause and effect. Negative feedback of information on deviations from the state to be maintained or a goal to be reached provides a circular causal chain enabling a system to operate in a purposive manner. Positive feedback of information, which serves to enhance or increase the original behavior, provides a circular causal chain which, if not constrained, drives a system out of control and, eventually, to its own destruction.

Thus, recognition of the operation of the twin principles of equifinality and multifinality, and of the dynamic, cybernetic operation of organic systems serve to indicate the complete inadequacy of any simplistic explanations of the causes of behavior of organic systems, particularly purposive systems such as human beings. Instead, we must recognize the possibility and probability of multiple causes and multiple effects interacting in a continuing cybernetic mode with both positive and negative feedback.

Unfortunately, when we are dealing with human beings the physiological and psychological subsystems with which we are concerned are not always amenable to detailed analysis at a level of resolution which provides the degree of understanding necessary for prescription of remedial treatment of pathological conditions. In such instances, we must resort to the use of "black box" theory.

BLACK BOX THEORY

2.18 The concept of the "black box" originally arose in electrical engineering schools where students were given sealed boxes that were painted black. Each black box had terminals for input and terminals for output. The student was allowed to apply any desired inputs, that is, voltages, shocks, or other disturbances. From the output, the student was required to make legitimate deductions about the structure and contents of the black box without breaking the seal.

From such investigations the systems sciences have begun to develop a "black box" theory, which deals with such questions as: 1) what is the basic approach to the study of a black box, 2) which properties of a black box are discoverable and which are not, and 3) how should the experiments proceed if the black box is to be studied efficiently.

The study of black boxes has wide application, and in fact, is the method sometimes called "systems analysis." Applications may be found in medicine, government, industry, and elsewhere.

For purposes of this study an executive is a "black box" and subject, therefore, to the laws of black box theory. (See: Ashby, 1956, esp. p. 86–117, and 244–272.) We dare not dissect a human being to see what makes one "tick," for the seal would be broken and we could not make the person operable again. This means that in our study of the human being as a system, we are largely constrained to observation of inputs and outputs; we are severely limited in any attempts to observe internal structure or processes. Those modern sciences and technologies that deal with human beings in all their manifest complexity are still woefully inadequate in predicting either human behavior or the myriad of internal states the individual human being can assume. While the physical scientist is generally free to assume that other conditions remain constant while one variable at a time is altered (the closed system approach), the behavioral scientist rarely enjoys this luxury. The living system is open, dynamic, cybernetic, and equifinal and, therefore, much less predictable. The black box approach, however, allows us to study systems without system destruction. Throughout the study, this will be our objective: to provide a means of discovering the reasons for an executive's behavior without destroying him or her.

MODELS

2.19 One way of studying "black boxes" is to simulate their behavior through the construction and operation of models. While we cannot demonstrate the operation of a model in this study, we can construct models, depict them in graphic form, and describe their operation.

The use of models is an effective aid in communication and is especially relevant to the systems approach which we have adopted in this study. We shall be resorting to the use of a number of models in parts II, III, and IV, in our discussion of executive stress and its causes, costs, and coping mechanisms. Accordingly, it is important that we explain in advance just what we mean by the term *model* and how we propose to use models for our purposes. We hope our more sophisticated readers will bear with us, therefore, if we begin with some fundamentals.

THE CONCEPT OF MODEL

2.20 We live in a world of infinite variety and constant change. The potential impact of stimuli from this infinite variety of objects and events and their continuing changes might easily overwhelm beings with our finite mental capacity. Fortunately, however, we have retained, from our evolutionary development, two mechanisms which enable us to cope with this potential overload. First, the physical limitations of our sensory receptors significantly delimit the number of stimuli we are capable of receiving. Secondly, as we shall develop in more detail in chapter 5, each of us has inherited or developed certain filtering mechanisms that enable us to screen out a large number of stimuli that are not of immediate interest or significance to our continued existence. This filtering process takes place on three levels: the conscious, the subconscious, and the unconscious.

In addition to controlling the input process, we also have the power to control the process of storing input in the brain—memory. Although we do not always consciously and effectively exercise this power of organizing our information input, it nevertheless has a significant impact on the way in which we view, and deal with, the world. Our recall of the stored information usually takes the form of symbols or images, which may be representations of long past events or of events that have just occurred.

Each such symbol or image is a mental model—a representation of an object or event in the outside world, an abstraction from reality. The model may be verbal or pictorial, it may take the form of a concept, an observation, an inference, a hypothesis, etc. Whatever its form, it is an abstract representation of some set of objects or events and their interrelationships, but the representation is highly selective and necessarily so, since we are incapable of comprehending the totality of any set of objects or events and their interrelationships even over a very limited period of time.

Even so, the susceptibility of such models to mental manipulation and verbal discussion, entirely apart from the objects and events they represent, provides us with a powerful tool for the advancement of our knowledge and understanding. For example, one significant advantage of this ability to mentally manipulate models is the power it provides for developing probabilistic predictions of future events on the basis of varying inputs to the model.

In fact, most of our daily behavior is guided in large part by such predictions based on our mental models; even such a simple act as crossing the street is governed by the predictions we formulate from our mental models of the behavior of the threatening traffic. We operate by selecting and emphasizing the significance of certain aspects of our environment and simplifying or ignoring others. This is the essence of model building.

TYPES OF MODELS

2.21 Model building is not merely essential, it is inevitable; it is our way of dealing with the environment in which we live. Because of the infinite variety and constant change, we are impelled to simplify and abstract. Our methods of simplification and abstraction, however, may range from the most crude and inelegant to the highly complex and sophisticated; from simple verbal analogies to esoteric mathematical formulae; from artless mental or graphic pictures to intricately designed, three-dimensional, operating, mechanical devices. Because of this infinitude of methods of model-building—that is, of methods of simplification and abstraction—there is no single, universally accepted scheme of classification of models. Rather, there are a variety of schemes of classification. For example: models may be classified by purpose (descriptive, prescriptive, predictive, etc.), by content (a specific variety of objects, events, or subject matter), by form (structure, shape, or configuration), by degree of abstraction (ranging from abstract to concrete), etc.* Despite the wide range of models available to us, however, we are unlikely to find any one of them ideal for any particular purpose; instead, they will vary in degrees of adequacy from completely useless (or even counterproductive) to adequate or optimum, at best. But the real test of the value of any given model is not its degree of approach to the ideal, rather, the test is its effectiveness in serving the purpose for which it is being used.

While the models we use for illustrative purposes in this volume are relatively simple, graphic representations, the process of model-building and the types of models available to an executive are impor-

---

*We discuss this topic of *Models* in greater detail in our *System Thinking for Managers*, forthcoming.

tant considerations in gaining an understanding of the phenomenon of executive stress and of the ways of coping with it. In fact, the success of executives in their work and in their every day living depends in large part on the appropriateness of their models and their ability to apply them properly.

MODELS AND REALITY

2.22 In his attacks on Aristotelian logic and traditional ways of speaking and thinking, Korzybski enunciated his principle of non-identity, which may be stated as "a map is not the territory it represents." (Korzybski, 1948.) Likewise, a word is not the thing it represents. Maps and words, of course, are, in a sense, models; they are symbols which represent other objects or events. Too often, we tend to forget this fact and to operate on the assumption that models are the reality.

The confusion of models and reality is vividly illustrated in the way in which we have organized our knowledge into disciplines, when, as a matter of fact natural events do not occur as purely physical, chemical, or biological. These disciplines are simply the way we have decided to organize our information; they depend upon the point of view of the observer.

This point applies with special emphasis to our topic of discussion—the causes of stress. Whether a given cause is classified as physiological, psychological, or environmental depends primarily on the point of view of the observer. Likewise, the behavior of the victims of stress depends on their points of view. In fact, our perception of all objects and events is affected by point of view. Further, humans can never know all there is to know—even about a single event. In other words, it is impossible for the model to include, or even represent, all of reality. Thus, we tend to develop concepts and make judgments based on limited information which is also biased by our point of view.

Of course, this weakness afflicts both the victims of stress and the observers who are studying them; we are all equally susceptible.

In summary, models have their uses, but they can never take us through the barrier that exists between humans and reality. If a model helps us to learn or serves some other useful purpose effectively, it is worthwhile. We need to remember, however, that there are no ulti-mate models of reality. Finally, the real danger lies in confusing our models with reality. Reality is always at the lowest level of resolution, models never. In communicating with each other and in observing reality many difficulties arise because of the various differences in level of resolution—differences between communicators, differences between observers and observed, and even differences in the point of view of an individual (observer or observed) at different points in time.

SUMMARY

2.23 This brief discussion of a few of the basic concepts of systems thinking obviously does not purport to constitute an adequate, much less a comprehensive, summary of systems theory. It should, however, provide a sufficient background for our presentation of a systems approach to the understanding and management of executive stress.

Executives who understand the role of perspective and the use of models in their perception of the world and the systems in it are in a better position to recognize why certain objects, persons, and events operate as causes of stress. Likewise, a consciousness of the constancy of change; of the inadequacy of linear habits of thinking—of single cause and effect reasoning; and of the problems involved in dealing with black boxes; all will contribute to their ability to understand the nature of stress and to better manage their own stress levels.

Chapter 3
The Nature of the Stress Response

3.0 As all executives know, there is a positive correlation between their effectiveness as managers and their understanding of the processes of the system being managed. Their understanding, to be at least adequate, must extend beyond mere descriptive knowledge of the characteristics of the system; they must comprehend the operations of the system and appreciate the significance of the interrelationships and interactions involved; their understanding must be operational in nature. Their effectiveness improves, at least up to a certain point, in direct proportion to the increase in their understanding of those processes and the system in which they operate. They further know that they need not be experts in any one or more of the processes, but, if they are to be effective, they must at least be capable of conducting intelligent discussion of these processes with the respective experts.

The same reasoning applies to the self-system—one's own body. Executives who wish to effectively manage their own self-systems must have an adequate understanding of the operations of that system and its significant processes. One of those significant processes is the stress response. Executives, therefore, need to understand the nature of stress and the operation of the underlying processes so that they may effectively manage their own responses to stress and their daily stress levels.

We have direct evidence from the fields of psychiatry and psychoanalysis of the value of self-understanding in the prevention or cure of psychological, psychosomatic, and even somatic disorders. Since executives are expected to operate, at least most of the time, as rational beings, the better they understand the operation of the self-system, the more likely they are to avoid such disorders, or to properly treat those they cannot avoid. Socrates' age-old advice is still sound: know thyself. Executives who understand their own self-systems and appreciate the strengths and limitations of such systems are much more likely to operate successfully. Executives who understand the nature of the stress response are much more likely to manage their own stress responses appropriately.

Such an understanding will also aid one in recognizing the symptoms of undue stress in others and in dealing with it appropriately.

This chapter lays the foundation for developing a basic understanding of the fundamental nature of the stress response in human beings. It provides an introductory, overall view of the nature of human stress in general and executive stress in particular. This brief discussion should facilitate understanding of the subsequent chapters on the causes and costs of executive stress and on the coping mechanisms which are available.

Neither this chapter, nor the book as a whole, however, will make any manager an expert on the subject of stress. Nevertheless, we believe that it will provide that degree of understanding required for effectively managing one's own stress levels and responses and for dealing appropriately with the symptoms of undue stress in others with whom one associates. When we say "dealing appropriately," we do not mean providing medical or psychological treatment or counseling, we mean fulfilling the responsibilities of the executive as a manager of systems.

Unfortunately, the literature on stress probably contains as much misinformation as information; much of the popular writing on stress is characterized by fuzzy thinking, obscure argot, irrational treatments, and worthless "remedies". Sifting the wheat from the chaff in this bounteous harvest would require more time than most executives would be willing to spend on the effort. We have tried to spare them this effort and to provide a summary of the information needed for a solid understanding. We have tried to remove some of the mystery from both the scientific research findings and the metaphysical approaches to the subject. We have sorted through the contradictory definitions and tried to restore to the term *stress* a more specific meaning, retrieving it from the morass of misusage into which it has fallen. When a word acquires too many meanings, it comes to have no meaning at all. Such is about to become the fate of the term *stress* in the popular literature. We begin by briefly tracing the genesis of the term as it is used in the sciences of medicine and human behavior.

GENESIS OF THE STRESS CONCEPT

3.1 There are numerous indications that even prehistoric humans had some awareness of the nature of the process of stress, even though they had no name for it. Archeological findings provide evidence of certain practices, still extant among some present-day primitive tribes, which were followed in the treatment of both mental and somatic disorders, utilizing stress-producing ceremonies, drugs, bandages, or poultices. Certainly Hippocrates, so-called father of modern medicine, and other early Greek physicians recognized the phenomenon of stress and its role in the treatment of certain disorders. The ancient Greeks were familiar, for example, with the process of bloodletting, which continued as a standard—if not always appropriate—medical practice until the early part of this century. They were also familiar with the beneficial effects of artificially induced strong fever in the treatment of both mental and physical ailments. Flogging and dunking in cold water were favored treatments for mental disorders for hundreds of years. All of these treatments involved the common element of the application of some type of stressor, the imposition of unusual physical or psychological forces so as to shock an individual out of a current undesirable state. (Selye, 1956, p. 7–10.)

This knowledge of the effects of stress, however, was not always applied for benevolent purposes; there are many examples, in divers parts of the world, of the deliberate application of extreme stress for purposes of ritual executions or for murder. (See: Cannon, 1942.) Thus, mankind has been aware of both the beneficial and the harmful effects of human stress for thousands of years.

Nevertheless, we did not have any clear idea of the operational nature of the stress response until the middle of the twentieth century when Hans Selye produced his monumental volume, *Stress.* (Selye, 1950.) (Selye published his first paper on Stress, in 1936.)

Two of Selye's predecessors deserve special mention for their contribution to the development of our current understanding of stress because of their recognition of the importance of viewing the body as a system. Claude Bernard was probably the first to identify one of the most characteristic features of all organic systems: their ability to maintain the constancy of their internal states ("milieu interior") despite changes in their environment. (Bernard, 1865.) Walter B. Cannon studied this characteristic of organic systems in depth and gave it a name: *homeostasis.* (Cannon, 1939, 1963.) The work of these two investigators, served to clearly establish the systemic nature of living beings and pointed up the role of the feedback process in maintaining the stability essential to the preservation and continuation of life. Cannon also made quite considerable contributions to our knowledge of stress and was one of Selye's teachers.

Building on the basic ideas of these investigators, Selye, after reviewing a mass of research results and conducting numerous scientific experiments of his own, came up with the concept of the "General Adaptation Syndrome" (G.A.S.) as the body's typical mechanism of response to disease and other stressors. He defined stress as the state which manifests itself by the G.A.S., and, alternatively, as the nonspecific response of the body to any demand made upon it. He also pointed out that stress is, in effect, the essence of life. Without stress there is no life (Selye, 1974, p. 32); failure to react to a stressor is an indication of death.

THE MANIFESTATIONS OF STRESS

3.2   The only way we can recognize the state of any system is by the evidence it provides through our sensory apparatus—its appearance or manifestations. Thus, we can recognize the state of stress only by the way it reveals itself to our senses, by its manifestations. If we wish to understand the several processes involved in the stress response we shall have to analyze the system—dissect it and examine (physically or mentally) the separate parts and their interactions. Selye and a number of other investigators have performed the physical dissections and provided us with verbal and graphic reports so that we need perform only the mental dissection, reading their reports. What follows is a synthesis, in layman's language, of the currently available information.

Probably the most dramatic example of the manifestations of stress may be found in an imaginative description of the phenomenon as it might have been experienced by one of our prehistoric ancestors. If a neolithic caveman unexpectedly encountered an aggressive wild animal—such as a sabre-toothed tiger—his body would immediately activate what psychologists today call the "fight or flight response" (also variously termed: the "alarm reaction," by Selye; or the "emergency response," by Cannon). The hairs on the caveman's head and body would tend to become erect, his heart would pound harder and faster, his breathing would become deeper, his pupils would dilate, and he would become mentally more alert. The reaction, including all these symptoms, would be almost instantaneous. If it were not, he might easily become a dinner instead of a diner.

While we rarely encounter a wild tiger unexpectedly these days, the symptoms mentioned above should be familiar to every adult human being. The same symptoms may be as easily aroused by hearing the sudden, unanticipated, loud barking of an aggressive dog as by the perception of a hint of disapproval in a remark by an authority figure (boss, parent, etc.), or by the perception of a feeling of disaffection in the remarks of a loved one. Such threats are merely perceptual in nature—a given event is perceived as a threat by the brain, even though it may, in fact, be entirely innocuous. There are, of course, innumerable other types of threats of a subliminal nature which may just as effectively serve to arouse the stress response, albeit with somewhat different superficial symptoms; for example, invasion of the body by stressor agents such as harmful viruses or bacteria.

The symptoms we have described, however, are merely the more obvious and superficial manifestations of stress at a macrolevel of behavior; they are fairly well known to almost everyone, but are actually not much above the level of understanding of our prehistoric ancestors, as mentioned above. Executives who intend to exercise some degree of control over their own stress levels, and perhaps those of others, should have a better understanding. They should have at least a fundamental acquaintance with Selye's concept of the G.A.S. and how it operates in the human body.

THE G.A.S.

3.3 The General Adaptation Syndrome (G.A.S.) is a highly complex series of interacting events which constitute the human response to any stressor. Even after fifty years of study the details are not completely understood, but we are learning more about it every day. The following sections summarize the principal findings of Selye and other investigators, omitting the highly technical clinical details.

Principal Stages

3.4 According to Selye, the G.A.S. consists of three principal stages. The first stage, the alarm reaction, is elicited upon sudden exposure to stressors to which the body is not qualitatively or quantitatively adapted. This stage has two distinct substages: 1) the shock substage, characterized by the above mentioned fight or flight reaction, and 2) the countershock substage, characterized by a reversal of the initial fight or flight symptoms, and certain internal organic changes described in more detail below. In the first stage the general resistance of the body to the particular stressor tends to drop below normal. In the second stage, the self-system begins to adapt to the stressor through a gradual increase in resistance to it and a decrease in resistance to other stimuli. The third stage is that of exhaustion; the self-system is no longer able to maintain the state of adaptation. If the stress continues for a long enough period, this third stage may be a precursor to death.

We shall be exploring, in Part II, the variety of objects and events which may act as stressors. Here let us note simply that any noxious agent which assaults the self-system or even any event which is perceived as a threat to the self-system may serve as a stressor which elicits the alarm reaction. Whether the stimulus involves physical assault or merely a perception (optical, auditory, olfactory, or other) of a threat, the response is essentially the same: the release of a complex set of neural and hormonal messages, which in turn, actuate a number of glands, organs, and other subsystems of the body. The general flow of events in somewhat simplified form is about as depicted in Figure 3.1 and further described below.

Sequence of Events

3.5 Although there is no doubt about the occurrence of the alarm signals, we still do not have complete information about their precise nature or chemical composition. The final word is not in on the

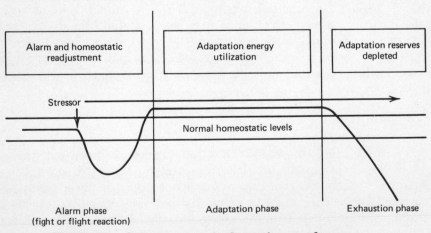

Figure 3.1   Selye's general adaptation syndrome.

neural or chemical nature of the messages going to the hypothalamus and the pituitary, the central control organs of the G.A.S. We do know that some type of neural or hormonal alarm signals flow from the site of the directly affected body cells when the stressor strikes—physically or perceptually.

If the stressor is perceptual in nature, the alarm signal is neural and flows from the directly affected sensory area of the cerebral cortex to the hypothalamus and then on to the pituitary.

If the stressor is physical in nature, the immediate reaction takes the form of a local adaptation syndrome (L.A.S.)—some of the cells or tissues of the directly stressed area may die and the surrounding tissues become inflamed. The blood vessels in the affected area are dilated, fluids and blood cells leak from the dilated blood vessels into the surrounding tissue. The cells of the fibrous connective tissue begin to multiply rapidly in response to the irritation from the stressor. The blood vessels and connective tissues secrete chemical substances which tend to offset the irritating effects of the stressor and to kill any invading microorganisms. As a result of this increase of cells and fluids, the area becomes swollen, reddened, and heated. The local nerve endings become irritated by all this activity causing the sensation of pain. The whole process constitutes the body's active defense against the stressor—the fight response. It tends to produce a barricade around the stressed area to prevent the spread of the invader.

In the meantime, one or more alarm signals flow from the directly stressed area. The neural signals of pain flow to the brain—perhaps first to the cortex then to the hypothalamus, perhaps directly to the hypothalamus; thence to the pituitary. The nerve endings in the locally stressed area also release certain hormones—noradrenaline, acetycholine—which act locally, but may also carry alarm signals directly to other organs and subsystems.

The hypothalamus is a small but vitally important organ in the brain, lying at the junction of the midbrain and the thalamus. It is probably the most important structure involved in the control of the autonomic nervous system and plays a major role in the experiencing of emotions and motivations. It is generally responsible for controlling body temperature, for example, but it also contains a number of other vital regulatory centers. When appropriately stimulated by an alarm signal, the hypothalamus neurally activates the adrenal medulla, the autonomic nervous system, and, through the pituitary gland, the endocrine system.

The pituitary gland, upon activation by the hypothalamus, secretes several hormones, three of which are significant in the G.A.S. One of these hormones (adrenocorticotropin—ACTH) activates the adrenal cortex. Another (thyrotropin—TTH) activates the thyroid gland. The third (vasopressin) tends to raise the blood pressure by acting on the unstriped muscles of, and thereby, constricting, the blood vessels.

The adrenals are endocrine glands, located one above each kidney. The outer layer (cortex) of each adrenal, when stimulated by ACTH, secretes two other types of hormones (anti-inflammatory corticoids— A−Cs; and proinflammatory corticoids—P−Cs). There are several hormones of each of these types (cortisone, aldosterone, etc.), but we need not be concerned with all their names. Although all their functions are not yet completely understood, we do know that the proinflammatory corticoids encourage inflammation and influence mineral metabolism, and the anti-inflammatory corticoids inhibit inflammation and raise the blood sugar level. While these two hormones sometimes oppose each other—as in their effect on inflammation—at other times they may act synergistically, for example, they may have a deleterious effect on the kidneys, producing inflammation, and renal lesions, which in turn cause a significant rise in blood pressure. Their specific activities depend, in each instance, on the nature of the threat and on the nature and degree of activity of other organs and glands.

The thyroid gland directly controls the metabolism rate, raising energy levels in the stress response by accelerating chemical reactions throughout the body. The thyroid also secrets thyroxin, which makes body tissues more sensitive to epinephrine (adrenaline), which is secreted by the adrenal medulla, as described below.

The autonomic nervous system consists of two separate structures: the sympathetic and the parasympathetic. The sympathetic nerve fibers secrete norepinephrine which tends to inhibit the activity of the smooth muscles of the alimentary canal; accelerate the heart beat; dilate the bronchi, so that more oxygen is drawn into the lungs; and dilate the pupils of the eyes, so that more light is allowed in. These nerve fibers will also act to dilate some blood vessels and constrict others. The parasympathetic nerve fibers secrete acetylcholine, which generally tends to offset the effects of norepinephrine, thus serving to restore normal functioning when the emergency has passed—the homeostatic effect.

The inner core of the adrenals (medulla), when neurally stimulated by the hypothalamus, secrets epinephrine (adrenaline), which tends to stimulate the heart, constrict the blood vessels, and postpone muscle fatigue. Incidentally, this hormone is identical with that secreted by the nerve endings, but while the latter has a purely local effect, the epinephrine secreted by the adrenal medulla has a general effect on the self-system because it is secreted into the blood which circulates it through the body.

As a result of all this activity, the body is in a heightened state of alertness, with an increased supply of blood, glucose, and oxygen to the brain, muscles, and other organs and tissues, and an increased efficiency of the perceptual apparatus. The body is ready to fight or flee, as further events may dictate.

Of particular significance is the fact that this sequence of events is nonspecifically produced. It occurs, to a greater or lesser degree, whenever the self-system is sufficiently disturbed or is required to respond to unusual demands. The stressor agent may be as apparently innocuous as strenuous exertion of the muscles, in work or recreational activities; or it may be in the form of mental or emotional demands associated with a new job or traumatic event; or invasion of the body by a noxious agent; or any other event which requires a significant adjustment of the internal operations of the self-system. Any damage, perceived threat, or activity of the body or one or more of its subsystems which is more intensive than normal may result in inflammation, with resulting stiffness and pain. This characteristic response is an essential feature of the self-system's ability to adapt to changes in its ambient environment or to internal demands. The self-system tends to constrain the stressful effects to the smallest area of the body consistent with meeting the requirements for restoring homeostasis; for example, inflammation serves to restrict an invader to the immediate area of attack and to remove the resulting debris. The more extensive the area of attack, and the greater the degree of tissue damage, the greater is the self-system response—in the production of ACTH and other hormones, etc.

Subsystems Involved

3.6 Of course, each of the above mentioned organs, glands, subsystems and hormones serves other functions as well as those we have specified. In addition, they interact in a variety of ways to produce a synergistic effect during the stress response. Consequently, this and any other proposed division of the self-system into subsystems for descriptive purposes is arbitrary and depends upon the perspective of the observer (see: 2.5–2.15).

Many organs, glands, and other parts of the body perform multiple functions and some functions are performed by a number of parts acting independently or in concert. Further, and a very significant aspect of Selye's concept, the G.A.S. involves, not merely the parts of the body we have mentioned above, but every other part of the body in one way or another, directly or indirectly. This becomes obvious, of course, when we realize that both the composition and rate of flow of the blood (which carries a number of hormones as well as other substances) and the degree of activity of the entire nervous system are involved in the G.A.S. and that every cell and organ in the body depend on these two integrators of bodily activities. Figure 3.2 provides a somewhat more detailed representation of the highly complex nature of some of the more significant interactions, but even this diagram is a drastic simplification of the entire process and omits some subsystems and many of the interactions involved in the G.A.S.

For example, it would be difficult, without unduly complicating our diagram, to depict the antagonistic forces which are released by both the nervous system and the endocrine system, the principal coordinating systems of the body. Yet it is these two systems, acting in concert, which control the signals to fight or flee. We would have similar difficulties in modeling the multiple functions of the proinflammatory and anti-inflammatory corticoids released by the adrenal cortex, which, independently or in combination, have such diverse functions as regulating sugar and mineral levels of the blood, pigmentation of the skin, blood pressure, and certain emotional reactions, as well as inflammation in stressed tissues. These regulatory functions depend on the body's ability to vary the proportions of the several hormones involved. Likewise, the kidney's several roles would be difficult to portray adequately in a simple model. In addition to its major role in maintaining homeostasis during the G.A.S., it participates in the regulation of the chemical composition of the blood by screening out certain substances (e.g., excess glucose), and it participates in regulating the blood pressure by secreting certain renal pressor substances into the blood. Part of our difficulty in adequately modeling these processes is the fact that some of them are, at this stage, only partially understood; for example, the roles of the corticoids and the renal pressor substances in regulating blood pressure. The regulation of the glucose level of the blood is likewise extremely complex and incompletely understood, with the liver, the corticoids, certain cells (islets of Langerhans) in the pancreas which secrete insulin, and other organs involved.

The liver, in addition to participating in controlling the glucose levels of the blood, is one of the principal controllers of the degree of concentration of a variety of other chemical substances—proteins, insulin, and certain hormones. It serves as a sort of warehouse, storing reserves of carbohydrates for conversion to glucose as needed; it also destroys excess quantities of the corticoid hormones.

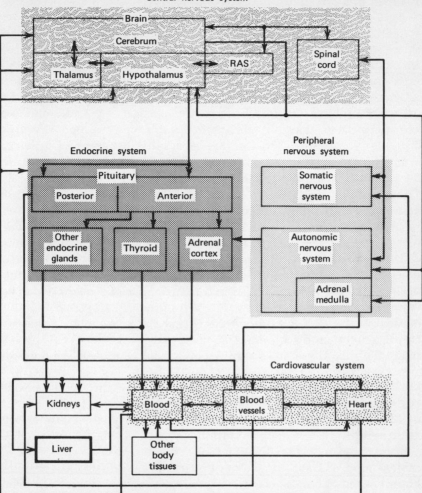

Figure 3.2   Body model for stress research.

Certain white blood cells (e.g., the lymphoid cells and the eosinophils) participate in the G.A.S. by regulating serologic immune reactions and the degree of sensitivity to allergens.

The listing could go on for many pages, but enough has been said to convey our main point that practically every element of the self-system is involved in the G.A.S., although the principal elements involved are the nervous system, the circulatory system, the pituitary gland, the thyroid gland, the adrenals, the liver, and the kidneys, in addition to the cells of the directly affected tissues.

Multiple Effects

3.7 Considering the potentiality for differences in stressors and individual differences in reactivity to stressors, tracing and identifying all of the various effects of the three stages of the G.A.S. throughout the body would be difficult, if not impossible. Some effects are specific, some non-specific; some local, some general; some benign, some malign; but in a biologic system as complex as the human body such distinctions may not always be clearly discernible. Any given effect may be, at once, local in one aspect and general in another; or beneficial to certain organs or tissues and harmful to others. Further, any time a stressor acts upon a specific target, there are both specific and nonspecific effects and certain specific effects may condition, or even completely block, certain nonspecific effects in any given instance. When a stressor acts upon multiple targets, each will produce both specific and non-specific effects; the latter will be additive because the alarm signals are the same, but the specific effects will not be additive because the individual responses are different. Fortunately, for our purposes, we need not even attempt any comprehensive survey of the multiple effects of stress. As will become increasingly clear in subsequent chapters, certain effects of the G.A.S. are more significant than others for our discussion of executive stress. At this point we shall simply identify these more significant effects as a basis for more detailed discussion in later chapters.

As with any other activity of the human body, the stress response does not always conform to the normal pattern. When it does deviate significantly, failing to cope adequately with a stressor, there may result certain diseases of adaptation. Successful adaptation signifies the attainment of a new level of homeostasis in consonance with the ambient environment, it involves a properly balanced combination of defensive and submissive measures by the body or the involved elements thereof. When the body fails to provide such a balance, when there is excessive defensive or submissive response, disease may result. The excessive defensive response may take the form of hyperactivity or overdevelopment of a particular element (e.g., allergic reactions); excessive submission may result from exhaustion or failure of the element to respond (e.g., renal failure). Such excessive responses—defensive or submissive—may also be emotional rather than physical in nature, taking the form of worry, anger, depression, etc.

Diseases of adaptation, therefore, are simply inappropriate responses by the body during the stress reaction; they are the indirect results of attack by stressors, in contrast to other diseases, resulting directly from such attacks. The distinction is, of course, primarily conceptual, since the body rarely, if ever, successfully responds to any significant stressors without some degree of maladaptation. Thus, there are no "pure" diseases, in which only the directly affected organ is involved, with no side effects on other organs—no pure heart disease, kidney disease, etc.

In effect, the characterization of any given condition as a *disease* is simply an indication that we have reached a terminal point in our current efforts to analyze the condition and trace its causes. This practice is the same in the field of medicine as in economics, sociology, business, or other fields of knowledge—witness such terminal point designations as inflation, poverty, personnel turnover, etc.

Among the most important effects of stress are the cardiovascular changes. The most obvious, immediate effect of stress is inflammation, a fundamental feature of all diseases, as well as the basic local reaction to injury. Inflammation is not a simple response of the body to attack by a stressor, but a syndrome characterized by a variety of symptoms, including swelling, reddening, heat, pain and general interference with function. These conditions result from a rapid infusion of blood and other body fluids into the affected area. As we have seen, this local response is accompanied by the secretion of a variety of hormones throughout the body, resulting in increased demands for blood in some places, decreased demands in other places, and significant changes in the chemical composition of the blood. There are also increased blood pressure, blood flow, and capillary permeability. These cardiovascular changes directly affect the oxygenation and nutrition of all bodily tissues, including those of the heart and blood vessels themselves. These increased demands on the cardiovascular system, plus the effects of the increased flow of pro-inflammatory and anti-inflammatory corticoids in the blood, cause significant inflammatory and other changes in the walls of the blood vessels themselves—conditions we call arteritis or arteriosclerosis. If such vascular derangements are severe enough, or occur often enough, they may result in numerous and diversified local lesions throughout the body, again including the heart and blood vessels themselves.

Likewise, excessive demands for oxygen may lead to congestion, edema (excess fluid), and other disturbances of the lungs, leading to pneumonia and other disorders of the pulmonary system, which, like other elements of the body is subject to inflammation when overworked. The adverse effects ramify through other elements of the self-system as the supply of oxygen is gradually reduced because of impaired lung functioning.

The entire nervous system, depending as do all other parts of the body upon the blood supply for nutrition and oxygen, and being particularly susceptible to biochemical changes which occur throughout the body during the G.A.S., is especially susceptible to the effects of systemic stress. Chronic involvement in the stress response, with increased activity in the secretion of noradrenaline and acetycholine at nerve-endings, may lead to inflammation (neuritis) and other serious structural and functional derangement of the nerve fibers and cells. In addition to these physiological effects, there are the psychosomatic effects of stress resulting from misunderstanding or inappropriate evaluation of the significance of other stress reactions, or from the fear of, or worry over, an inability or failure to understand bodily conditions or reactions.

The gastro-intestinal tract is also extremely sensitive to the effects of stress. This is due, in large part, to intense neural discharges from the autonomic nervous system during the G.A.S. At the same time, the hormones being released tend to stimulate the production of peptic enzymes thereby increasing the attack of the digestive juices on the stomach lining. The results frequently take the form of bleeding ulcers in the stomach and adjacent areas of the alimentary canal.

While these are probably the most significant for our purposes, they are by no means the only adverse effects of the stress response with which we must be concerned. As we have seen, the G.A.S. involves an almost total mobilization of the body's resources, so that the strain of increased demands on the self-system is realized in almost every subsystem of the body. The kidneys, for example, are subject to greater demands in disposing of the increased volume of waste products resulting from the higher rate of metabolism, and in regulating the heightened blood pressure. The strain of these demands makes the kidneys more susceptible to the damaging effects of the corticoid hormones, resulting in irritation, inflammation, and renal lesions. The lesions, in turn, constrict the blood vessels of the kidneys causing further damage, including permanent histologic changes. This constriction of the blood vessels in the kidneys tends to further increase the secretion of renal pressor substances, which in turn raise the blood pressure still more by further constricting the blood vessels, and so on in a positive feedback cycle.

The sensory subsystems of the body are also made more susceptible to inflammatory, allergic, and other disturbances because of the increased demands of the G.A.S., and the concomitant destruction of certain white blood cells (lymphoid and eosinophil) which are essential for production of immunity and in certain allergic reactions.

The heightened degree of tension also adversely affects muscle tonus and fatigability as well as the epidermis, hair, and nails—

resulting in excessive wrinkling, loss of hair, premature graying, etc. The skeletal system may lose valuable minerals, resulting in osteoporosis. Even the sex organs may suffer some diminution of activity. The rheumatic and rheumatoid diseases are also the result of maladaption, of inappropriate reactions to stress. The anti-inflammatory corticoids also weaken our defenses against certain, usually innocuous, microbes which inhabit our lungs, skin, and gastrointestinal system and aid the body in disposing of dead cells and tissues.

Individual Differences

3.8 Of course, while the basic pattern of the G.A.S. is always the same, there are significant variations in the degree of response and in the after-effects among individuals, and for any one individual from time to time. There are also wide variations, in any one person, in the reactivity of individual subsystems, organs, glands, and cells. These variations are due to such factors as heredity, diet, the current state of health (generally and of individual organs), previous exposure to stress in general, the specific nature of the stressor, and other individual, cultural, and environmental factors. There is also the possibility that repeated exposure to a given, specific stressor may result in selective conditioning of the individual or of certain of his or her subsystems. Such selective conditioning may be either positive or negative, increasing or decreasing susceptibility to the specific stressor, raising or lowering the reaction threshold, enhancing or reducing one's tolerance of stress in general, and in improving or impairing the rate of recovery from stress. Hence the wide variation in the nature and degree of response to specific stressors, in the long range effects of continued or repeated exposure to stress, and in the ability to manage one's stress levels. In addition to these individual differences in susceptibility, tolerance, and recovery, there is the factor of the duration of exposure to the stressor. For example, repeated brief exposures may tend to increase the degree of tolerance or resistance, while exposures of longer duration may tend to be additive in nature, lowering resistance and increasing the adverse effects. Finally, the individual's way of coping (or failing to cope) with stress will significantly influence the effects.

Summary—The G.A.S.

3.9 In summary, we see that stress is a state of the body manifested by a general adaptation syndrome—the G.A.S. The stress response—the G.A.S.—is essentially a defense mechanism of the human body, a means of coping with stimuli which threaten either the maintenance of stability (homeostasis) or the preservation of life. It is a very complex mechanism involving, in one way or another, every part of the body in a sequence of interactions, many of which are, as yet, but dimly understood at the microlevel of resolution. The basic pattern of the response is always the same, although there are wide variations in degree of reactivity, depending upon individual, cultural, and environmental differences, as well as upon the number and duration of exposures to a particular stressor and to stress in general.

As a defense mechanism, the G.A.S. is beneficial; it prepares the body for fight or flight in emergency situations, thus tending to ensure self-preservation as well as stimulating the self-system to higher levels of performance in challenging situations.

We must note, however, that, even though it is essentially a defense mechanism, the G.A.S. places such severe demands on the body, in the total mobilization effort it calls forth each time, that it inevitably results in some systemic damage. Each incident of stress leaves some irreversible trace of damage, and these scars accumulate over time to constitute the process of aging. The accumulation of the undesirable by-products of stress-induced chemical reactions in the tissues of the body and the cumulative effects of the continuing loss of body cells (particularly in the brain and heart) constitute the process of exhaustion, the inability to adapt. Thus, the process of aging is, in effect, the gradual exhaustion of the body's resources through the cumulative effects of irreparable wear and tear on the tissues. Further, chronic or repeated stress has significant adverse effects of a widely varying nature on the human body, and accelerates the exhaustion of body resources, diminishes the ability to adapt, and speeds the process of aging.

These adverse effects take the form of diseases of adaptation; they result primarily from inappropriate or inadequate responses by the self-system to stressful stimuli. Of course, some stressors—for example, X-rays, extremes of temperature, severe physical blows, and certain microbes—cause disease regardless of the body's response. Generally, however, the disease is the product of interaction between the stressor and the self-system. Thus, in addition to the direct effect of the stressor on the body there are the defensive and defense-inhibiting responses of the self system. The interaction of these three forces in appropriate proportions provide the necessary balance for resistance and adaptation of the self-system to the stressor.

Of course, not every deviation from homeostasis constitutes disease. Only when the adaptive mechanisms fail to adequately counteract the stressor, or when the self-system over-reacts does disease result. Disease is not a state, or condition, but a dynamic clash of the opposing forces of aggression and defense; it is a struggle to maintain or regain the homeostatic balance of the self-system.

Nor does every deviation from homeostasis constitute stress; rather, every stimulus received by the self-system causes a deviation of some degree from the normal level of homeostasis. In contrast, stress is the state manifested by a specific syndrome—the G.A.S.—which consists of all the nonspecifically induced changes in the self-system responding to a specific stressor. Because of the alarm signals involved, it is the common denominator of all the adaptive reactions of the body. While it has its own characteristic form—the G.A.S.—it has no single cause. Further, while its manifestations change from moment to moment during the three stages of the G.A.S., stress exists throughout the process. In fact, not every instance of stress will progress through all three stages; only the most severe stress progresses to the third stage of exhaustion, or death. In most instances of stress, the G.A.S. progresses through only the first two stages; even when it does progress further the exhaustion is only partial or temporary, it is not necessarily irreversible.

From this brief description of the manifestations of stress it should be clear that so long as we continue to live we cannot avoid stress. The best anyone can do is to learn how to control its adverse effects and to manage his stress levels so as to minimize the degree of wear and tear on his self-system.

THE NATURE OF EXECUTIVE STRESS

3.10 Since our principal topic is executive stress it behooves us to indicate in what respects executive stress differs from the stress to which other individuals are subject. We have already indicated that the stress response is always basically the same, differing only in the degree of reactivity of individuals and individual organs. This leaves open two possibilities for significant differences. First, there is the possibility that executives as a class may be subjected to exposure to certain types of stressors to a greater extent than other individuals. Secondly, there is the possibility that executives as a class may be peculiarly susceptible to certain of the adverse effects of the stress response which we have discussed above. As subsequent chapters will demonstrate, we believe there is evidence to support the actuality of both of these possibilities.

First, however, let us note that when we speak of executive stress, we are not speaking of a singularity. There are many varieties of stressors impinging on the executive and the adverse effects are as many and as varied as the number of executives. In other words, no two executives are exactly alike either in the combination of stressors to which they are exposed or in the combination of adverse effects to which they are susceptible.

We take up in Part II of this volume some of the more significant causes and effects of executive stress. Here let us simply indicate the general nature of those causes and effects by way of differentiating executive stress from the stress of others.

EXECUTIVE STRESSORS

3.11 Depending upon one's philosophical or ethological concepts, one may view the struggle for existence as competitive, cooperative, or an alternation or combination of the two. Whatever the choice, we believe it is fair to assert that most people will see executives as being, or at least tending toward, the competitive end of any continuum representing all of mankind. By the very nature of their work, executives are seekers after power. Power is of the essence of the executive function; without power, the executive ceases to function as an executive. This is not true of other types of work, or at least not true to the same degree. Hence, executives differ significantly from their fellow human beings both in the drive for power and in the power dimension of their interrelationships with others, both in their own organization and in other organizations with which they deal. As we shall see in more detail in Chapter 5, this characteristic of executives constitutes a fruitful source of stressors for them.

Another aspect of the executive function is the propensity for risk taking, a part of the very fabric of the executive life. Of course, all of us, every day of our lives take untold numbers of risks—from falling out of bed in the morning, to drinking polluted water from the tap, to eating contaminated foods, to venturing out on the street, to using any form of transportation, to subjecting ourselves to occupational hazards, to having an airplane crash into our home during the night. A few venturesome souls even seek out special dangers—mountain climbers, daredevil circus performers, stuntmen in the movies. But all such risks involve danger to only oneself, or perhaps a few others. Executives bear the responsibility for taking risks involving the wealth or welfare of many others—employees, stockholders, taxpayers, customers, other organizations, etc. Executives differ from most of us in the degree to which they seek out risk as part of their daily work and in the magnitude of the risks they take. Herein lies another major source of stressors for executives.

Their responsibility for interpersonal relationships constitutes still another major source of stressors for executives. Again, all of us, in varying degrees, have some responsibility for interpersonal relationships—within the family; within the work group; among our relatives, friends, and associates in the variety of activities in which we engage from day to day. Some of us, such as foremen and supervisors at various higher levels in an organizational hierarchy, have additional special responsibilities for maintaining harmonious relationships while ensuring effective, efficient, and economical achievement of production goals. This responsibility necessarily entails some involvement in the resolution of personality and other conflicts of an interpersonal nature. The general tendency is to refer to higher levels of authority the more difficult and the wider ranging problems of this nature. Thus, the higher the organizational level, the more difficult the nature of the problems and the greater the impact of the solution. Further, the higher the level, the greater the responsibility for establishing guiding policies for others at subordinate levels. The executive, therefore, serves as legislator, educator, mediator, and judge all at once with all of the attendant frustrations involved in each such occupation. The possibilities for generation of stressors becomes obvious.

Somewhat related to the executive responsibility for management of interpersonal relationships is the responsibility for the management of change. Human beings are somewhat ambivalent in their attitudes to change. We have mentioned above the process of homeostasis, the innate tendency to strive for a state of internal stability. Contrasted with this is a characteristic which humans share with all other animals, an inherent curiosity, a drive to continually explore the environment—whether it be only a tiny mud puddle or the entire cosmos. The biologists tell us that even in the microscopic animalcule the constant probing is not entirely explained by the drive for nutrition. In humans, this curiosity takes the form of seeking information, ever-increasing knowledge. Perhaps this ambivalence, this continuing contest between the curiosity and the homeostatic drives constitutes a source of tension or stress in all of us. If so, executives must share it with the rest of us. In addition, however, they bear the burden of managing, not only a certain number of subordinates afflicted with this ambivalence, but also the very process of change itself. Their responsibility for managing change is not, however, limited to their own organizations, but extends to some degree to a variety of other organizations—suppliers, customers, government regulators, etc. At every point, in their own organizations and in others with which they deal, they will encounter these conflicting tendencies—curiosity and homeostasis, the desire for change and the desire for stability. Because of their wider responsibilities, these conflicting drives constitute a more fruitful source of stressors for executives than for most of us. Furthermore, in our Western culture at least, the very life of the organization is seen as being dependent on its ability to maintain a reasonable rate of progress. Every organization must keep up with the times or die. Thus, executives must continually seek to stimulate change and to encourage this tendency even at the risk of losing some degree of stability. Calculating and maintaining the optimum rate of change without unduly challenging the desire and need of others for stability probably serves to multiply the possibilities for engendering executive stressors.

There are a number of other sources of stressors which are either peculiar to executives or are more productive of stressors for them than for the rest of us. For example, their "summit isolation," the higher executives rise in the organizational hierarchy, the more likely they are to encounter the phenomenon of loneliness. They have fewer and fewer peers with whom they can confer, on whom they can depend for support in their decisions. Further, the very process of progress up the executive ladder is likely to require such devotion to work as to entail increasing loss of time for, and communication with, one's family. The result is not only summit isolation, but isolation from the family as well.

The application and dedication to their work lead not only to a lack of sufficient time to spend with their families, but also to a lack of sufficient time for a number of other activities—recreational, educational, cultural, and even health care. Eventually, it may even lead to lack of sufficient time to perform all of the work activities in which they feel impelled to engage. The very problem of managing their time begins to become a source of stressors. We could mention other sources of stressors for the executive, and there are probably a number of sources of which we are unaware, but enough examples have been given to demonstrate that the executive is subject to certain stressors, perhaps greater in number and variety than, but certainly different from those to which most other members of our society are exposed. In fact, certain stressors arise from the very life style of executives. Not only do executives have a stronger tendency to deliberately seek out certain forms of stress, but the characteristic life style of the executive in itself seems to lead to the development of undue stress.

EFFECTS OF EXECUTIVE STRESS

3.12 Our subjective analysis, above, of the executive life style revealed a number of sources of stressors to which executives seem to be particularly susceptible. We cannot similarly identify any particular types of the adverse effects of stress. We are not saying that there are no such effects peculiar to executives. We are simply saying that our analysis does not reveal any. Nor do we find any reliable morbidity or mortality statistics which suggest such a result.

There are some writers on the subject of stress who seem to indicate that executives are perhaps more prone than others to cardiovascular diseases, gastrointestinal diseases, alcoholism, and suicide, but we fail to find any supporting statistics for such claims.

Our assumption at this time, therefore, must be that executives as a class are subject to the same types of adverse effects, and probably to the same degree, as others who are subjected to undue stress.

DISTRESS AND EUSTRESS

3.13 One finds in the literature on stress a number of attempts to distinguish between bad stress and good stress, between distress and eustress. Distress is reputed to have detrimental, even pernicious, effects; eustress, beneficial, even exhilarting, effects. The matter requires some clarification.

While stress is essential to life, it has, as we have seen above, both beneficial and adverse effects. In fact, the very same incidents which serve to protect the body against a specific stressor have at the same time a detrimental effect as a result of the severe demands placed on the body's defensive mechanisms. Thus, every event which serves as a stimulus to the self-system requires some degree of adaptation and, therefore, produces some degree of nonspecific stress in addition to its specific effects. Whether the stimulus is perceived as pleasant or unpleasant is irrelevant; the significant factor is the degree of adaptation required for adjustment. Hence, any kind of activity—normal or unusual—produces some degree of stress, ranging from negligible to severe. Even in sleep, when the body is about as relaxed as it can get, there is some degree of activity—the heart continues to pump blood, the alimentary canal continues to digest food, the muscles continue to move the diaphragm in breathing, and the brain may be active in dreaming—and, therefore, some degree of stress. Conversely, prolonged deprivation of external stimuli may also produce stress, resulting from the emotional tensions of fear, worry, anxiety, etc. Accordingly, the terms *distress* and *eustress,* which seem to imply that there are actually two different kinds of stress, are misleading. There is only one kind of stress, that exhibited in the G.A.S., and it has both beneficial and detrimental effects. For example, exposure of the entire self-system to intense stress may be beneficial in shock therapy, but detrimental in traumatic incidents. Exposure of only a portion of the self-system to intense stress may result in greater resistance through adaptation or inflammation, or it may result in tissue destruction. In each instance, the result depends on a variety of circumstances, including the intensity of the stressor, the conditioning factors within the self-system, the timing, the point of impact of the stressor, the sensitivity or degree of reactivity of the target area, etc. The result is largely a matter of chance, with the possibility that the weakest link in the self-system may break down.

To avoid this confusion, in this volume, we shall use the terms *distress* and *eustress* to refer to the effects of stress, not to different kinds of stress.

Since stress is essential to life, and, indeed, unavoidable in any event, executives should strive to so manage their stress levels and stress responses as to minimize the distressing effects and maximize the eustress effects. As a general guide, they may assume that successful activity, even if very strenuous, may result in temporary exhaustion, but will produce little long term damage or distress. Continual frustration, however, even though not involving strenuous activity, may produce both temporary exhaustion and the permanent damage of distress. In Part IV, we explore these alternatives in more detail. But if stress is both essential and unavoidable, how does one manage it?

MANAGING STRESS

3.14   We believe it is both feasible and advisable for executives to manage their own stress levels and responses as well as to exercise some significant degree of influence over the stress levels and responses of their organizational subordinates, peers, and others with whom they deal on a business or social basis. As Selye suggests (Selye, 1974, p. 17–18), the basic principles of defense against stress are essentially the same at the intercellular level, the interpersonal level, and the intersociety level. A sound knowledge of these basic principles and of the nature of the stress response will, therefore, equip the individual to effectively manage his or her own stress levels and responses as well as to deal appropriately with the stress levels and responses of others.

As we examine the causes, effects, and coping mechanisms in subsequent chapters we shall see that there are several points at which executives may intervene in the stress process. Further, they may control their intervention so as to decrease the distress effects and increase the eustress effects for themselves and the others with whom they deal.

The first, and probably most important, step executives may take in this direction is to improve their knowledge and understanding of the stress process, its effects, and the available coping mechanisms. We have already mentioned the value of this step in the opening paragraphs of this chapter. For their own benefit, for the benefit of other members of the organization, and for the benefit of the organization itself, they may also provide opportunities for others in the organization to gain such knowledge and understanding. The more everyone understands the nature of the stress process, the more they become capable of controlling their own stress levels and responses and the general stress levels of the organization as a whole. Control over the stress levels, as we shall see in later chapters, is an effective means of reducing distress and increasing eustress effects.

With a deeper knowledge and understanding of the causes of stress, executives may more easily evaluate in advance the stress-producing potentials of given situations. Then, recognizing their own proclivity for seeking out stress-producing activities, they may regulate their participation so as to minimize the distress and maximize the eustress effects for themselves, and perhaps for others. In addition to regulating their own participation in stress-producing activities, executives may also exercise some degree of control or influence over the participation of others in such situations.

Further, they may recognize in advance the role of specific stressors in any given activity or situation and evaluate the possibilities for eliminating them or regulating the severity of their effects on themselves or others. Others in the organization who gain the necessary understanding of stress may do likewise.

These and other methods of regulating the stress-producing stimuli provide only one approach to the control of stress. Another avenue of approach lies in the response of the individual to stressors and stress-producing situations. The individual who has a knowledge and understanding of the G.A.S. may utilize that information to gain some degree of control over his or her own responses to stress stimuli. In other words, he or she may consciously intervene to regulate some of the otherwise autonomic activities of his or her own body.

Finally, individuals who gain adequate knowledge and understanding of the stress process will find themselves in a better position to evaluate the potential benefits of specific coping mechanisms. Thus, they may avoid the counter-productive quackery and concentrate on those mechanisms which they believe will be most appropriate for their own circumstances. We shall return to this topic in chapter 13.

PART II
THE CAUSES OF STRESS

To the best of our knowledge, there is not currently available for the interested layman any systematic treatment of the causes of stress. This lack may be due, in part at least, to the diversity and multiplicity of objects and events which may serve as stressors and the conditions which predispose an individual to stress. In the next four chapters we propose to remedy that deficiency.

For this purpose, we have chosen to classify the multitudinous causes of stress into three major categories: physiological, psychological, and environmental. Obviously, this, and any other, categorization is bound to be arbitrary; it is imposed on the data, rather than arising from it. Further, it is overly simplistic, as may be inferred from our discussion of cause and effect thinking in chapter 2 (2.17). Suffice to say, at this point, that any given incident of stress arises, not from any single cause, but from a constellation of interacting causes.

In addition, we know from the discussion in chapter 3 (3.1), that the human being is an open system, equipped with homeostatic mechanisms which tend to maintain a relatively stable state within the organism and to return it to a stable state whenever it has been disturbed. As we shall see, disturbances of the stable state may arise from within the body or from without. The stressors which give rise to these disturbances constitute the provocative causes of stress.

The internal disturbances arise from a multitude of more and less subtle and insidious stressors, including a wide variety of genetic disorders, congenital conditions, and bodily states which develop in the normal course of living. We discuss these disturbances in the chapters on physiologial and psychological causes. We take up the external sources of disturbance in chapter 6, Environmental Causes of Stress.

There is one further categorization of the causes of stress to which the reader may find references in the literature: the division into primary and secondary causes. A primary cause of stress consists of any stimulus or combination of stimuli which triggers the G.A.S. A primary cause may be either internal or external. The secondary causes of stress consist of those bodily states and activities which are at once the effects of one or more primary causes of stress and, as a result of positive feedback, the cause of additional stress. In other words, certain bodily states and conditions which constitute the effects of one or more primary causes of stress may, in themselves, provide positive feedback to amplify or exacerbate the stressful conditions. Obviously, the secondary causes of stress are purely internal.

Some stressors by their very nature tend to produce effects which, in turn, constitute the secondary causes of stress; and some individuals appear to be highly susceptible to such primary causes and also prone to produce the very effects which constitute the secondary causes of stress.

Selye calls these secondary causes of stress *diseases of adaptation*. They may take one of two forms: lesions in the organs involved in the G.A.S., or abnormal responses of such organs. The reader will recall that we previously mentioned (3.13) that every stress response has both beneficial and adverse effects. The secondary causes of stress constitute the principal source of the adverse effects. We discuss these causes in Chapters 4 and 5.

Since any given stress condition arises not merely from any one or more of the variety of potential stressors occurring within the body or outside of it, but from the interaction of the body with that potential stressor, whether any given cause is physiological, psychological, or environmental will frequently depend on the perspective of the observer. Nevertheless, some type of classification of the causes of stress is essential for bringing some degree of order to an otherwise chaotic array of data as a basis for our discussion and for use as a diagnostic tool in understanding the process of stress.

Again, so long as we remember the interacting nature of these causes and their systems effects on the human body, the categorization we have adopted will probably serve as well as any.

Chapter 4
Physiological Causes of Stress

4.0 Rather than attempt to deal with specific stressors, which would involve us in an effort to present an endless enumeration, we have selected for discussion ten categories of the physiological causes of stress. Obviously, our categorization is not exhaustive, but it will aid us in ordering and presenting the available information on the subject. We have selected these particular categories because they are the ones most prominently and frequently mentioned in the literature on stress and because they appear, also from the literature, to be the categories of most significance in executive stress. The stressors comprised in the categories listed below may indirectly affect or directly involve any one or more of the bodily subsystems mentioned in chapter 3.

1. Genetic and congenital factors
2. Life experience
3. Biological rhythms
4. Sleep
5. Diet
6. Posture
7. Fatigue
8. Muscular tension
9. Disease
10. Diseases of adaptation.

GENETIC AND CONGENITAL FACTORS

4.1 Certain physiological predispositions to (or causes of) stress are the result of factors which develop before birth; one of these prenatal factors is the individual's genetic composition. For example, the susceptibility to hypertension and a variety of other diseases may be inherited traits. In fact, all of the physical and mental characteristics of each individual, including all of his or her strengths and weaknesses, are controlled to some degree by the instructions contained in his or her particular genetic code. Of course, some individual traits are influenced by environmental factors also, but the genetic composition constitutes a significant factor in predisposing the individual to certain types of stress.

A second factor that predisposes one to stress is the process of fetal development during pregnancy. Ingestion by the child-bearing mother of certain medications, drugs, poisons, alcoholic beverages, and allergenic foods may serve to produce congenital defects in the baby. Certain diseases—notoriously, rubella—may also produce such effects. In fact, any internal or external stressor which affects the mother may affect the unborn child, and the effects may last the lifetime of the child. The effects may take the form of a variety of tissue weaknesses, organ dysfunctions, and abnormal behavior of many kinds.

By affecting the total life experience of the individual, both the genetic composition and congenital conditions affect all of the other factors discussed below.

LIFE EXPERIENCE

4.2 Each individual has his or her own unique life history, his or her own particular collection of events; it is this entire history that we refer to as *life experience*. During childhood we suffer the ravages of the usual childhood diseases, for example, measles or scarlet fever; plus a host of accidents, which may include broken bones; and a myriad of other conditions which range from pinworms to heart murmurs. During the adolescent years, children have the problems of adjusting to a developing feeling of independence and the phenomena of sex. Some of the physical changes that take place during this period may lead to emotional stress.

A number of researchers have also sought to identify various specific stages of adult life; some of these ideas, such as that of the "managerial middle-age crisis," may be of interest to executives. (See: Levinson, 1973 and Levinson, 1978.) Others are of significance only in that they underline a point we have previously made: the ubiquity and constancy of change (2.16). We live in a universe of constant change and we, ourselves, are constantly involved in effecting changes in that universe, but our minds and bodies are no exceptions to this inexorable law. The suggestion of some of these researchers is that certain types of changes occur at certain stages of life and that such changes constitute crises. Our life experience determines how we deal with such crises. We return to this topic in chapter 5.

In summary, life experience is a process of transitions; some of these transitions produce crises for the individual and these are, to some degree, always stressful. Further, these crises affect, directly or indirectly every one of the other factors discussed below.

BIOLOGICAL RHYTHMS

4.3 Currently, there is a significant amount of research being undertaken and reported in the field of biological rhythms. The term *biological rhythms* applies to a subject of scientific research; it is to be distinguished from a similar term, *biorhythms,* which is generally applied to a popular fad without scientific foundation (see: Luce, 1971). The basic idea behind biological rhythms research is that the process of change, which we have been discussing, is neither irregular nor chaotic, but rhythmic in nature. The universe is permeated with various types of forces—gravitational, electromagnetic, physical—each of which has a rhythmic character of its own. Further, all forms of organic matter, including human, conform to such rhythms and develop biological rhythms of their own.

The rhythmic processes range from cycles of a few milliseconds for cells to much longer ones for the body as a whole. Most forms of life, including human beings, exhibit circadian rhythms. The term *circadian* is a neologism, adapted from the Latin, meaning about a day. It is applied to those cycles which approximate either the solar day of about twenty-four hours, or the lunar day of about 24.8 hours. The menstrual cycle of women more nearly approximates the lunar month. Less well known is the fact that men also have a monthly cycle, involving bodily weight and other biological processes.

Rhythms with a cycle of less than a day are called *ultradian.* These include, among others, the pulse rate and the respiration rate. Normally, the human resting pulse rate is about four times the respiration rate, which ranges from about fifteen to twenty breaths per minute, with some variation according to the time of day. The variation follows a circadian rhythm which rises to a peak by day and drops to a low point during nighttime sleep. If a person's normal rate is four to one, any significantly higher or lower ratio may be a signal of body malfunction and, as we have seen, body malfunction leads to stress.

So far, over one hundred internal functions of the human body, ranging from pulse rate to temperature to mood and physical and mental performance, have been recognized as operating in a rhythmic mode. These biological rhythms are intricately interrelated and synchronized to ensure an appropriate state of homeostasis. When the body is subjected to stress, however, they may become uncoupled, thus disturbing the normal balance. The disturbance of the normal balance serves as positive feedback to provide secondary symptoms of stress. Both the primary disturbance and the positive feedback affect the sleep patterns and fatigability of the individual; in addition, through the life experience, any disturbance in the biological rhythms is likely to have some effect on the other factors discussed below.

SLEEP

4.4 The most noticeable feature of sleep is that it fits into our daily life as part of the circadian cycle, but sleep itself is also rhythmic in nature. Current researchers divide sleep into four stages. The completion of the four stages in sequence constitutes a sleep cycle. Although it varies by individual, for most people the length of the complete cycle ranges from ninety to one hundred and twenty minutes. Throughout the night, the normal, healthy person will repeat this cycle four to six times. The four stages of the sleep cycle are:

Stage I: Rapid Eye Movement (REM). This stage is sometimes called paradoxical sleep because of the similarity of the brain wave patterns to those of the waking brain (four to seven cycles per second).

Stage II: Brain waves shift to about twelve to fourteen cycles per second and the eyeballs stop wandering. This stage makes up about fifty percent of all nocturnal sleep.

Stage III: This stage is characterized by high voltage (300 microvolts, five times the alpha voltage), large, slow waves, about one per second. During this stage there is a slowdown of the body's activity: heart rate slows, blood pressure and body temperature drops.

Stage IV: Deep sleep is characterized by slow waves of about 0.5 to 3.5 cycles per second. Sleep researchers find that certain individuals are especially prone to bedwetting, sleepwalking, or night terrors that are not recalled upon awakening, even if the individual screams out in his or her sleep; and that among such individuals, these phenomena generally take place during this fourth stage.

The normal, natural time allocations for a healthy person for Stage IV sleep are largest soon after retiring and the time spent in Stage IV is a lot less as sleep progresses. The reverse is true for Stage I (REM) sleep, which has its larger allocations towards morning.

Deprivation of Stage I (REM) sleep results in mild behavior changes, including sexual tension and increased appetite. Subjects participating in sleep laboratory experiments who have been awakened as REM sleep starts, complain, after a few nights of this treatment, of apathy, bodily malaise, and depression. As deprivation of REM sleep continues, subjects become anxious and on some occasions mentally disturbed.

REM sleep is not equivalent to dreaming; in fact, there is some evidence to indicate that dreaming is a secondary rather than a primary biological process. Mentation, however, apparently takes place throughout the entire sleep period, increasing in intensity towards the end of the sleeping period, that is, the morning for most people. Stage I (REM) sleep appears to be a time when the drive centers in the brain discharge excess energy. Apparently this is a safe time to discharge such energy since the brain is active while the body is almost paralyzed by a lack of muscle tone, thereby preventing the individual from acting out any part of his or her dream.

Human beings need sleep; without adequate sleep they perform poorly at work, they cannot sustain concentration, they become irritable, and eventually begin to suffer from hallucinations, which may result in deranged behavior. Conversely, stress encountered during waking hours may manifest itself in different ways during sleep. For example, some sleep laboratory subjects who encountered stress during the day displayed shortened sleep cycles (approximately sixty minutes, instead of ninety to one hundred and twenty minutes, for the complete four stages) and researchers have speculated that this is a form of regression to an infantile state. (Luce, 1971 a and b.) Other sleep research subjects who were subjected to stress (in group therapy or surgery) tended to cope with stress by dreaming; at least, this is what the researchers conclude as a result of dream analysis. (Berger, Hunter, and Lane, 1971.)

Sleep deprivation studies show that individuals attempt to make up for the loss of Stage I and Stage IV sleep just as soon as opportunity offers.

Two other disturbances associated with sleep are insomnia and narcolepsy (inability to stay awake during normal waking hours). Narcolepsy has been found to begin after a particularly stressful situation, while insomnia has been traced to abnormal body rhythms.

In general, anyone who is suffering from body rhythms that are out of phase is a candidate for poor (nonrestful) sleep or insomnia.

In summary, sleep is part of the human being's biological rhythm process and is in turn affected by other biological rhythms. If sleep is interfered with by abnormal working hours, jet travel to remote parts of the world (jet lag), or by stress, it can throw the entire biological system of rhythms out of order, which in turn can exacerbate the stressful conditions. Further, irregular or abnormal sleeping patterns predispose the individual to fatigue, muscle tension, poor posture, various diseases, and some diseases of adaptation.

DIET

4.5 By the term *diet* we mean the foods, food supplements, and vitamin preparations ingested by the individual for nutritional purposes.

Although nutrition is far from being an exact science, there are certain basic facts which have been established and certain basic principles which have been demonstrated to be essential to human health. We know, for example, that a normal individual requires a well-balanced diet, including specific proportions of protein, carbohydrates, fats, vitamins, certain essential minerals, and water. The proportions may vary from individual to individual depending on body weight, degree of activity, physical condition, etc., but some amount of these essential nutrients must be included in every diet. Special adjustments must be made for those individuals with food allergies or metabolic diseases. Any significant departure from these basic requirements, any severe quantitative or qualitative nutritional deficiency, may produce a bodily condition which acts as a stressor. Overeating, too, may serve as a cause of stress.

As we saw in Chapter 3 (3.6), during the General Adaptation Syndrome (G.A.S.), there are significant changes in the blood sugar level, with the body calling strongly on its glucose reserves. Hence, any pre-existing metabolic disorders or deficiencies would tend to exacerbate the effects of stress, and vice versa, in a positive feedback cycle. Further, dietary deficiencies and overeating tend to interfere with normal metabolic processes, to disturb the normal blood sugar levels, and to place undue stress on the homeostatic mechanisms of the body. Such disturbances tend to disrupt other biological rhythms and to predispose the individual to fatigue, irregular sleep patterns, and disease. Definite links have been established between certain diseases and dietary excesses of fat, sugar, and salt; too much fat, too much sugar, and too much salt, all have been shown to be contributory to heart disease, cancer, obesity, and stroke, among other killing diseases. In all, six of the ten leading causes of death in the United States have been linked to diet.

POSTURE

4.6 Posture is a function of the skeletal framework and the general body musculature. Poor posture interferes with proper functioning of a number of the normal reflexes and may also adversely affect some of the other internal organs and subsystems, such as the cardiovascular system, the respiratory system, and the digestive system. It may also adversely affect the individual's psychological well-being and his or her social intercourse.

The erect posture of mankind, which is unique in the animal kingdom, is well suited to locomotion, but poorly suited to standing. From this fact arise many of the stress stimuli generally attributed to poor posture.

Actually, poor posture may be due to one or more of three causes: (1) diseases of the skeletal framework of the body or the related musculature; or (2) inappropriate use of the muscles; or (3) disturbances of the vestibular apparatus of the inner ear, through which we regulate our balance against the force of gravity.

Deformities or diseases of the bones and muscles may be due to genetic or congenital defects or to subsequently acquired injuries or diseases. Whatever the cause, the resulting conditions may constitute a source of stress by placing undue demands on certain parts of the body, thereby disturbing the normal homeostasis.

A more frequent source of stress is the inappropriate use of the muscles of the body. The maintenance of proper posture is an acquired trait, and improper posture (in the absence of deformity or disease) is, therefore due to lack of adequate training or learning. Many bad habits of posture are developed in childhood and carried over into adulthood. Few of us habitually maintain proper posture when sitting, standing, or walking. In some instances, the work environment contributes to poor posture. For example, the type of desk chair used by most white collar workers, including executives, is poorly designed for maintenance of good sitting posture—the seat is usually too soft and too deep, and the back of the chair fails to provide adequate support for the base of the spine. Most of our beds are too soft and fail to provide adequate support for the spine. Few of us are familiar with the most relaxing positions for sleep. In some instances, as we shall see in the next chapter, inappropriate use of the muscles may be related to certain emotional disturbances. Most of us are familiar with the unnecessary muscular contractions accompanying fear and anxiety; we call it *tension* and attribute headaches and other pains and troubles to it. (See 4.8, below.)

Frequently posture is simply a reflection or expression of certain emotional attitudes; thus, good posture is indicative of self-confidence or extroversion, poor posture of lack of confidence and introversion. Disturbance by injury or disease of the vestibular apparatus of the inner ear may result in inability to sit, stand, or walk without assistance.

Poor posture, whatever the cause, tends to arouse muscular tension and to predispose the individual to fatigue, irregular sleep patterns, and certain diseases; it may also interfere with other biological rhythms.

FATIGUE

4.7 Technically, fatigue is the name applied to a condition in a sensory receptor or motor end organ characterized by a temporary loss of power to respond because of repeated or continued stimulation. More generally, it connotes weariness from physical overexertion or nervous exhaustion. At a lower level of analysis, fatigue is characterized by either, or both, excessive accumulation of waste products (e.g., lactic acid) or inadequate supplies of blood sugar and oxygen to the affected part.

The condition may be brought on by one or more of a variety of causes in addition to simple overexertion; for example, excessive smoking or drinking, inadequate rest, prolonged muscular tension, anemia, heart disease, or tuberculosis, any of which may induce fatigue directly or predispose the individual to fatigue upon mild exertion.

Prolonged fatigue may lead to sleep disturbances, muscular tension, poor posture, improper diet, and other forms of secondary stress. It may predispose the individual to a number of diseases and interfere with other biological rhythms.

MUSCULAR TENSION

4.8 Muscular tension is intimately related to nervous tension. In fact, the two terms are merely different names for two different aspects of the same psychophysiological phenomenon. Here, we focus on the physiological aspect—muscular tension; we shall treat the psychological aspect—nervous tension—in the next chapter.

Muscular tension is simply a prolonged contraction of the muscles in response to certain emotions (nervous system adjustments to life experience) or to postural defects or other pathological conditions. Contraction of the muscles automatically shortens the connective tissue (fascia). Permanent fascial shortening or thickening results from habitual muscular tension; tearing of the fascia results from sudden or undue stretching of the muscles. Both result in pain and other secondary stresses.

A significant source of muscle tension resulting from emotional disturbances is the wide array of petty annoyances and irritations each of us experiences every day—missing a traffic light when you are in a hurry; having someone cough or sneeze in your face; loud talk, raucous laughter, or other unnecessary noise in a quiet place (for example, a library); having someone stand too close or too far away during an attempted conversation; a nervous tic of another person; a missed putt from six inches on the golf green; a wrong number on the telephone. Each time we experience such a petty annoyance or irritation certain muscles become tense; if these petty stresses continue to occur throughout the day, the muscles remain tense and fail to relax as they should in the normal cycle of tensing and relaxing, they lose resiliency, they become tight and inelastic. When a muscle becomes thus permanently shortened it loses its capacity to release tension. This results in back pain, stiff neck, headaches, and a variety of other complaints.

Conversely, muscles which are insufficiently exercised tend to become flabby, shortened, and equally inelastic. Then when the tensions resulting from petty annoynaces and irritations occur, the weakened muscles may go into spasm or even tear.

Emotional habit patterns resulting in muscular tension frequently carry over into sleep, depriving the victim of needed rest. The resulting fatigue stimulates further tension in a continuing cycle of positive feedback and secondary stress. Thus, emotional responses to any form of stress tend to become habitual, establishing such positive feedback cycles.

DISEASE

4.9 Disease is an impairment or disturbance in the function or structure of the body, or one or more parts thereof, due to the failure of the adaptative mechanisms to adequately counteract one or more varieties of stressors. As we saw in chapter 3 (3.1), according to Bernard, health is a matter of balance, which in turn depends on a relatively constant composition of the inner medium—the "milieu interieur." The organism's ability to resist disease is based on a number of complex balancing actions—the homeostatic process of dynamic stabilization that involves many parts of the body working together cooperatively.

When the homeostatic mechanisms are not operating properly, the body is more susceptible to stressors such as infectious microbes. When the homeostatic mechanisms are working properly, the body is able to resist or overcome invading microbes.

Thus, in the modern view, disease is not a simple state or condition attributable to a single cause; rather, it is a bodily process involving the efforts of the homeostatic mechanisms to deal with the disturbances caused by one or more stressors. The specific bodily response depends on a number of factors, including the individual's genetic composition, previous experience with the specific stressors, current physical and emotional state, etc. In some instances, these responses (the G.A.S.) are abnormal and then constitute diseases in themselves—the diseases of adaptation, discussed next below.

Any disease interferes with normal biological rhythms and tends to induce fatigue, which leads to irregular sleep patterns, muscular tension, and other disturbances.

DISEASES OF ADAPTATION

4.10 The capacity for adaptation is one of the distinguishing characteristics of organic systems. While some man-made inorganic systems may have built into them a limited capacity for adaptation, natural inorganic systems do not have such capacity. Adaptation consists in self-modification to meet the requirements for continued existence under the prevailing conditions of the environment. One of the essential features of the adaptive process is the restriction of the stress response to the minimum amount and area of the body required for maintaining homeostasis. Any failure in this process of coping with a stressor results in one or more of the diseases of adaptation.

Any abnormality of the adaptation process itself—any maladaptation—constitutes a disease of adaptation. The abnormality may take any one of three forms: (1) inadequate adaptive response (hypoadaptation); (2) excessive adaptive response (hyperadaptation); or (3) inappropriate response. Inadequate adaptive response may take the form of insufficient secretion of the anti-inflammatory hormones, resulting in such conditions as the rheumatic and rheumatoid diseases, certain inflammatory diseases of the skin and eyes, and arthritis. Excessive adaptive response may take the form of overproduction of corticoid hormones, leading to such conditions as cardiovascular disease, and kidney disease. Inappropriate adaptive response consists of any unusual or extraordinary hormonal secretion, or any unusual or extraordinary response to stress, and may lead to such conditions as nervous and mental diseases, sexual derangements, digestive diseases, metabolic diseases, cancer, or shock. In fact, many of the most common human maladies are diseases of adaptation, consisting of abnormal adaptive responses to stress by one or more organs or subsystems of the body.

The diseases of adaptation are a form of secondary stress and as such interfere with the body's ability to provide a normal response to future stressors, thus predisposing the body to the stress involved in all of the factors discussed above.

INTERRELATIONSHIPS OF THE PHYSIOLOGICAL CAUSES OF STRESS

4.11 In this chapter, we have considered ten of the more significant physiological factors that may act as causes of stress. They are by no means the only physiological factors, but they are probably the most general and the most pertinent to the subject of executive stress. We have also mentioned some of the interrelationships among these factors.

The intricate complexity of these interrelationships cannot be clearly depicted, but only suggested in two dimensional graphic representation (Figure 4.1). This greatly simplified model does, however, serve to remind us that stress has no single cause or effect. All of the factors we have discussed, as well as many others, are in some way related to each of the other factors. Further, these interrelationships are closely coupled and either a negative or positive influence on any one may start a series of cascading effects on the others. Thus, stress begets stress in a continuing cycle.

This discussion of the physiological causes of stress is, however, only a beginning and, complex as they are, the interrelationships among these factors will seem relatively simple in our final model which includes the psychological and environmental causes of stress, to be discussed in the next two chapters.

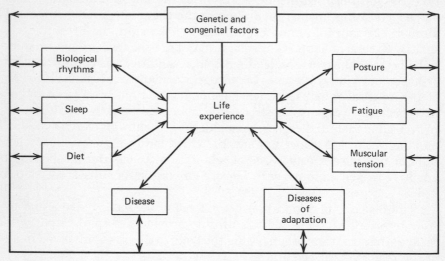

Figure 4.1   Interrelationships of the physiological causes of stress.

Chapter 5
Psychological Causes of Stress

5.0 In the previous chapter we developed a model to facilitate our understanding of the systemic nature of the physiological causes of stress. In this chapter, we shall again utilize the modeling process, this time as a basis for making clear the systemic nature of the psychological causes of stress, which are, in fact, the most common and the most significant stressors for human beings. This chapter is, thus, doubly important to our principal theses. First, because of this high level of significance of the psychological causes of stress. Secondly, because the model we present here serves as a basis for our treatment of the management of stress in Part IV. Unfortunately, however, the development of a model of the psychological causes of stress poses certain difficulties not encountered in the development of our model of physiological causes.

First, the science of psychology is relatively immature compared to the physical sciences and biology; therefore, the concepts and theories are more fluid, less generally accepted. For example, there continue to be fundamental disagreements on such a basic matter as the relationship of mind and brain, with leading neurosurgeons as well as psychologists taking opposing views on the subject. Some insist on a physical identity of the two, the singularity of mind and brain; others are equally insistent that there is no physical basis to be found in the brain for a directing agent such as the mind; still others are uncertain or unwilling to take a position absent more definitive research findings. (See: Penfield, 1975; Aron, 1975; and Arbib, 1972.) There are equally fundamental disagreements about the nature of consciousness and the validity of the concept of altered states of consciousness. (See: Ornstein, 1968, 1972; Tart, 1975.) This controversy has a direct bearing on some of the coping mechanisms (e.g., relaxation and meditation techniques) to be discussed in Part IV.

Secondly, there are still a number of schools of thought or varieties of approaches to the study of behavior (e.g., behaviorism, gestalt psychology, psychoanalysis, and the controversial new discipline of sociobiology), a situation which tends to condition both experiments and the interpretation of their results, leading to some degree of confusion and disagreement.

Thirdly, and perhaps most importantly, we are seriously hampered by the fact that our analysis of the internal operations of the human mind and brain depend, in the end, on the analytical ability of that same device, the human mind and brain. This involves inherent difficulties of perspective and level of analysis—we cannot rise to view the operation of mind and brain from a higher level. We cannot gain the perspective which presumably would be available from a metalevel of existence. While we can probe and test the brain of another individual with electrodes and surgery, we cannot observe the internal operations of this black box, only the inputs and outputs. The only brain we know from the inside is our own and, so far, we have not found any way to secure an objective view of its operations.

Despite these difficulties, we must, in our systems analysis of the psychological causes of stress, be concerned with such matters as mind, brain, consciousness, and behavior. Further, the term behavior must include mental and emotional as well as physical behavior; rational as well as irrational behavior, normal as well as abnormal behavior; conscious as well as unconscious and subconscious behavior; covert as well as overt behavior, that is, internal processes and operations of the central nervous system and other bodily systems as well as publicly observable behavior.

We embark on this venture not without some hesitation and concern lest we mislead an innocent reader. However, if the reader will be forewarned that our discussion of the psychological causes of stress is not entirely based on scientifically demonstrated facts and theories, but as well on the best informed opinion currently available, the dangers will be minimized.

Our model will be constructed on the basis of a concept of the self-system. The self-system in our model is a highly abstracted representation of the individual unit of psychological study: the human organism.

THE SELF-SYSTEM MODEL

5.1 First, we need to set forth certain assumptions about the operation of the human nervous system which underlie our model of the self-system. The fundamental assumption is that the human nervous system is basically cybernetic in its mode of operation; that is, a part of the output of the nervous system flows back to serve as input, thus providing a measure of self-control. A second assumption is that our self-system has inherent powers of self-reorganization. We expound briefly on these two assumptions in the following two subsections, before discussing the elements of our self-system model.

CYBERNETIC MODE

5.2 For the purposes of our discussion, we shall assume that the human organism—and, therefore, our self-system model—operates generally in the manner of the cybernetic model proposed by William T. Powers in his highly original approach to the psychological functioning of the human body. (Powers, 1973.) Of course, we could not hope to do justice to Powers' richly detailed account in these few pages, but we hope to provide the general idea of it as a basis for our own rudimentary model. The description which follows, although owing its basic ideas to Powers, is in fact liberally adapted from his account and he should not be held responsible for our description or our model.

Powers proposes the novel thesis that our nervous system is constructed hierarchically so that each level (except the lowest) provides a measure of control which specifies the behavior of lower levels and thus controls its own input. The inputs, as modified by the controls, constitute our perceptions—the only "reality" we can know. The lowest level of the hierarchy receives input in the form of sensory stimuli, whose sole characteristic is intensity; that is, all stimuli, internal or external, are distinguishable at the lowest level of the nervous system in terms of intensity only. All other distinctions—quantitative or qualitative—are made at higher levels in the neurological hierarchy and, therefore, are conditioned by the internal states and processes of the nervous system at those levels.

Within the neurological system there are continually flowing reference signals which are constantly being modified in a cybernetic manner. Each level, except the lowest, provides the reference signals for the next lower level and is dependent on that next lower level for its input. In many instances, two or more levels provide reference signals for a single lower order level. If these reference signals are compatible they will serve to reinforce each other, thus providing a stronger input to the lower order level. If these reference signals are in conflict, however, they will tend to offset each other. When the conflicting signals are equal in strength, they effectively eliminate control within the range defined by their reference levels, thus resulting in a strong avoidance of either reference level. We shall return to this phenomenon in our discussion of conflict, below (5.10).

Each level, including the lowest, provides input to the next higher level. Each level compares its input from the next lower level with the reference signal from the next higher level; any difference between input and reference signal constitutes an error which serves to increase the tension in some particular muscle or muscle-group. This change in tension stimulates effort to reduce or correct the error, thus restoring the normal level of control—the homeostatic function suggested by Cannon (see section 3.1). The whole process is cybernetic in nature, so that both the output and the input signals serve to modify the continually flowing reference signals.

These reference signals derive, in part, from retrieved recordings of past perceptual signals—in a word, *memory*. Memory, therefore, is not just a mental property, but is distributed throughout the body, residing in every synapse. While the precise microphysical nature of memory is not yet completely understood, one hypothesis, which will serve our purposes as well as any, suggests that it consists of information stored through modification by neural signals of RNA sequences (specific proteins) in the nerve cells. (Nathanson and Greengard, 1977.) These RNA sequences, in turn, participate in the release of neurotransmitters, which determine the specific neural pathways that are activated. The same process accounts for at least one form of learning.

These same reference signals derive also, in part, from recordings from our genetic heritage—inborn tendencies, drives, or instincts, the label varying from one school of psychological thought to another. Such signals would be stored in the DNA as well as the RNA.

There is at least one other component of the reference signals which, for lack of a better term, we shall call motivation. (In psychology, the term *motivation* has no fixed meaning; it may range from the basic appetitive drives to the "best laid plans." We use it here loosely, and advisedly, to cover any type of internal process which serves to energize and direct the self-system toward a given goal.)

In a sense, both genetic heritage and motivation may be subsumed under the term *memory*, if that term is used to embrace all of the stored information in the self-system—whatever form it takes and wherever it is stored. We single out these factors for specific mention merely to insure that the reader understands the comprehensive coverage we intend by these neural reference signals.

The act of retrieving such stored information—variously termed remembering, recall, or recollection—is, of course, itself the product of the flow of neural signals, whether it is performed voluntarily or involuntarily. The resulting neural signals may serve in any of the various roles of other neural signals, producing perceptions in the afferent channels, or functioning as reference signals for lower order levels.

While Powers speculates that there may be even higher levels of control, he limits his model at this stage of development to the nine levels for which he can account on the basis of available knowledge of the neurological system. These nine levels range from the lowest—the spinal reflex—to the highest—self-control of the system, in which the system selects principles to fit self-system concepts.

Our model will not attempt to account for each of these nine levels, but will subsume their existence and the general method of operation described by Powers, in summary, a cybernetic mode.

SELF-REORGANIZING

5.3 We shall also assume that the self-system of our model has inherent powers of self-reorganization. One characteristic of a self-reorganizing system is the capacity to alter its own structure or behavior to permit continued survival in an otherwise hostile environment—a process commonly called adaptation. The following continuum indicates in a general way the relationships among regulation, homeostasis, and adaptation:

	Regulation	Adaptation	
Highly passive or static		Homeostasis	Highly dynamic with varying degrees of reorganization

Any living system is engaged in one or more of these processes throughout its life cycle. The elements of such a system are its variables, which are of three kinds: (1) identifying variables (the factors which makes the system what it is), (2) transformation variables (which serve as buffers between external stimuli and the identifying variables), and (3)other variables (which may perform a variety of functions). If a system is to survive, it must keep each of its identifying variables within certain limits. If any one of these identifying variables undergoes changes which exceed these limits, the system will not survive—at least, not as the same system. Figure 5.1 shows the schematic of system survival, the relationships among the environment and the three types of variables in the system under conditions of survival—that is, with the identifying variables remaining within the required limits. (The dashed lines indicate an incidental relationship.) As may be seen from this schematic representation, the important relationships are those involving the effect of the changing environmental parameters, operating through the transformation variables, on the identifying variables.

When regulating, the transformation variables prevent the parameters from unduly affecting the identifying variables. When the transformation variables are unable to prevent the parameters from unduly affecting the identifying variables, either the transformation variables or the identifying variables will undergo transformation. If the identifying variables are transformed and take on values beyond the defining limits of the system, the system will have failed to survive—it will have adapted. Adaptation, therefore, implies internal reorganization

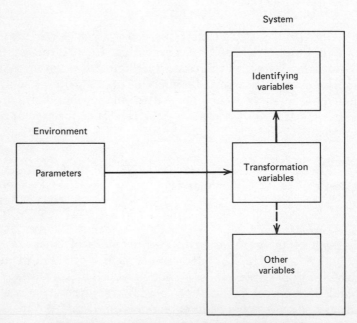

Figure 5.1   Schematic of system survival.

of the parts of the system itself, which, indeed, changes the system.

This view of adaptation regards the self-system as essentially reactive and is probably fairly accurate for most forms of life. In humans, however, adaptation may be active as well as reactive; the human being has the capacity for creative adaptation. Humans may, and do, seek, not merely to survive, but to improve their way of life. Thus, the human self-system is not only homeostatic, but also homeokinetic; it has the capacity to regulate its internal variables so as to produce, not simply a return to the status quo after any disturbance, but an advance to an improved state or level of existence.

Further, humans have the capacity to change their environment as well as themselves, for purposes of survival or improvement of their standard of living. (This is not to suggest that humans are the only organisms endowed with these capacities, but the human being is the focus of interest in this volume.)

Throughout this continuum of activity from regulation to creative adaptation, the self-system effects internal changes, not merely to fit the environment, but to control its own perceptions. This concept is central to Powers' view of the process of behavior and to the theme of this chapter.

ELEMENTS OF THE SELF-SYSTEM

5.4 Within our self-system model we posit for discussion nine elements:

1. Sensory receptors
2. Cognition and appraisal
3. Sensations
4. Perceptions
5. Feelings and emotions
6. Situations
7. Life experience
8. Life decisions
9. Behavior.

With these nine elements we propose to account for at least the more significant psychological causes of stress. We emphasize, again, that these elements do not directly correspond to any of the nine hierarchical levels posited by Powers, but do subsume the general system of operation which he proposes.

The accompanying diagram (Figure 5.2) of our basic model of the self-system and its nine elements indicates their major interrelationships. As our discussion proceeds, it will become apparent that the interrelationships are actually immensely more complex than could possibly be depicted in any diagram.

The self-system in our model is enveloped in its ambient environment. Of the infinite number of events in that environment, some are perceived and some are not. Some nonperceived events impact directly on the self-system; for example, certain forms of electromagnetic radiation—ultraviolet, X-ray, gamma ray. Other nonperceived events have an indirect influence on the self-system; for example, the effects of electromagnetic radiation on the plants and animals which become our food. The events in the ambient environment which are perceived are those which register in one or more of the sensory receptors of the self-system. We shall return to a discussion of these environmental events—perceived and nonperceived—in the next chapter.

As Powers indicated, the stimulation of a sensory receptor produces an input signal which has intensity only. As this signal is transmitted through the neural hierarchy it is controlled by the neural reference signals at one or more levels and becomes output in the form of a sensation, a perception, a feeling or emotion, an action (behavior), etc. In a sense, of course, a perception, a sensation, or an emotion is a form of behavior, but it is internal or covert, although it may be accompanied by certain symptoms in the form of overt behavior. In our model, however, we distinguish among these several types of activities and reserve the term *behavior* for the overt variety.

Overt behavior constitutes and produces further events in the ambient environment, some perceived, some not. The perceived events are those which are observable by the producing self-system or some other self-system. Some of the nonperceived events merely escape observation, some are unobservable—such as the internal (black box) effects of the self-system behavior on some other self-system.

Our concern at the moment is, not with the effects of overt behavior on the ambient environment or on other self-systems, but with the internal events in the self-system of our model. We shall consider each of the nine elements listed above. Six of those elements are merely aspects of cognition and appraisal; we have shown them in the diagram of our model as ovals. They should properly be represented within the box for cognition and appraisal; we have displayed them separately for

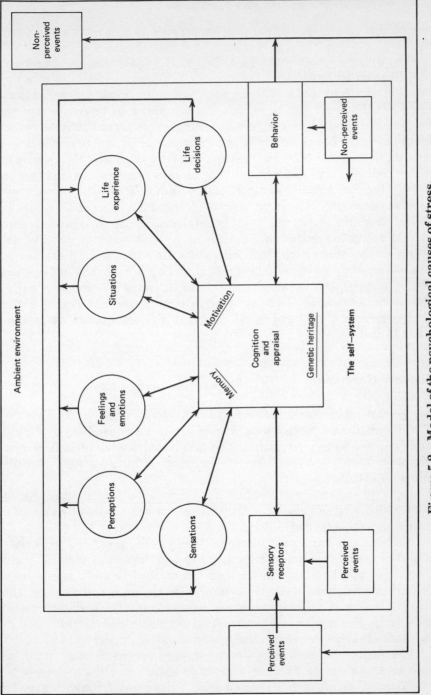

Figure 5.2   Model of the psychological causes of stress.

purposes of emphasis and because we propose to discuss them in some detail.

The direct flow of events, as indicated (in highly simplified form) in our diagram is: from either within the self-system itself or from the ambient environment to the sensory receptors; input to the sensory receptors produces signals which are compared to reference signals from higher neural levels; the resulting error signal may serve as input to higher neural levels or to certain motor control nerve endings, or both; the signals to higher levels may serve similarly; the signals to motor control nerve endings activate certain muscles; the changes in muscle tension serve to control further input. The self-system, how-ever, is not merely a passive, reactive mechanism, responding only to stimuli from the environment. It is a dynamic creative organism, cap-able of initiating action on its own as well as reacting to external stimuli. The source of such initiative lies in the higher neural levels—what we have called cognition and appraisal. The self-system acts in a cybernetic manner to maintain its input at some internally-selected reference level. That level in turn is the net result of the phylogenetic and cultural development of the self-system up to that point in time.

Sensory Receptors

5.5 Our senses include the well-known five—sight, hearing, taste, smell, and touch—plus five or six more depending on defini-tions and the source consulted. The additional senses include: kines-thesis (motion), temperature, pain, balance, nausea, and possibly hunger and thirst.

Input to the sensory receptors may come from the environment or from within the self-system itself. The input stimulates the flow of a neural signal—a flow of electrons.

Such signals vary only in intensity and in the number and variety of higher neural levels to which they flow, in the spinal column, brain stem, or cerebral cortex. Thus, a signal from the eye and a signal from the ear are fundamentally the same, differing only in intensity, the areas of the brain to which they are referred, and the levels of neural processing. The higher level processing, not the initial stimulus makes the distinction between sight and sound—and other perceptions.

The degree of sensitivity of the sensory receptors may, in some instances, determine whether a given event constitutes a stressor or not. Thus, a sound with a given decibel rating and frequency may be sensed as a stressor by one individual and be completely ignored by another individual with less sensitive hearing. Bright sunlight is, in general, more stressful for blue-eyed persons than for brown-eyed persons. Any bright light is more likely to be stressful to a person with normal sight than to one with well-developed cataracts. Similarly with certain odors, a hot plate, a spicy food, etc. For most individuals with normal sensory receptors, however, what happens to the input signal at the second and higher levels of neural processing is of far greater importance. The reference setting determines, in effect, whether any given stimulus will be perceived as a stressor.

Cognition and Appraisal

5.6 In our model, we include the activity of cognition and appraisal all of the activities encompassed by Power's levels two through nine, and any higher levels which may be identified. Thus, as indicated above, and in the diagram of our model, the activity of cognition and appraisal accounts for the effects of genetic heritage, memory, motivation, and any other internal factors or vectors which influence or affect the neural reference signals.

The simplest effect of this neural processing issues in the form of the spinal reflex (e.g., the knee-jerk). From there the range is infinite—from simple sensations and perceptions on up to the highest forms of creative thinking and activity. In the intermediate levels of such activity we find the complete range of feelings and emotions as well as the activities of planning, programming, and decision making. Also included in this range are the self-organizing activities and the initiation of action. In sum, cognition and appraisal embraces all of the psychological activities of the self-system between sensory reception and overt behavior. Some of these activities we single out for special attention in this discussion because of their significance to our principal topic—executive stress.

Sensations

5.7 Sensations constitute one form of output resulting from the neural processing, at one or more levels, of afferent neural currents (input signals) from sensory receptors which have been activated by stimuli from within the self-system or from the ambient environment. For the most part, the neural reference signals which establish the reference settings for sensations flow from the lower brain stem. Sensations involve primarily the lower neurological levels of the self-system and may or may not correspond directly to an entity or event in the physical world. In themselves, sensations may or may not produce noticeable stress in the normal individual, depending on the accompanying circumstances.

Historically, psychologists attempted to maintain a distinction between sensations and perceptions. The term *sensation* was applied to any impression resulting from direct stimulation of a sensory organ. The term *perception* was reserved for higher level interpretations of such sensations. The distinction was at best fuzzy and few scientists continue to seek to maintain it. Old habits die slowly, however, and the two terms continue to be used, albeit almost interchangeably now. In some instances, the term *sensation* may be used specifically to identify the physiological manifestations of the sensory process.

Acknowledging the lack of a scientific distinction, between the two terms, we choose to treat them separately here because we believe that in layman's language there probably is still a tendency to recognize a difference. The term *sensation* appears to be favored when referring to those reactions or experiences which are more general and less localized in nature, such as vertigo, temperature changes, hunger, thirst, pain, nausea, pressure from internal organs (bladder, bowels), etc. These experiences arise from stimulation of the interoceptive or visceral senses. The term *perception* is usually reserved for those experiences arising from stimulation of the exteroceptive sensory organs. Such experiences are usually more precise in nature and more specifically focused; they include sight, hearing, taste, touch, smell.

In effect, then, sensations are more direct, immediate, and elementary in nature. Perceptions are somewhat more complex in nature and include a higher level of conditioning by learning, motivation, and other cultural influences. Both types of experiences, however, are the product of some degree of psychological conditioning at some level of the neural hierarchy, a fact which we shall find very significant when we come to deal with the management of stress.

Whether one may validly maintain a clear distinction probably depends on one's perspective and purpose. In any event, we shall not attempt here to deal with the subject exhaustively, specifying every type of sensation or perception.

One type of experience, whether categorized as sensation or perception, which is highly significant in any discussion of stress is that of *pain*. Pain is at once a primary and a secondary source of stress. It may be experienced at various levels in the neurological system. At the lowest levels, there is the instantaneous response of withdrawal from a painful stimulus such as a pin prick or intense heat. At higher levels, we may have to concentrate attention and thought to identify the location and nature of a given pain, which is otherwise experienced as vague, but nagging discomfort.

Pain is certainly one of the most highly significant types of the secondary causes of stress. Anyone who has ever suffered with a migraine headache, a throbbing toothache, or a festering boil will readily understand the nature of positive feedback in the amplification of the stress that results from some entirely different primary cause (digestive disturbance, exposure of a nerve ending in a tooth, or a bacterial infection). Not only does stress cause pain, but pain causes stress, each reinforcing the other.

The stimulus for pain may be internal or external. Muscle spasm, stomach gas, coronary infarct, all may cause pain as severe as or more severe than, that induced by a bruise or a burn resulting from an outside stimulus. One of the most common manifestations of undue stress is the tension headache brought on by prolonged contraction of the muscles of the face, head, and neck. The tension headache, in addition to being a symptom of stress, is also a source of further stress. Even the anticipation of pain is sufficient to create emotional disturbances thus tending to intensify perceived pain. (Melzack, 1973.)

Pain and certain other simple sensations when prolonged or repetitively experienced may lead to feelings or emotions of anxiety, worry, and even fear (fear of disease, weakness, or debilitation). (Mines, 1974.) Such sensations may also lead to stress-producing behavior—over-dependence on drugs, alcohol, tobacco, or other types of escape mechanisms; aggressiveness, hostility, or other types of fight mechanisms; or to immobility—all of which we shall discuss in slightly more detail below.

Perceptions

5.8 Contrary to widespread popular belief, there are no immaculate perceptions. Every signal produced by the sensory receptors is simply the initial stimulus in a series of higher level, neural processing activities which may or may not eventuate in a perception. At each successive level of this series the incoming signal from the next lower level is compared with a reference setting established by the reference signal from the next higher level. This interaction produces a new signal which is further processed at the next higher level.

The reference signals, and thus the reference settings at each level, are the product of the genetic and cultural development of the individual up to the moment of interaction and thus are constantly changing. Thus, memory, motivation, genetic heritage, and inferences drawn from the sensory signal combine to form the perception. The sensory signal is only one of many factors involved in perception. From these facts, Powers draws the conclusion that behavior controls perception. The term *behavior,* in this sense, includes the internal behavior of our neural hierarchy.

If, then, we control our own perceptions, we have the power to control one very considerable source of stress because much executive stress derives from what we see or hear. Every executive is fully aware of the fact that mere observation of what others are doing or saying (or even writing) can produce varying degrees of stress for the observer. What the executive is probably not aware of is the fact that the source of that stress is not in the acts of others, but in the observer's own perception of those acts, which, in turn, depends on the particular reference setting for that perception. One's perceptions constitute one's only reality, but since one controls one's own perceptions, one can control this source of stress.

Feelings and Emotions

5.9 The terms *feelings and emotions* are not scientific terms and have no precise meanings in psychology. Furthermore, and unfortunately, there are no generally accepted terms which encompass the psychological phenomena suggested by these terms. Accordingly, one still finds the terms used, sometimes apologetically, and with widely varying meanings, in modern psychological texts and research reports.

In general, the term *emotion* denotes a complex physiological disturbance of the normal homeostatic state which originates from a psychological stimulus—an affective process. The disturbance is subjectively experienced as an awareness of a bodily (neural) state. It is objectively manifested in specific bodily changes in the smooth muscles, glands, organs, blood composition, blood pressure, galvanic skin response, and overt behavior changes. Emotion is generally distinguished from simple sensations, organic feelings, sentiments, attitudes, moods, and temperaments—all of which are also affective processes of varying degrees of complexity, but which are not necessarily disturbances of the homeostatic state.

Some sensations may arouse certain feelings and emotions, but, as may be seen in Figure 5.2, above, all other elements of the basic model also influence feelings and emotions, either directly or indirectly. Thus, feelings and emotions arise from the interactions of a complex flow of neural currents in the nervous system, involving a wide variety of positive and negative feedback circuits.

Although the pattern of development is far from clear, there is some evidence to indicate that the ability to experience and differentiate specific feelings and emotions is not innate in the human organism, but is learned or developed as a product of the interactions of the normal process of biological maturation and gradually accumulating experience.

Two emotions which become differentiated in the early months of the infant's first year are fear and anger. These two and five others are most frequently mentioned in the literature as being significantly related to stress. Recognizing that these seven feelings and emotions represent only a very small portion of the total spectrum of human experiences, we nevertheless restrict our discussion to these as being sufficiently representative for our purposes and as probably being the most significant for executive stress. The seven are:

1. Anxiety

2. Guilt

3. Worry

4. Fear

5. Anger—Rage

6. Jealousy

7. Loss and bereavement.

As our subsequent analysis will show, none of these feelings and emotions is either simple or elemental in nature. Rather, each is a complex, dynamic process resulting from the interaction of a number of neural currents with a variety of organs and other subsystems of the body. Further, each neural current, each organ and subsystem, and every interaction involves a complex pattern of positive and negative feedback cycles, which, in turn, serve to stimulate reinforcing and counteracting currents in endless variety. Thus, no two individuals can have the same reaction to any one event and no single individual will ever have two identical reactions. We mention this complexity, not because we have any intention of getting involved in such clinical details, but simply to emphasize the systemic nature of the phenomenon with which we are dealing—stress. Our principal concern will be with the macrolevel manifestations and interrelationships of these internal activities.

Anxiety. Anxiety is essentially a reaction of the self-system to perceived but unspecified threats. When it becomes severe enough to disrupt normal functioning, it is considered pathological. It is a chronic, complex process which is characteristic of various nervous and mental disorders. The physiological symptoms include disturbed breathing, increased heart activity, vasomotor changes, musculoskeletal disturbances such as trembling or paralysis, increased sweating, etc. Psychologically, it is characterized by a distressing and depressing awareness of imminent, but unspecified, dangers accompanied by a feeling of powerlessness, of inability to cope with the threats. Untreated, the feelings of apprehension tend to magnify, to become all-absorbing; there is a felt demand for alertness which leads to muscular and nervous tension, physical exhaustion, increased uncertainty, and an inability to deal with reality—a neurosis.

One potential source of anxiety for many of us is the awareness of death, with all of its uncertainties. But the uncertainties of life also serve, for some, as a source of anxiety. The very life style of the executive, for example, tends to produce a susceptibility to anxiety because of its inherent uncertainties. The constant upward mobile striving, with recurring job changes and relocations, frequent job related travel, and weakened family ties tend to foster feelings of impermanence. Restrictions on one's freedom of action imposed by higher officials, boards and committees, unions, government, etc., all conflict with one's desire for autonomy and tend to lead to feelings of inadequacy (see Schoonmaker, 1969) and fear of failure. Prolonged feelings of anxiety lead to worry, fear, and other stress-producing behavior.

Guilt and Worry. Guilt and worry are generally classified in current psychological writings as subcategories of anxiety, but, unlike general anxiety, guilt and worry involve specified or specifiable threats. Guilt is usually characterized by a decrease in self-esteem and an urge to expiate, or make retribution for, a real or imagined wrong—a breach of some ethical, moral, or religious standard. The guilty person usually feels unworthy, bad, evil, or remorseful; the individual may develop feelings of self-blame or self-hate for such a transgression.

Worry is characterized by continuing and repetitive return to a particular thought in a wholly unconstructive manner; baffled mental activity constitutes worry. The etymology of the word accounts for the connotation of repetitiveness and agitation in popular usage; one "worries" an idea or feeling as a terrier worries a rat.

Guilt focuses on past events, worry on anticipated events. Both tend to lead to immobility as the victim, feeling powerless to act or uncertain about what action to take, becomes absorbed in the feeling to the neglect of other activities. The futility of both is epitomized in Mark Twain's comment: "I am an old man and have known many troubles, but most of them never happened." Both guilt and worry lead to other forms of stress-producing behavior.

Fear. Fear, like worry, is a future oriented state. Although both anxiety and fear are reactions to a feeling of threat, anxiety is an emotional response to a nonspecific threat, while fear is the response to a specific threat. Most of us have fears of many types—fear of failure, fear of rejection, ego damage of one sort or another, etc. Many of us spend our lives avoiding achievement because of the fear of failure. The fear of rejection stems from our sensitivity to what others do or say; we tend to interpret innocent or humorous actions or remarks as criticism of ourselves. When we make ourselves vulnerable in this way, we set ourselves up for rejection. The fear of having our egos damaged generally results from the process of setting and attempting to achieve goals. We know that if the goals are not achieved we will encounter ego damage, so, to protect our egos and to avoid rejection, some of us tend to avoid setting goals.

The potential fears of mankind are innumerable: the fear of pain, the fear of punishment, the fear of losing one's mind, to mention just a few. Uncontrolled fears lead to worry and other stress-producing behavior.

Anger—Rage. Anger is an intense emotion characterized by acute reactions of the autonomic nervous system and by overt or covert agonistic behavior. It generally takes the form of a temporary outburst with possible loss of emotional control. In its more violent form, with an even higher degree of autonomic activity and definite loss of self-control, it becomes rage; with its elevated adrenal and other autonomic activity, rage dissipates more slowly and, hence, is usually more stressful.

Anger, while stressful, is not necessarily harmful in itself, but its repression is definitely stressful, both emotionally and physically. Executives whose interpersonal relationships require frequent repression of anger, may incur such adverse results as high blood pressure, ulcers, and other psychosomatic disorders all severely detrimental to health. Frequent experiences of anger, or rage, or its repression may lead to feelings of guilt and other forms of stress-producing behavior. The repression of anger or rage—or any other strong emotion—constitutes an interruption of a normal biological cycle and leads to frustration and other adverse effects of stress (see 5.10, below).

Jealousy. Jealousy is a form of envy and entails feelings of possessiveness; a loved person is essentially viewed as property or chattel and any degree of affection shown by the loved one to a third person, or by a third person to the loved one, arouses feelings of envy, hatred, and suspicion. Thus, jealousy involves a desire to dominate, control, or enslave another person, to assert complete possession. The problem with possessiveness is that it tends to produce the exact opposite of what is really wanted, namely, stress instead of tranquility; and it adversely influences the loved one, with negative feedback for the possessor. Overcontrol tends to destroy the personality of the loved one with the result that he or she becomes uninteresting, and possibly full of resentment.

Jealousy and envy stem from a basic desire to overcome inherent feelings of insecurity, and we are all vulnerable to such feelings from time to time. The harmful effects derive primarily from chronic attacks which may lead to feelings of worry, fear, and anxiety, or anger.

Loss and Bereavement. Loss is a feeling of harm or privation resulting from change. Any change may stimulate the feeling of loss: changes in personal relationships (love, support, etc), changes in personal capacity (sensory abilities, power to act, etc.), changes in material circumstances (income, residential or occupational location, material possessions, etc.), even unavoidable developmental changes (maturing, promotion, demotion, transfers, reorganizations, etc.).

Bereavement is a more specific term. While loss conveys the general meaning of harm or deprivation, bereavement specifies the grief feeling due to the loss by death of a loved one. The loss of a spouse by death is probably one of the most severe forms of psychological stress to which human beings are subjected, yet many of us will experience such a loss at some time in our lives.

Feelings of loss or bereavement may lead to any one or more of the other six feelings or emotions discussed above or to other forms of stressful behavior.

Interrelationships of Stress-Related Feelings and Emotions. The above listing of feelings and emotions includes those most frequently mentioned in the literature as being stress-related. Although the definitions and descriptions are less than comprehensive, they will probably suffice for our purposes. More important, at this point, than comprehensive descriptions or definitions (which may easily be found in the literature of psychology and psychiatry) is the recognition of the way in which these feelings and emotions may lead to stress. A first step in this direction is the identification of the interrelationships of these affects. Figure 5.3 suggests the main lines of such interrelationships.

Jealousy leads to fear of being left alone, crimes of passion (based on anger or rage), worry, or general anxiety. Two of the most common reactions to bereavement are guilt and anger, but both loss and bereavement lead to anxiety, fear, and worry. Anger leads to guilt; fear and anxiety lead to worry. Thus, all the other stress-related feelings and emotions eventually lead to terminal feelings of guilt and worry.

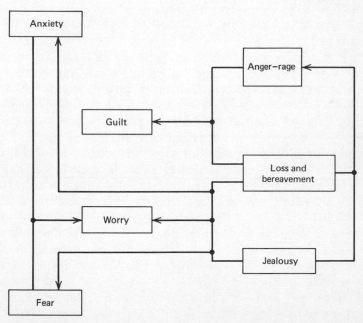

Figure 5.3   Interrelationships of stress-related feelings and emotions.

Situations

5.10 A situation, as we use the term, is simply an individual's conception of a particular state or condition in which one perceives oneself to be at any given time or times. One's conception of the situation is a product of some combination of sensations, feelings, and emotions, as conditioned by temperament, mood, memory, attitude, inference, etc.

The important point to recognize is that "situations" do not necessarily correspond to reality, but are the result of cognition and appraisal and are, therefore, highly individual in nature. Thus, one particular combination of sensations, feelings, or emotions may be experienced as a stressful situation by one individual while it is not by another.

While there may be more, we shall restrict our attention to only four types of stressful situations: 1) threat, 2) the "near miss phenomenon," 3) frustration, and 4) conflict.   -

Threat. An inference drawn from some set of events (which may be inherently neutral in nature) of impending unpleasantness—of evil, injury, damage, loss, disaster, etc.—may be experienced as a threatening situation.

Any given individual may interpret as a threat some completely innocent statement by another individual. More impersonally, one may see as a threat some combination of natural events which have absolutely no direct bearing on one's future. The anticipation of any painful or harmful experience is experienced as a threat, and the anticipated pain or harm need not even be directed at oneself.

Grinker and Spiegel found that for men under the stress of combat fear is cumulative. (Grinker and Spiegel, 1945). Janis found little relationship between the objective seriousness of a surgical operation, as judged by surgeons, and the fear that was reported by the patient. (Janis, 1958). Wolff found that patients could be threatened by non-sympathetic attitudes of an interviewer. (Wolf and Goodell, 1968). Lazarus and, independently, Levi found that the viewing of certain types of films can induce physiological manifestations of stress. (Lazarus, 1966; Levi, 1967).

The perceived sources of threat are unlimited, but the perceptions of threat are all internal—the products of the self-system, itself.

The Near-Miss Phenomenon. One type of "situation" which has not been investigated to any significant extent is termed by Lazarus, the "near-miss phenomenon." (Lazarus, 1966). An individual successfully copes with an emergency which, in itself, has imminent possibilities of danger or disaster, and only after the danger has passed exhibits the normal symptoms of stress. Lazarus asks why the stress reaction is delayed in such instances until after the confrontation with danger. The occurrence of the phenomenon is sufficiently common to require no further elaboration. Most of us have either experienced it ourselves or have witnessed its occurrence in others—the peak of excitement and immediate let-down following the near-miss of an automobile accident, a precipitous fall, an encounter with a vicious animal, etc.

One possible answer to Lazarus's question may be that the individual's initial reaction to the perceived threat is subconscious, automatic, or autonomic in nature. When the danger has passed, the individual actually relives the experience consciously and again goes through the triphasic general adaptation syndrome—alarm, defense, exhaustion. Another possibility is that the individual's initial reaction to the perceived threat may constitute the first stage of the G.A.S. (the alarm or fight reaction)—with heightened alertness, muscle tension, keen perception, improved coordination, etc. The apparent symptoms of stress which follow the confrontation may be simply the let-down of the third stage (exhaustion). In any event, the "near-miss" phenomenon, as a perceived situation, deserves further study as an obvious source of stress.

Frustration. When individuals perceive some (specific or nonspecific) interference in their efforts to effect a course of action which will result in a desired goal, or if they encounter undue delay in the fulfillment of the desired goal, then they experience frustration.

Whereas threat involves potential or future harm, frustration involves present or past harm.

Although even those most expert in the study of stress have failed to provide a complete explanation for the fact, frustration is actually more likely than excessive muscular exertion to produce some of the diseases of adaptation—peptic ulcers, migraine, hypertension, psychosomatic pain. In fact, physical exercise may actually aid in relieving or help the stressed individual to resist the adverse effects of mental frustration.

There is, however, some indication that frustration may result from interference with an innate cyclicity of biological activity. As we saw in our discussion of biological rhythms (4.3) there are a number of regular cycles in human existence. These cycles are, apparently, due in part to the periodic, alternate accumulation and exhaustion of chemical energy sources in the cells and tissues of the self system. Any interference with the completion of one of these normal cycles means that accumulated waste products are not properly eliminated or that necessary energy sources are not replaced on a timely basis. The inevitable result is damage to the involved cells or tissues. Since our behavior depends on, or consists of, these flows of energy, any interference with the completion of the normal cyclicity of such behavior produces similar damage.

Conflict. The activity of opposing forces constitutes conflict. Human conflict may be interpersonal or intrapersonal. We discuss interpersonal conflict under the heading of Behavior, below (5.13). Our concern at this point is with internal conflict—a process involving the perception of two incompatible goals, both of which the perceiver wants to attain at once, but neither of which can be attained without foregoing the other.

In terms of Powers' model (discussed above, 5.2) internal conflict may be explained as an encounter between two control systems, both of which attempt to control the same lower order system, but in opposite directions. Thus, each conflicting control system effectively prevents the other from attaining a zero error level. The lower order system, receiving opposing signals, acts on the average or vector sum (which becomes the virtual reference signal) and is, accordingly, reduced to immobility or a narrow range of activity—at least with respect to the quantities or reference levels being controlled by the conflicting signals. Conflict, in these terms, may occur at any control level in the neurological hierarchy, but only when the two control systems control the same kinds of variables and in opposing directions. The net result of such conflicts is behavior (and, therefore, perceptions) which is not intended by higher order systems; lower order systems will tend to avoid intended perceptions, and will behave in ways that interfere with achievement of the higher order goals. Chronic, severe conflict of control systems produces a state of anxiety (discussed above, 5.9)

The individual suffering from inner conflicts may develop certain defenses or may reorganize internal control systems. The defenses may take the form of avoidance of situations requiring use of the conflicting systems, imaginative substitution of information for the uncontrolled perceptual signals, or attempts at rationalizing away the conflict. Such defenses will not resolve the conflict, but will, in the long run, tend to exacerbate the intrinsic errors. Any attempt by the self-system to defend itself against the threat of experiencing the intrinsic error due to conflict is bound to fail. The only solution lies in reorganization of the conflicting control systems, that is, a transformation of the identifying variables (see 5.3, above).

Life Experience

5.11 We used the term *life experience*, in our model of the physiological causes of stress to comprise the entire set of events which constitute the individual's own unique history—a process of transitions. (See 4.2). We indicated there that some of the events were traumatic in nature and constituted passages from one stage of life to another. Any of these events might have emotional implications and any of them might be stressful. As we use the term in our model of the psychological cause of stress, life experience comprises the entire set of psychological events in an individual's lifetime. Any of these events may also have physiological implications and any of them may be stressful.

For purpose of discussion, we divide life experience here into three categories: life changes, life passages, and life crises. These three categories overlap somewhat so that for the present, crisp definitions are not possible, but they, nevertheless, do provide a convenient basis for our discussion.

In this discussion, we emphasize the traumatic events. The pleasant experiences which occur within an individual's lifetime are less significant than the traumatic events for purposes of stress analysis.

Life Changes. The original work on life changes was done in the 1930's by Adolf Meyer, of Johns Hopkins University, a research physician. His life-chart idea was refined and expanded during the 1950's and 1960's by a group of scientists under the leadership of Thomas Holmes and Richard Rahe, of the University of Washington's School of Medicine. (See Holmes and Rahe, 1967). Since then, many researchers have been investigating the effects of life changes on individuals; much of this work is related to stress research. For example, NATO sponsored a symposium on "Life Stress and Illness," and investigators from Finland, Great Britain, Greece, Norway, Sweden, Switzerland, and the United States participated. (Gunderson and Rahe, 1974). The report of this symposium tends to confirm the findings of Holmes and Rahe.

Life changes are incidents which require a coping response of some magnitude. The life changes that have been studied are common to the Western way of life. They include divorce, marital separation, jail term, injury, illness, being fired from work, business readjustment, changes in work hours or conditions, and various other changes. Some researchers assign each such event a point value in terms of life change units (LCU's). The point values, or LCU's, are intended to indicate the degree of coping response required; for example, the point value of 100 is assigned to the "death of a spouse," which has been confirmed in most studies as the event which requires the highest degree of coping response. In contrast, a change in sleeping habits has a point value of only 16, while a minor violation of law is only 11. (Holmes and Masuda, 1972).

Life change units are cumulative and there is a limit to the lifetime coping ability of an individual. Each stress experienced by the individual depletes a fixed reserve of adaptability. This conforms to Selye's findings (see 3.9). Further, there are certain critical threshold levels; the accumulation of a certain number of points tends to predispose the individual to more serious stress in the form of physical or mental illness.

Life Passages. Each individual's personality continues to evolve throughout his or her lifetime. During this period there occur certain relatively stable intervals and certain critical turning points. The stable periods constitute stages and the turning points are the transitions or life passages. Studies by Gould (1974), Levinson (1978), and others (e.g., Veiga, 1973; Davitz and Davitz, 1976) indicate that certain stages are predictable and that most normal individuals will pass through each of these stages at the appropriate age level.

Some writers identify as many as seven stages, each characterized by certain critical psychological states of mind, beginning at age sixteen and ending at age fifty. The particular stages and their characterizations are not strictly relevant to our discussion, but the basic idea of life passages is.

Life passages, in this sense then, are the critical turning points in life. They are stressful to the extent that they require significant changes of attitude. Old solutions to problems do not seem to work, so there is the stress of finding new solutions. At mid-life, new quandaries arise with the realization that there is only so much time left. Identity, authenticity, and personal renewal problems badger us. If we are already under stress, these critical turning points tend to intensify it.

Life Crises. A life crisis may be defined as a radical change of status in a person's life, taking on emergency proportions, and potentially leading to a catastrophe. Life crisis depends on individual cognition and appraisal (as discussed above, 5.6) because what one individual sees as a radical change or life crisis, another individual will take in stride. Alternatively, the same individual at a different time in life will react differently to very similar conditions. For example, the loss of a job may not be a crisis for a young unmarried man living with his parents, but after he is married and loaded down with heavy financial commitments, this same person is likely to respond as if it were a crisis. As another example, a traffic violation citation is not a crisis to some people, but if this particular traffic violation means loss of driving privileges, then it could adversely affect the individual's life style, and, therefore, may be perceived as a catastrophe.

The life changes list of Holmes and Rahe represents a potential menu of stressful items which are candidates for life crisis. Applicability for life crisis status from the life changes list, however, depends upon the individual's cognition and appraisal of the events.

The incidence of life crises appears to be highly correlated with killing or crippling problems like heart disease, and other diseases of adaptation.

Life Decisions

5.12 This part of our model relies on the psychological technique of transactional analysis and is made up of two parts: life positions and life scripts. Life decisions are not to be confused with decisions that are routinely made on a daily basis or tough decisions that individuals occasionally make when it is difficult to select between alternatives. Rather, life decisions have long term psychological consequences that will determine the course of an individual's life and mental health.

Life Positions. The transactional analysis school of thought claims that fairly early in life we take one of four positions, with respect to ourselves and other people:

1. I'M NOT OK—YOU'RE OK

2. I'M NOT OK—YOU'RE NOT OK

3. I'M OK—YOU'RE NOT OK

4. I'M OK—YOU'RE OK. (Harris, 1967).

According to Harris, sometime during the first three years of life a child makes final the decision to take a chosen position from one of the first three categories above. At this stage of life, the decision is undoubtedly made on emotional grounds. The most common choice is: "I'M NOT OK—YOU'RE OK." The fourth position is more likely to be based on a rational process of determining how the individual is going to cope in life. Rarely is this position taken before adulthood, if then.

Our interpersonal relations can be smooth or stressful, depending on the life position we adopt. The "I'M NOT OK"—position handicaps the individual when dealing with others, especially when others are seen as "OK". When one operates in the "I'M NOT OK" position one invites more stress due to interpersonal relations than is necessary. For the executive, who is continually relating to others, this is an important aspect of the stress problem.

Figure 5.4, presents a graphic model of life positions. As may be seen from the model, the most common position involves life scripting.

Life Scripts. The work on life scripts had only started when Harris wrote his book. He mentioned that Claude Steiner was then one of the principal investigators. Steiner suggests that a script is essentially a blueprint for a life course. He develops three categories of life scripting:

1.   Banal scripts
2.   Tragic scripts
3.   Script-free living. (Steiner, 1974).

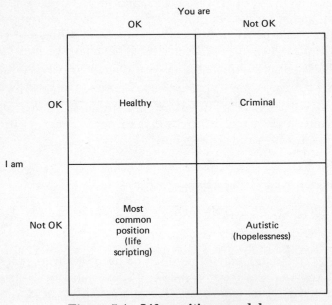

Figure 5.4   Life positions model.

According to Steiner, most people live banal scripts, a minority of people live tragic scripts, and those living script-free lives are the exceptions.

In a banal script, the autonomy of the individual is restricted (there appears to be no choice open to the individual); this is generally due to parental injunctions and attributions. Tragic scripts are more severe and dramatic, as opposed to the melodramatics of a banal script. A tragic script, such as living the life of an alcoholic or drug-addict, is a script that leads to self-destruction.

Becoming script-free means living a life of choices rather than following preordained scripts; freedom from scripts can be based only on an "I'M OK—YOU'RE OK" position. In addition, Steiner believes that the following factors (or ideals) contribute to a healthier life style: truthfulness (rather than lies, secrets, and games), cooperation (rather than competition and power plays), and love.

Life scripts appear to restrict an individual's ability to function in a completely free way. For the executive living with a life script, any loss of freedom to act is going to inhibit effectiveness, and will eventually manifest itself in terms of stress.

Effect of Life Decisions on Self-System. As a result of taking positions, and consequently adopting scripts, significant definitions of one's own self-system are formulated by the individual. These self-definitions, in turn, influence the other components of our self-system model.

Both life positions and life scripts have a bearing on the mental health of the executive. By taking the healthy life position and developing a script-free life, mental health is improved and the ability to manage stress would seem to be enhanced. But taking a life position not conducive to mental health and living with a life script would appear to exacerbate even small stresses.

One consequence of this line of reasoning is that the executive is more likely to discover the principal sources of stress in his or her own life style rather than in his or her ambient environment. We have, so far, identified a significant number of physiological and psychological *potential* stressors. What we are now suggesting is that the greatest of these lies in the executive's own attitudes—the decision as to whether these potential stressors become actual stressors depends upon his or her own attitudes and life style. The executive alone controls the effects of the potential stressors on himself or herself. We shall return to this theme in Part IV.

Behavior

5.13 Beyond the definition of behavior as the activity of an organism, there is no general agreement among psychologists about specifically what phenomena should be included in the coverage of the term. The behaviorists would, in general, limit the term to overt or publicly observable activities of an organism. Others would include introspectively observable processes or phenomena—pain, hunger, worry, fear, etc. While still others would include, as well, unconscious processes, those not normally directly accessible even to the experiencing organism. Since the G.A.S. includes a number of processes and effects in all three categories, we adopt the broadest definition for purposes of our discussion. At a relatively low level of resolution, we may define behavior as the output of any of the nine or more hierarchical levels of (Powers' model of) the neurological system. In a sense, then, any of the processes we have been discussing so far—sensations, feelings, emotions, cognition and appraisal, etc.—constitute behavior of one type or another. Further, each of these processes may be stress-producing and may also be a result of stress. At this point, however, and at a somewhat higher level of resolution, we are going to focus on those types of behavior which we have previously identified as the basic response of the organism in the first stage of the G.A.S.: the fight or flight reaction. As we have seen, these types of behavior result from stress and are, in themselves, stress-producing.

Reverting to our model of the self-system (Figure 5.2), we may observe a number of inputs to behavior. Certain sensations produce immediate, autonomic behavior—the spinal reflex, the tendon reflex—but perhaps the sensation of most interest in terms of its relation to stress is that of pain. We have also identified a number of stress-producing feelings and emotions which lead directly or indirectly to stressful behavior. In addition, we have seen how the cognition and appraisal of certain types of "situations" lead to stressful behavior. As indicated above, while each of these inputs to behavior itself constitutes a type of behavior, our interest now focuses on the fight or flight response and its after effects.

The Fight or Flight Response. The fight or flight response may best be represented, in diagrammatic form, as a continuum:

Flight   Fight
◄──►
                              Immobility

The categories of behavior represented on this continuum comprise what some psychologists now term agonistic behavior—a somewhat more precise scientific term for what is more popularly and generally known as hostile behavior.

Agonistic behavior is adaptive activity in response to injury or the threat of injury, whether from the physical environment, predators, or members of the same species. Avoidance of injury is a behavior trait found throughout the animal kingdom—probably an aspect of the basic drive for self-preservation.

The Fight Reaction. The fight reaction may take a variety of forms within the limits of the above mentioned continuum: aggression or attack, defensive fighting, defensive posturing, defensive vocalization. Fighting, offensive or defensive, appears to be the almost universal response to injury or any other painful stimulus. (How many times have you kicked a stool or rock which you stumbled over in the dark?) In fact, the basic adaptive function of all agonistic behavior appears to be to repulse the individual (or object) who (or which) threatens to produce, appears to have produced, or has produced the painful or unpleasant stimulus. Thus, pain and fear (of pain or other harm) are the principal stimuli for agonistic behavior.

The processes of evolution and cultural development, however, have produced significant diversity in the adaptive response of human beings to injury or the threat of injury. In modern humans, the fight reaction may manifest itself in varying degress of aggression ranging from simple self-assertiveness, through gentle verbal criticism and competitiveness, to active hostility and physical assault. The locus of the threat or injury which may serve as a stimulus has been extended considerably. Defensive fighting has come to be accepted as the normal response to injury or threat of injury to a spouse, offspring, sibling, friend, associate, acquaintance, or any other member of a given society, as well as oneself. There have been changes, too, in the human view of the nature of the threat or injury which serves as the stimulus to agonistic behavior. The stimulus need no longer involve bodily harm or possible death. We have become conditioned to respond in the same manner to symbolic or psychological stimuli. For example, the loss or threat of loss of the companionship of another individual (wife, husband, child, sweetheart, friend, etc.) is usually viewed as an injury to one's ego (if not one's body) and frequently stimulates agonistic behavior. In its early stages, we call such behavior jealousy, but as we saw above (5.9), it may lead to anger and rage.

The human being's highly developed reasoning powers and linguistic ability also serve as fruitful sources of stimuli to agonistic behavior. We experience a considerable degree of comfort and satisfaction in those unusual periods of concord when we find ourselves in the company of others who express agreement with our ideas, but even slight differences in the way of expressing congeneric or isomorphic ideas may lead to agonistic behavior ranging from mild expressions of disagreement to violent actions. Any attack on, or threat to, the sanctity of one's beliefs, values, or knowledge is seen as an attack on oneself and arouses the same type of reaction. The inherent tendency is to drive away the offending view or the individual who holds it. When such disagreements occur at high enough levels in the social or political hierarchy they may even erupt into warfare; at lower levels, the reactions are basically the same, but less widespread. In fact, in the historical period, ideas have probably been the most fruitful source of agonistic behavior among human beings. Disagreements over ideas—one's view of the truth or matters of doctrine—have resulted in long-lasting and violent struggles which continue to this day. Such struggles have been more frequent, and more violent, than any which arose from territoriality or threats or injuries of a physical nature.

Freud saw aggression as one of the primary instincts; Adler viewed it as a basic drive to overcome feelings of inferiority. Regardless of its phylogenetic origin or the nature of the immediate stimulus, we now know that agression is accompanied by heightened activity of the neuroendocrine systems of the body and may lead to certain diseases of adaptation, of either an organic or psychosomatic nature.

However, the conscious or unconscious inhibition (suppression or repression) of aggression may also lead to quite similar results. We have already recognized the role of the hypothalamus in the G.A.S. (3.5); its activity serves to magnify and prolong the internal effects of the stress stimulus. Long continued or often repeated experiences of agonistic behavior may lead to a condition of irritability, of a lowered threshold to further stimulation and the establishment of a vicious cycle. Continued or repeated stress cybernetically conditions one's cognition and appraisal, life experience, and life decisions, tending to narrow one's perspective by increasing anticipation of agonistic behavior, thus leading to further stress. The process is reminiscent of the old Chinese saying: "Insanity consists in doubling one's efforts, while forgetting the goals." In this manner, a series of even weak stimuli may result in a state of heightened emotional response. The normal emotional reactions of anger or fear may become magnified as a result of repeated reinforcement. Eventually, the response may reach intolerable levels. The net result, obviously, is the production of the same diseases of adaptation as are produced by the original stimulus when the response is uninhibited. These include, but are not limited to: migraine headaches, hypertension, hyperthyroidism, cardiac neuroses, fainting spells (the vasodepressor syncope), rheumatoid arthritis, and diabetes. (Alexander, 1950, p. 67.)

The Flight Reaction. Whether the initial arousal stage of the G.A.S. leads to fight or flight appears to depend upon whether anger or fear emerges as the predominant feeling. This alternative depends, in turn, on the assessment of the situation resulting from the interaction of the higher level neurological processes with the stimulus input. This assessment, of course, may be instantaneous, or may take a considerable length of time, again depending on the individual's further assessment of the urgency of decision. Obviously, if this latter assessment is inappropriately delayed, the results may range from unfortunate to fatal. The entire process depends on the nature of the reference signals circulating in the nervous system and their interaction with the afferent signals arising from the stress stimulus. When fear emerges as the predominant emotional response, there is still an alternative; the resultant behavior may take the form of defensive fighting, immobility, or flight. Unsuccessful flight—failure to escape the noxious stimulus—may result in defensive fighting or immobility.

Successful flight—escape from the stress stimulus—will probably produce relief from stress, but may be followed by feelings of anger, guilt, worry, anxiety or some combination of these depending on one's subsequent state and one's review and reassessment of the original stressful situation and one's reactions to it. Such feelings, as we have seen, lead to further stress from internal stimuli, thus continuing the reaction cycle.

Therefore, whether the behavioral outcome of the stress response is fight or flight, the emotional arousal pattern and the subsequent psychological and physiological effects are essentially the same—the diseases of adaptation: somatic, psychosomatic, and psychological. Likewise, the inhibition of the flight response will have similarly adverse results for the same reasons.

Immobility. In other species, the adaptive mechanism of "freezing" or feigning death emerged as a third alternative in the fight or flight response to stress. Absolute immobility is apparently much less stimulating to the attacker in most species and, therefore, has obvious adaptive value as a means of self-preservation and avoidance of injury. As with the other forms of agonistic behavior, this tactic, too, has undergone some changes as a result of our evolutionary and cultural development. For example, in addition to physical immobility we may respond with psychological immobility.

Psychological immobility may take the form of refusal to make a decision, vacillation (wavering between contradictory decisions), or inability to make a decision. In refusing to make a decision, one consciously adopts an attitude of dependency—looking to others to make decisions for one and to provide needed psychological support in the form of advice and guidance. In vacillating, the individual appears desirous of making a decision, but uncertain about which of two or more contradictory or conflicting decisions to adopt; the individual is ambivalent, torn between opposing or mutually inconsistent attitudes or goals. While the ambivalent individual can at least entertain the possibility of choosing between conflicting decisions, there are some individuals who, in certain situations, are simply unable to reach even that stage of decisiveness; they are overcome by feelings of helplessness. In effect, psychological immobility constitutes the interruption of a biological cycle leading to frustration and the adverse effects discussed above (5.10). Long continued or repeated incidents of psychological immobility lead to pathological feelings of dependency and helplessness, with the tragic consequences indicated below in chapter 8 (see: 8.6 and Figure 8.2).

Psychological immobility is the antithesis of the stereotyped picture of the hard-driving, action oriented, executive. Yet, under severe psychological stress, such as double-bind situations, the executive may be unable to act, perhaps hoping the situation may resolve itself. It rarely does.

Purposeful Aggression. The types of agonistic behavior discussed above constitute the normal human response to stress. Our discussion does not pertain to instances in which aggression is purposefully used to achieve ends completely unrelated to the phylogenetic and culturally developed functions of adaptation to injury and threats of injury. Purposeful aggression may, however, serve as a source of stress and, therefore, as a stimulus to the adaptive forms of agonistic behavior discussed above.

Levels of Existence. Looking at human development through the historical stages of hunting, farming, and urban settlement, one may easily detect differences in the levels of existence—ranging from mere subsistence to the higher levels of intellectual and artistic expression. Likewise, looking at cross-cultural comparisons, one may also detect similar differences in the levels of existence. Some observers suggest that even restricting our view to modern humans in the Western world of abundance, it is still possible to observe similar differences. There is no need, at this point, to explore these views comprehensively; our purpose will be served by citing a few examples to illustrate the basic thesis.

An early observer of this phenomenon, Aristotle, distinguished four levels of life: intellect, sensation, nutrition, and motion; or, alternatively, three levels in man: reason, spirit, and desire. The lowest level of life is exhibited in nutrition and reproduction—for example, in plants. In animals, the levels of sensation, motion, and desire are superimposed; while in humans there is added the level of reason or mind (self-direction in accordance with a rational formula). While modern scholars have elaborated on this basic hierarchy in various ways, the fundamental idea remains essentially unchanged.

Riesman, Glazer, and Denny (1961), McClelland (1961, 1975), Bois (1969), Manslow (1970), and Graves (1970, 1974) have all contributed to the discussion of this matter and each has proposed his own schema of levels of existence. In general, the levels range from a low of relatively primitive existence with an emphasis on satisfaction of basic physiological needs to a high of a transcendental level of existence with recognition and appreciation of the importance of self-actualization and of harmony—both internal and with the physical and social environment. Each of these observers has analyzed the human condition at a different level of resolution and from a different perspective. Although all seem to recognize the role of evolution in the development of these levels, some see the level of any given individual as relatively static and fixed for a lifetime, while others see possibilities for psychological growth and movement from one level to another (within limits) with the exercise of conscious effort.

All seem to agree that the general behavior and the values of an individual tend to conform to those of others at the same level. As a result, an individual at any given level cannot understand or successfully communicate with individuals at higher levels.

The implications of this type of hierarchy for executive stress appear to be plain and clear: any subordinates, peers, superordinates, customers, vendors, etc., operating at a level higher than that of the executive will maintain values and behave in ways that are incomprehensible to that executive. Further, that executive, in dealings with individuals operating at such higher levels of existence, may employ tactics that produce ineffective results. In addition, the executive will not understand the really meaningful communications directed towards him or her from others existing at higher levels.

Although an individual may not be confined for life to any one of these levels of existence—and lives in a potentially open system of values—nevertheless, most individuals tend to settle into what appears to be a closed system. Some crisis and a special insight is necessary for a change to take place. We shall return to this topic in our discussion of coping mechanisms.

SUMMARY

5.14. Our model of the psychological causes of stress has now served its purpose; it allowed us to focus on the nine major elements within the self-system, to identify and describe those elements, and to discuss their interrelationships. Having established at least a limited understanding of the internal operations of the self-system as they pertain to the psychological causes of stress, we may now, with somewhat greater assurance, recognize the fact that the self-system is not a closed system, but an open, dynamic, cybernetic system in continuous interaction with its ambient environment. Our discussion of the environmental causes of stress comes in the next chapter. Here, however, we must take cognizance of the existence of that environment and its general impact on the self-system.

We may observe that the self-system is subject to two types of input from its ambient environment: 1) perceived events, and 2) nonperceived events. Perceived events are those sensed by the self-system, stimuli which trigger sensations; the best examples are those which affect the so-called five senses—sight, hearing, taste, smell, and touch. There are, of course, other types of perceived events; for example, changes in temperature, changes in position, or motion. The nonperceived events which serve as input to the self-system occur below the level of awareness, they do not trigger sensations; they include, for example, cosmic rays of various types with which the self-system is being constantly bombarded; radioactive fallout; air, food, and water pollution of various types; X-rays; changes in barometric pressure; and, generally, the force of gravity. (Of course, we may become painfully aware of the force of gravity upon specific occasions of awkardness, clumsiness, or accident.)

One other class of nonperceived events which is very important to a self-system operating in a social environment includes what we have previously referred to as Black Box operations—the events and activities which occur within a system and which cannot be observed without interfering with, or destroying, the system. Included in this latter category, of course, are the events which take place within the minds of other human beings, and which may serve as the source of highly significant input, albeit indirectly, to the self-system. This fact leads to the observation that both perceived events and nonperceived events consist in part of output from the self-system; the flow is two-way.

We may further observe that these two classes of events (perceived and nonperceived) may occur within the self-system as well as in the ambient environment. Perceived internal events might include: pain, changes in heart beat, changes in blood pressure, changes in blood-sugar level, dehydration, changes in body weight or size. Nonperceived internal events would include: cell growth, osmosis, normal blood flow, normal breathing, some digestive processes, many glandular operations. Many or all of these may, at one time or another, have specific stressful effects as indicated in our discussion of the physiological causes of stress, and some of these effects may also be psychological in nature. In fact, for human beings, the psychological causes of stress are more frequent and more severe than the physiological or environmental causes. Perceived "situations" of threat or frustration, interacting feelings and emotions leading to helplessness, hopelessness, depression, and various psychosomatic illnesses, all are among the most damaging of stressors, yet all of these may be attributed to our own internal processing of perceived events and are, therefore, subject to control. We note again that the flow is two-way; both perceived and nonperceived internal events may constitute either input or output from one or more elements within the self-system.

Thus, we see that the self-system operates cybernetically both internally and in relationship with its ambient environment; there is a variety of continuing input, and a variety of continuing output, some of which serves as feedback.

Similarly, the nine elements of our self-system are in continuing interaction among themselves, each element is continually receiving input from one or more of the other elements, continually providing output to one or more of the other elements, and continually receiving feedback from its own output. This continuing flow of energy and information constitutes the dynamics of our cybernetic self-system.

Given this type of open, dynamic, cybernetic operation, it becomes apparent that almost any type of stimulus, internal or external, may serve, directly or indirectly, as a psychological cause of stress under appropriate circumstances. Upon any given occasion of input of a perceived event, both the physiological and psychological condition of the self-system will have a direct, and controlling, effect on the resulting response.

As Powers suggested, the sensory input signal is compared with a continually flowing reference signal to produce the perception, sensation, feeling, etc. Similarly, the internal operations of each successively higher level in this hierarchy are governed by an analogous reference signal which is also continually flowing. Thus, the feelings and emotions which arise within the self-system affect and are affected by continually flowing reference signals; likewise, the cognition and appraisal of the sensations and resulting feelings and emotions both affect and are affected by continually flowing reference signals and, accordingly, determine the perception of a "situation." The resulting behavior, life experience, and life decisions also both affect and are affected by continually flowing reference signals at the appropriate hierarchical levels. With each of these nine elements providing input to the various reference signals, and with that input varying as the element changes its output based on its own input and feedback, it is obvious that the continually flowing reference signals at each hierarchical level are also subject to continuing change.

Thus, any given event may have stressful effects for one individual and benign or neutral effects for another, solely because of individual differences in the continually flowing internal reference signals. Further, and as pointed out in our discussion of the stress response in chapter 3, regardless of what particular stressor sets the G.A.S. mechanism into motion, the basic result is always *essentially* the same, although the particular manifestations will depend on the variable effects of the specific actions of the stressor, the integrity and responsiveness of each intermediate physiological subsystem, and the relative responsiveness of the target organs themselves.

Chapter 6
Environmental Causes of Stress

6.0 The environmental causes of stress include all those objects or events which precipitate, or contribute to, the stress response in the individual, but which originate outside of the individual. Such objects and events constitute noxious stimuli, but, as we saw in chapter 5, these stimuli do not necessarily have to penetrate the self-system to initiate the stress response. Sometimes the mere perceived threat of such a stimulus will trigger a stress reaction and avoidance behavior. Thus, the significant feature of an encounter with a noxious stimulus is not whether the stimulus is invading the self-system, but the nature of the reaction to the stimulus, whether there is actual penetration or mere percetion.

We may divide an individual's ambient environment into three categories: physical, biotic, and social. Although these categories may not be precisely differentiated, they will serve to categorize our discussion of environmental stressors and potential stressors.

THE PHYSICAL ENVIRONMENT

6.1 Among the more obvious physical stressors are those which cause wounds, bruises, or other lesions—objects which cause injury when they strike or penetrate the borders of the self-system— including knives, bullets, rocks, and other solid objects. Such objects may be directed at us purposely by an aggressor, or may strike us accidentally. The results are the same in terms of stress.

In the accidental category also are the many occupational health and safety hazards—the buildings we work in; the machinery, equipment, tools, and furniture we use; the corrosive, poisonous, and debilitating substances we work with or absorb through our lungs or skin; the power lines we may contact, etc. Less obvious, but, as we are beginning to learn, perhaps more significant, are the allergens, pollutants, additives, and pesticides which we take in with our breath, food, or drink. Even more insidious are the by-products of nuclear fission—whether from bomb tests or power production—which penetrate the self-system unperceived.

One long neglected cause of stress which appears to be an unavoidable consequence of modern urban living is the high level of low fidelity, almost continuous sound to which most of us are now subjected. By low fidelity we mean an unfavorable signal to noise ratio. (See: Schafer, 1977). From the drone and sonic booms of aircraft overhead to the roar of motor traffic on the road, from the din of machinery in the workplace to the clang and clatter of road and structural building activities, from the ceaseless chatter of radio and television to the cacophony of rock and roll, we are veritably drowned in a sea of noise.

Wide variations in temperature or altitude are also a source of stress, especially to those individuals with predisposing physical conditions (for example, heart and lung ailments). Catastrophic geological and meteorological events—earthquakes, tornadoes; hurricanes; blizzards; extremes of heat, cold, and wind speed; drought; flood; fire—may be sources of stress to many individuals at the same time. The ceaseless barrage of electromagnetic waves and particles from outer space; the gravitational forces which cause the tides and govern the orbits of the earth and other planets and satellites; ultraviolet rays from the sun—all these have known and unknown effects on the self-system. Who knows, for example, what effects the phases of the moon have upon the circadian rhythms and mental stability of the self-system.

THE BIOTIC ENVIRONMENT

6.2 Modern humans are more predator than prey, in the usual sense of that relationship, but we are still vulnerable. Our predators now, however, are no longer the wolf or sabre-toothed tiger, but mostly microscopic creatures—bacteria, viruses, and other infectious agents. These are the stressors, the causes of disease and debilitation.

Dermatologists estimate that the average human being may harbor as many as 25 million organisms per square centimeter of epidermis in the more populous areas of his skin—the armpits and the groin. Not all of these parasites are pathogenic. They range from harmless yeasts, bacteria, and mites to potentially harmful staphylococci, streptococci, and viruses. Some of these same types of organisms also inhabit the mucous membranes of the nose and throat; many more reside in the alimentary canal and perhaps elsewhere in the human body. Some of the harmless varieties assist in certain bodily processes—such as digestion. Others are ready to strike at any time, causing irritation, infection, inflammation, pimples, boils, and other lesions—perhaps even cancer.

Of course, in addition to the microscopic creatures there are a wide variety of animals and insects which may occasionally serve as stressors through bites and stings, or indirectly as carriers of disease organisms, or through the destruction of food and other supplies. In addition, certain plants (e.g., poison ivy, poison oak, poison sumac) may occasionally cause stress through skin contact; others (e.g., toadstools, mushrooms) through ingestion; still others (e.g., ragweed) through dispersion in the atmosphere of allergenic pollens which are drawn into the lungs.

THE SOCIAL ENVIRONMENT

6.3 By far the most prolific source of stress to humans are humans themselves—humans in organized society. In our listing above of the physical stressors, we have included a number which are direct or indirect consequences of social or urban living. Other consequences of the modern life style also constitute stressors. Both the scientific and the popular literature are replete with reports of the stressful effects of the workplace (monotony, production pressures, inept bosses, etc.), of the home (generation gaps, violence on television, wife and husband beatings, child neglect, divorce, etc.), of the leisure world (insufficient leisure time for some individuals, ineffective use of leisure time by others, overexertion in some activities, excessively vigorous pursuit of some avocations, etc.), and of the natural environment (despoliation, devastation, pollution, etc.).

The crowded conditions of some of our cities lead to stress; there is a source of stress in simple over-population. The very pace of urban living leads to stress, and that pace appears to be accelerating. The increasing mobility of the population leads to stress—increasing frequency in changes in jobs, occupations, employers, places of residence, all lead to lack of personal stability, to lack of stable relationships, and to stress. The rate of innovation and the sheer volume of innovation lead to stress—to what Toffler calls "future shock." (Toffler, 1970).

For the executive, the problems involved in the management of change constitute a source of stress; any break with tradition, any discontinuity, serves as a source of stress for employees and, hence, for the executive. The executive's management of his or her own time, including his or her leisure time, is a source of stress. Although we are hearing less about it recently, the increasing ubiquity of the computer tends to produce an information overload which still constitutes a problem and a source of stress for the executive.

Certain individuals, groups, organizations, and institutions are more significant than others as sources of stress for the executive—those who interact with him or her continually or frequently. This category of "significant others" includes: bosses, family members, colleagues, business associates, friends, acquaintances, neighbors; as well as informal groups (of friends, associates, etc.) and formal groups (employing organizations, religious and fraternal organizations, civic organizations, etc.). It also includes other groups and organizations of which the executive is not a member, but with which he or she interacts as customer, rival, client, patron, citizen, etc.

Some observers maintain that the bureaucratic milieu (governmental or corporate) is in itself stressful whether one is working in it or dealing with it from the outside. (See: Glass and Singer, 1972; Quick 1972). Established social institutions (rules, laws, folkways, mores, etc.) impose restrictions on the individual and limit freedom of action in a wide variety of ways, many of which may be perceived as stressful; for example, the simple activity of driving an automobile in traffic requires the careful observation of a number of laws, rules, and customs, and numerous interactions with others (pedestrians, drivers, traffic regulators, etc.)—all of which constitute sources of stress. Rules and customs of etiquette or protocol are simply prescriptions for conduct which, if not followed, constitute a source of stress.

Even the time-honored "principles of management," whose virtues have long been extolled in the literature of the classical approach to management, may serve as sources of executive stress. Some of these principles or guidelines may be traced back to the Bible (hierarchical organization), while others are of more recent origin, stemming from writings of the turn of the century. These so-called principles are still taught, unchallenged, in some of our better business schools. Specifically, one may refer to the works of Frederick W. Taylor and Henri Fayol, who laid down for posterity some basic precepts which many modern managers try to follow today. We suggest that these principles of management, in certain contexts and given a sufficient degree of vulnerability, constitute significant stressors for the executive.

In the world of management, these principles have the same standing as the laws, rules, and customs of society in everyday life. Thus, the executive who is familiar with these principles and fails to follow them may have feelings of guilt, leading to stress. Another reason for the stressful effects is the fact that within the generally accepted body of principles one may find numerous inconsistencies, pairs of principles which are mutually contradictory. Some principles, for example, advocate punitive measures to secure compliance or conformity, while others favor a more humanistic approach. Thus, the executive may find himself or herself caught between conflicting guidelines; the resulting uncertainty may lead to immobility and the consequent stressful effects we observed in chapter 5 (5.13). However, any managers who blindly try to follow these principles, without giving sufficient thought to the consequences, may find themselves in even deeper trouble when they discover either that the principles do not apply to the given situation or that they have misapplied them. The results may be equally stressful.

Similar types of prescriptions for executive behavior may be found in numerous, popular, "how-to" books which have appeared in recent years. Some of these books purport simply to describe executive behavior for the guidance of younger executives; others claim to instruct the reader in the art of exploiting a variety of types of situations. If our description of the psychological sources of stress is accepted, the conclusion is inevitable that some, probably many, if not all, of the recommended behaviors will prove to be stressful, not only for individuals following the recommendation, but for others with whom they interact. This is especially true of some of the more extreme types of self-assertive behavior.

Of course, all executives indulge in some amount of self-assertive behavior, otherwise they would never become, or continue to be, executives. We are, therefore, not suggesting that such behavior is to be avoided because it is stress-producing—any more than we would suggest that tennis or swimming be avoided because they are stress-producing. All we are suggesting, at this point, is that executives recognize the stress-producing potential of the other elements in their environment which we have been discussing. We shall return to this matter in Part IV.

The self-assertive tendency accounts for competition, aggression, defense, and other types of behavior conducive to survival of the individual. Opposing this tendency is the integrative tendency which accounts for cooperation, compassion, devotion to the group, and other types of behavior conducive to survival of the group. This tendency to subordinate one's own desires and interests to those of the group makes an individual more susceptible to influence by unscrupulous leaders and may lead to irrational behavior and further stress. Either of these two tendencies, when exaggerated, may become stressful and detrimental to the interests of both individual and group. In both instances the source of stress lies, not in the individuals themselves, nor in the social environment, but in the interaction of the two. (See: Koestler, 1967, p. 225–226.)

Of course, the self-system interacts with the ambient environment in many other ways; in fact, in an infinite variety of ways, including all the ways mankind has devised for working, playing, loafing, eating, and sleeping. For the executive, work probably provides the most opportunities for interaction, and may well be the major source of environmental stress. Although most individuals exercise a considerable degree of control over the activities in which they engage, the noteworthy activity of exception is the world of work where the individual's behavior may be programmed to a far greater extent than many are willing to admit. For example, one major activity of lower management is to propose to higher management the future activities of the organization; one of the activities of higher management is to determine the appropriate disposition of such proposals; the interactions involved in this hierarchical propose-dispose system may be a source of considerable stress for all concerned. (See: Schon, 1967, p. 78–92.)

The above discussion applies primarily to the interactions of individuals within their own culture. In these days of increasing mobility, the individual is more frequently subjected to cultural shock—encounters with alien cultures, where the known rules of behavior do not apply. The term (cultural shock) also applies to one's own society when the rules are changing so rapidly that even one's own cultural milieu becomes alien. (See: Hall, 1959, 1966, 1976.)

Even absent significant change, and whether interacting with members of one's own or an alien culture, the modern executive is subject to considerable stress attendant upon the difficulties of effective communication. There is a wealth of literature on the subject, even a whole school of thought on the importance of communication in the organizational environment, so we need do no more than mention the stress-producing potentialities of efforts at successful communication. (See Drucker, 1974; Groen and Bastiaans, 1975; Stieglitz, 1958; Lee, 1952; and Johnson, 1946.)

SOURCES OF ENVIRONMENTAL CAUSES OF STRESS

6.4 The above listings of stressors and potential stressors in our physical, biotic, and social environments is not intended to be comprehensive, but merely suggestive. In fact, a comprehensive listing would be impracticable for several reasons. First, there is the fact that we can never perceive all aspects of any given object, event, or set of objects or events. Our perceptions of reality are severely limited by the constraints of our sensory apparatus; for example, we cannot perceive the interior of solid objects; we cannot perceive a motionless, colorless, odorless gas; we cannot observe the internal operation of "black boxes." (See: Section 2.18). Secondly, no two individuals can share the same position in time and space so as to receive the same sensory stimuli. Nor can they share the same sensory apparatus so as to process those stimuli in precisely the same way. Whatever sensory stimuli each of us may receive is influenced by a different memory store and set of inferences (Powers' continually flowing, neural reference signals.) Thus, no two individuals will ever have precisely the same perception of any given object, event, or set of objects or events.

Further, perception involves a certain degree of selectivity; as Powers suggests, each individual's behavior determines his or her perceptions. Granted, of course, that at successively higher levels of resolution, we may find increasing degrees of consensus—that is, agreement is easier at macrolevels of perception (we can usually agree on whether a given structure is a house, or a warehouse), but when we become very specific about such details as color, shape, size, precise boundaries, composition of materials, etc., the area of agreement tends to lessen. The more detailed our perception, the less the agreement.

Finally, the self-system is the continuing recipient of an unknown number of stimuli which are not consciously perceived, but which may nevertheless be stressful—irradiation by unidentified particles, subliminal perceptions, the influences of gravitational and electromagnetic force fields, etc.

The effect of these inevitable differences in the receipt and internal processing of sensory stimuli is that any given stimulus may be a stressor or potential stressor to one individual, but not to another. Thus, the ultimate determinant of whether a given stimulus is a stressor or not is the state of the recipient of that stimulus. Given the range of individual differences (physiological, psychological, social, geographical, cultural), and given the range of possibly different reactions to similar stimuli among different individuals, and different reactions to similar stimuli by the same individual at different times, there would appear to be little choice in accepting the proposition that *every event is a potential source of stress to someone, somewhere, sometime.*

Thus, the inherent impracticability of any comprehensive listing of environmental stressors. Fortunately, such a listing is not essential to our purposes, but our model of the environmental causes of stress must take into account this indeterminacy. Our model must recognize the stressful potentiality of every event and therefore it deals with the sources of the environmental causes of stress rather than with specific stressors or types of stressors.

Figure 6.1, is a graphic representation of our model of the environmental sources of stress. The outer circle, representing time, indicates not only that all events take place in time, but that time, itself, is one of the sources of stress for the self-system. While there is no interaction with time, it is an element with which the executive must contend. We equate time with the Aristotelian concept of the dynamics of change, the flow of events. Every event is a change in the state of a system or its environment. So that even the very process of change itself may serve as a source of stress. More significantly, the individual's concept of time and certain drives related to the use of time frequently lead to stressful behavior. The sense of time urgency is one of the factors identified by Friedman and Rosenman in their analysis of coronary prone behavior. (Friedman and Rosenman, 1974). The individual's perception of time limitations tends to be stress-producing, especially when differing activities compete for attention without sufficient time to attend to all of them. One result of this situation is the unthinking substitution of increased activity for steady progress toward a manageable number od goals. Many executives appear to be particularly susceptible to the frustrations arising from their inability to control their use of their own time. (Drucker, 1967; Engstrom and Mackensie, 1967; Odiorne, 1974; Lakein, 1973; Webber, 1972; McCay, 1959).

The ambient environment consists of physical events, biotic events, and social events—all of which we have discussed above as potential

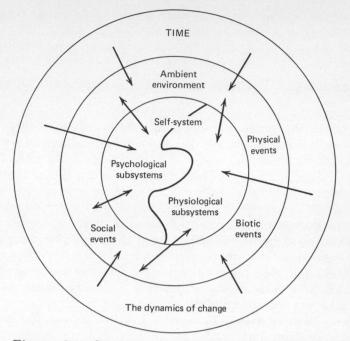

Figure 6.1   Sources of environmental causes of stress.

stressors. Note that there are no well-defined boundaries separating these types of events.

The inner circle, representing the self-system, consists of physiological subsystems and psychological subsystems, which we discussed in chapters 4 and 5. Note that, while the impact of time on the self-system may stimulate a reaction, the flow is strictly one-way, but the self-system interacts with its ambient environment and therein lies an additional source of stress. In other words, time and the ambient environment are sources of stressors for the self-system, but the self-system is not simply a passive recipient and reactor; it is in dynamic interaction with that environment and that interaction may, in itself, stimulate stress.

As we indicated in our model of the psychological causes of stress (chapter 5), events which impact on the self-system may be either perceived or nonperceived. Whether a given perceived event serves as a stressor will depend, in large part, on the perspective of that self-system—whether it perceives the event as significant input.

SUMMARY

6.5 Given the range of individual differences (physiological and psychological) discussed in chapters 4 and 5, given the range of possible different reactions to the same stimulus among different individuals, and given the range of different reactions to the same stimulus by the same individual at different times, there appear to be reasonable grounds for accepting the proposition that every event in the environment constitutes a potential cause of stress.

Our model, of course, can only hint at the richness and complexity of the interactions and other events which are continuously occuring and at the infinitude of potential stressors. Fortunately, as we shall see in Part III, no greater degree of detail is necessary for our purposes. Rather, the mediate effects of the great variety of the causes of stress, which may be more readily susceptible to classification, are more pertinent to our discussion.

Chapter 7
Summary: Causes of
Stress

7.0 Our analysis and our models of the physiological, psychological, and environmental causes of stress all suggest that any event—within the self-system or in the ambient environment—and even the very process of change itself may operate as a stressor on the self-system. Rarely, if ever, however, is there a single stressor triggering the G.A.S. More typically, a combination of stressors operate in concert to trigger the reaction.

Not only do stressors act in concert to trigger the G.A.S., but, as we have noted earlier, there is often a cascading of effects, with one stressful physiological or psychological condition leading to another; for example, poor posture leading to fatigue, muscle tension, sleeplessness, etc.; improper diet leading to nutritional diseases and diseases of adaptation; jealously leading to anger or rage, worry, and anxiety; loss or bereavement leading to worry, fear, and anxiety. Likewise, some of the physiological conditions lead to psychological effects and vice versa; environmental causes lead to both physiological and psychological effects.

In each instance, of course, the underlying basic stress reaction is the same—the G.A.S. Only the mediate effects are different—for different individuals, and for the same individual at different times. The reasons for these differences, as we have indicated, are several. First, because of the constraints of time and space and the inherent nature of the perceptual process, no two individuals can ever experience precisely the same micro-level event. Secondly, because of individual differences in the content of the memory store and in the internal operation of the self-system (the nature of the internally flowing neural reference signals) no two individuals will ever experience precisely the same perception of any two or more similar events. Thirdly, because each individual, and his or her memory store are continuously changing with each new experience, no individual will ever have two precisely the same perceptions or experiences.

Thus, whether any given event (or series of events) operates as a stressor depends, not only on the nature of that particular event (or series of events), but on two other factors as well. One of those factors is the vulnerability of the individual to that particular event at the time of its impact (perceived or nonperceived). The other factor is the context, that is the individual's perception of the ambient environment in which the event occurs.

Alan McLean developed a model to illustrate this relationship of the three factors in the stress situation: stressors, vulnerability, context. He represents the relationship in a Venn diagram (Figure 7.1). (McLean, 1975). As indicated in this diagram, stress occurs only when there is sufficient overlap among the three factors. The circles in the diagram should, of course, be viewed as representing dynamic states and dynamic relationships; they vary in content and in their relationship to each other from moment to moment as the flow of events— potential stressors, vulnerability, and the context—change.

The individual's vulnerability to a particular stressor depends, as we have suggested, on the state of his or her self-system—his age,

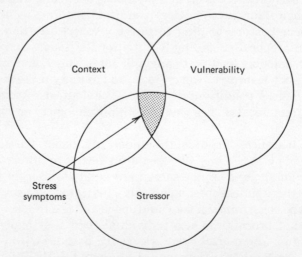

Figure 7.1   The McLean model of stressful events.

genetic and cultural development, occupation, education, memory store, physical condition, psychological mood, etc. The context of a particular potential stressful event depends on the nature of the potential stressor itself and the perspective of the individual. For example, one individual might experience a significant stress reaction to a drop in the foreign exchange value of the dollar, while another individual might not even be capable of appreciating the possibility, much less the nature, of the stressful effect of such a development on anyone. Similarly, within the family, the workplace, or any other organization, the context of any potential stressor depends on the particular perspective of the individual. Each individual is a unique product of genetic, physical, psychological, and cultural development; therefore, vulnerabilities and contexts will vary from individual to individual, and from moment to moment. This unique quality of each stressful event may provide us with a lead to developing the means of controlling, or managing, stress, as we shall see in Part IV. First, however, we shall consider the effects and costs of stress in Part III.

PART III
THE COSTS OF STRESS

So far as we know, there have been no attempts at developing any systematic approach to estimating the economic costs of executive stress, much less the organizational and social costs. In the next few chapters we offer a tentative model as a basis for developing such estimates. First we make an effort to reduce the number of variables for relating the immediate effects of stress to certain categories of mediate effects. We then identify certain selected cost factors which stem from the mediate effects and for which data are either available or can, in principle at least, be developed. We find the available data rather sparse, but, limited as it is, it still reflects the enormity of the individual, organizational, and social costs of this strange phenomenon. Of even greater significance, however, are the longer range and ultimate implications of the costs and effects of stress, as we point out in chapter 10.

Chapter 8
EFFECTS OF STRESS

8.0 The principal aim of this chapter is to propose a model that will bridge the gap between our discussion of the causes and immediate effects of stress in Part II, and our discussion of costs in the next chapter. Any attempt to assign specific cost estimates to each of the specific immediate effects would obviously entail an endless task. We have, therefore, adopted the standard scientific practice of reducing the number of variables with which we are dealing. In this instance, we accomplish this reduction by arbitrarily classifying the effects of stress into six categories of mediate effects—categories that appear to be the most significant for management purposes.

The adoption of this model is not intended to imply that our proposed six categories constitute the only mediate effects of stress. We believe, however, that these six categories will provide us with a resonable basis for identifying the significant costs of stress.

MEDIATE EFFECTS

8.1 In the broad spectrum of electromagnetic radiation, a human being's direct experience is limited to a very narrow range of phenomena—wavelengths somewhere between 10^3 and 10^4 angstrom units, the visible light spectrum. With the aid of instrumentation, we may extend our observations to wavelengths ranging from about 10^{-4} angstrom units (gamma rays) to about 10^{17} angstrom units (alternating current waves). Beyond these limits we may only speculate. We are similarly limited in the identification of causes and effects. In tracing any chain of events, we eventually reach a point beyond which we can only speculate about ultimate causes. In predicting and prognosticating effects, we may effectively utilize the laws of probability, but again only within limits—the vast future is entirely uncertain.

Our exploration of the causes and effects of executive stress is no exception to this general rule. Accordingly, we have tried to avoid speculation and limit our discussion to those causes of stress—physiological, psychological, and environmental—which are immediate and identifiable. Likewise, we have limited our identification of the immediate effects of stress to only those which are more significant for our purposes, out of the multifarious possibilities. Even so, we have seen that both the causes and their immediate effects are practically limitless in number.

Considering the rather formidable array of causes and effects of stress, one might be deterred from making any attempt at classification were it not for one fact: the underlying uniformity of the stress reaction. To reiterate, although the particular manifestations of stress will depend on the variable effects of the specific actions of the stressor, the integrity and responsiveness of each intermediate physiological subsystem in the self-system, and the relative responsiveness of the target organs themselves, regardless of what particular stressor sets the G.A.S. mechanism into motion, the basic result is always essentially the same. (See 3.2) But the mediate effects are different.

Our focus will be on the principal mediate effects of stress on executives, as these have been identified in the literature. Because of the above mentioned complexity of interaction among the various types of causes and consequent cascading effects, any attempt to relate our categories of mediate effects to specific causes, or to specific categories of causes, or even to immediate effects would be futile. As we shall see, any one or more of the immediate effects which we have identified in Part II may lead to one or more of the mediate effects we identify below. We limit our categories to those which have been generally recognized in the literature as significant and at least potentially measurable. The principal mediate effects identified in the literature are six in number, as described below.

We have already suggested the tremendous variety of physiological and psychological illnesses produced by undue stress. These then constitute our first category of mediate effects: illness, physical and mental.

That some of these illnesses may make the subjects accident-prone is fairly obvious; indeed, some of the underlying causes—fatigue (mental and physical), sleeplessness, anxiety, fear, etc., are clearly indicated as predisposing their victims to higher accident rates. Our second category is, then: accidents.

That some of the illnesses may result in suicide or death by other means has already been demonstrated. Death is the third category.

Almost equally obvious, many of these causes and immediate effects may lead directly to lowered effectiveness and efficiency—our fourth category.

Perhaps less obvious is the way in which the causes and immediate effects lead to the two phenomena of turnover and nonturnover, our final two categories of mediate effects. However, the literature is re-

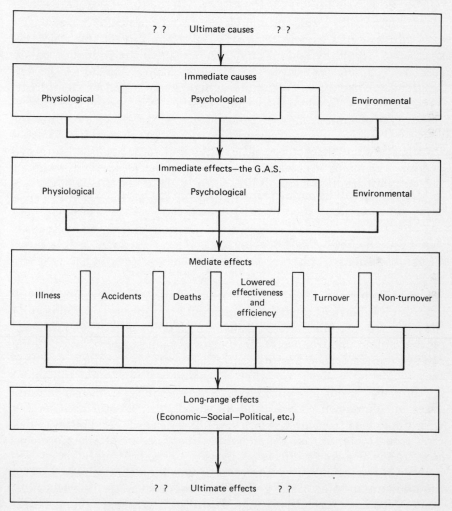

Figure 8.1   Causes and effects of stress.

plete with examples of these effects, both of which are discussed in more detail in chapter 9.

These then are the six principal mediate effects of executive stress. Their relationship to the foregoing models of the causes of stress is illustrated in Figure 8.1.

ILLNESS

8.2 As we saw in Part II, there are two basic types of stress-related damage to a self-system: (1) direct mechanical damage to tissues which occurs almost regardless of the nature of the stress response; and (2) the diseases of adaptation, resulting from inappropriate responses by the self-system to a stressor. Strictly speaking, the distinction is primarily conceptual; in actual practice it becomes difficult, if not impossible, to relate the various effects to their respective causes. Either type of damage may take one or more of three forms of illness or disease: (1) physiological, (2) psychological, (3) psychosomatic. The distinctions are not clear-cut in either the medical or popular literature and we shall make no attempt to remedy that defect. Instead, we adopt the standard practice of simply designating any given illness or disease as either physical or mental, reminding the reader here that the classification is arbitrary.

Physical Illness

8.3 In chapter 4, we identified ten major categories of the physiological causes of stress, and in Figure 4.1, we suggested the potential cascading effects of either a negative or positive influence on any single disturbance of the normal homeostatic balance of the self-system. Improper posture, fatigue, muscular tension, improper diet, inadequate sleep, or other disturbances of normal biological rhythms may predispose an individual to a variety of disease and diseases of adaptation. These conditions, in turn, create disturbances which may lead to other diseases and other diseases of adaptation in a continuing cycle, so that the individual becomes more and more susceptible to the adverse effects of stress.

We do not intend to go into clinical detail on this subject, but we should mention some of the generally recognized stress-related conditions which have a relatively high degree of prevalence among executives. The literature on stress-related research is replete with evidence of the stress-related nature of such disease conditions as: migraine, hypertension, hyperthyroidism, heart disease, arthritis, asthma, colitis, diarrhea, constipation, peptic ulcer, insomnia, and possibly diabetes. This listing is not exhaustive, but it is enough to indicate the wide ranging adverse physiological effects of stress. (Alexander, 1950.)

Mental Illness

8.4 Some, or possibly all, of these physical ailments may, in any given instance, be psychosomatic in nature—they may have no discernible organic basis, but may be apparently due to some emotional disturbance resulting from stress.

Such emotional disturbances may in themselves constitute, or may lead to, diseases or diseases of adaptation of a psychological nature, that is, to mental illness. Of course, some mental illness may also be organic in nature—somatogenic disorders. The various mental disorders number in the hundreds, most of which have no relevance to this discussion. Stress-related mental disorders may include certain psychoses, certain neuroses, certain personality disorders, and certain psycho-physiologic disorders, none of which may be attributed to stress alone, and all of which may occur without appreciable stress. (At this writing, the nomenclature and the symptomatology of mental illness is in somewhat of a disarray as practitioners try to agree on a revision of the standard reference on the subject: *Diagnostic and Statistical Manual of Mental Disorders,* American Psychiatric Association, 1968. There is, however, agreement on the fact that stress can lead to mental illness.) (See: Freedman, Kaplan, and Sadock, 1972.) There is one form of mental illness which very frequently results from undue stress: depression. (See: Flach, 1974.)

Depression. Actually, depression is not a single disease or mental disorder, but a syndrome—a set of symptoms characteristic of a variety of mental disorders. The debate over the appropriate classification of this mental disorder need not concern us here, but its significance as a mediate effect of stress and as a cause of other more serious effects—including suicide—should give us pause.

The symptoms of depression vary from person to person, and from time to time. They may include: a general lowering of mood-tone, including feelings of painful dejection, sadness, loneliness, or apathy; difficulty in thinking; and psychomotor retardation, including anorexia, insomnia, and loss of libido. Sometimes, they include: worry, anxiety, guilt, and a variety of regressive and self-punitive desires. Occasionally, the general retardation may be disguised by periods of restlessness or agitation. Some or any of these symptoms may occur, to some degree, in the normal state. Some or all of these symptoms may occur in any of a variety of neurotic or psychotic states. Hence, some of the difficulty in classification.

The duration of the condition also varies; it may last for just a few weeks or it may persist for months, sometimes remaining chronic indefinitely with periods of only temporary remission. Likewise, the intensity of the depression may vary from mild discouragement, through despondency, to utter despair; or it may fluctuate from one level to another. The rapidity of onset also may vary, being either sudden and immediate (e.g., following a specific loss or bereavement), or gradual, building up over several weeks or months.

One of the most significant features of the illness is the frequency with which it leads to attempted suicide. The motivation may vary from a desire for relief from the accompanying anxiety to desire for attention, or the attempt may stem from the victim's feeling of sheer hopelessness. One of the underlying reasons for the frequent attempts at suicide by depressed persons may be the distorted image they have of themselves, or their unrealistic view of the environment, or of their future. Depressed individuals tend to see themselves as unattractive and failures; they are deeply pessimistic about their opportunities for the future—the prospect is one of endless misery. (See: Seligman, 1975.)

ACCIDENTS

8.5 Any condition—physical or mental—which interferes with an individual's full and free exercise of his or her normal abilities and faculties will predispose him or her to accidents. Thus, certain of the causes of stress (e.g., sleeplessness, fatigue, poor posture), stress itself, and certain effects of stress (various physical and mental illnesses), all may lead to the development of a proneness to accidents.

Numerous studies show that the overly aggressive, the frustrated, the more passive, and the over-stressed have more frequent automobile accidents. The stress may even be the result of an actual or impending happy event (a promotion, a marriage, etc.) as well as a traumatic one. In each of these types, the behavior appears to stem from an underlying anxiety produced by the individual's fears or worry about his or her ability to measure up to expectations, to perform adequately.

Other studies also relate accident-proneness to stress. The accident-prone individual is, in general, emotionally less mature, less responsible, more antisocial, and not so well adjusted as those who are less accident-prone. Anxiety resulting from emotional disturbances and conflicts appears to lead to an increased number of accidents producing bruises and broken bones. (See: Dudley and Welke, 1977.)

DEATHS

8.6 Any of the diseases (including the diseases of adaptation) mentioned in chapter 4, may, of course, result in the death of the victim. Alexander (1950) and others have identified certain of these stress-related diseases, some of which are among the leading causes of death in the United States—cardiovascular diseases, cancer, etc. The evidence appears overwhelming for the stress-related nature of the conditions predisposing to fatal heart attacks. (See: Pelletier, 1977.)

In Chapter 5, we saw how the various types of psychological causes of stress lead to one or more of the three types of agonistic behavior: fight, flight, or immobility. We saw, too, that both the fight and the flight reactions lead to a wide variety of somatic, psychosomatic, and psychological illnesses, while the third type of agonistic behavior— immobility—may lead to feelings of dependency or helplessness. Dependency, in turn, may lead to some of the same types of diseases of adaptation as the more active responses to stress. Helplessness, however, tends to lead to hopelessness, depression, and suicide, as indicated above. Further, a variety of stress-producing events may lead to psychogenic death. Figure 8.2 suggests the relationships of the several types of reactions and their eventual result in death.

Almost any type of traumatic event may produce the conditions leading to suicide or psychogenic death. The sudden disruption of a close human relationship—for example, the death of a spouse, a divorce or separation, the breaking of an engagement, the loss of a job, retirement—may produce any of a variety of somatic, psychosomatic, or psychological disorders which lead to sudden death. The newspapers carry such stories almost every day—spouses who die within hours of each other, rejected suitors who die of a "broken heart", the long-time employee who just goes to bed and dies after being fired or retired. In most instances, there is no other apparent reason for the death. Events involving sudden or extreme danger, struggle, or attack produce deaths which we usually attribute to "shock". A variety of types of

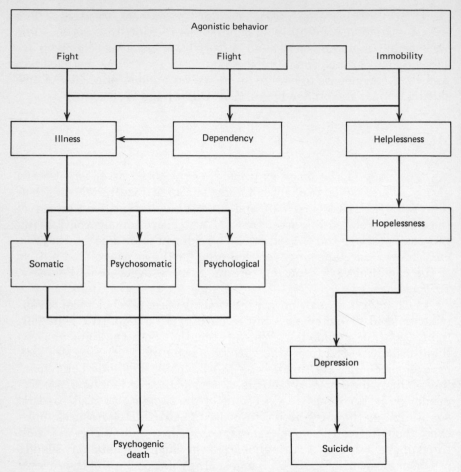

Figure 8.2   Some mediate effects of reactions to stress.

losses—of status or material possessions—and failures or defeats, disappointments, and humiliations also may frequently result in psychogenic death. Even otherwise happy events—unexpected triumphs, reunions, public recognition—may produce similar results. George Engel has compiled an inventory of such incidents. (Engel, 1977.) He further suggests that the normal reciprocity of the fight or flight reaction may break down under either extreme or conflicting stimulations, producing essentially the same results; even minor uncertainties may cause momentary cessation of motor activity and cardiac deceleration because of the excess secretion of certain hormones during the stress reaction. (See also: Cannon, 1942.)

Several studies linked suicide with stress and its resultant condition of depression. Many popular accounts of specific suicides trace them directly to particular stressful events occurring just before the suicide. Paykel suggests that depressives accumulate more life change units (see section 5.11) than other individuals, but those who attempt suicide have the most. (Paykel, 1976)

LOWERED EFFECTIVENESS AND EFFICIENCY

8.7 There is a large and growing literature on the subject of executive productivity, most, if not all, of it speculative in nature. Nevertheless, even though objective studies are lacking, we feel safe in joining other writers on the subject in asserting, on an intuitive basis, some correlation between the factor of impaired effectiveness and efficiency and some of the stress-producing elements of modern life.

Our readers, themselves, can attest to the fact that, generally speaking, their effectiveness and efficiency on the job are usually higher when they are "up" than when they are "down." Distress of any kind—mental or physical—tends to be distracting. There are exceptions, of course; witness the stories of the great artists who were lifelong invalids or neurotics, continually racked by pain or other forms of distress—Sand, Tennyson, Poe, Van Gogh, and others.

The accident-prone, obviously, are less effective and efficient when their labors are frequently interrupted by accidents. Feelings of guilt, worry, and anxiety interfere with productivity by diverting one's thoughts to matters other than work. The depressed individual, obsessed with feelings of helplessness, hopelessness, and possible suicide will be much less productive than the individual who can keep his or her mind on his or her work. Death, of course, is likely to be severely disruptive.

TURNOVER

8.8 A number of studies (e.g., Peskin, 1973; Flowers, 1975; Uris, 1972) have identified stress as a significant, if not leading, factor in the causes of executive turnover. In many instances, departures are voluntary—efforts to escape from stressful situations. In other instances, the exits are stimulated by the employing organization—getting rid of deadwood, executives whose peformance has been impaired by some of the mediate effects of stress.

NONTURNOVER

8.9 As we saw in chapter 3, and in Part II, stress may lead to contrary responses in different individuals, or in the same individual at different times. The same type and degree of stress which leads one individual to leave an organization (the flight reaction) may produce immobility in another. Overwhelmed by fear and anxiety, one may cling to one's job as the only safe refuge in a world of adversity. Likewise, one's bosses may be incapable of decisive action regarding one's tenure because of their own feelings of fear, guilt, or anxiety. Firing subordinates may be seen as a reflection on their own competence in personnel selection, or in executive direction. Better not to draw attention to an unsatisfactory situation. The net result: lowered productivity for the whole organization, with an increasing number of executive dropouts who go on drawing salary.

LONGER RANGE EFFECTS

8.10 All of the above mentioned mediate effects of stress lead to increased costs of operation for the employing organizations. We shall explore this matter in the next chapter. Here, we need but mention the positive feedback effect of such increased costs. Any increase in the costs of operation of an organization tends to increase the internal, and sometimes the external, pressures for improved effectiveness and efficiency. Such pressures, of course, merely exacerbate the already stressful environment and increase the stress on individual executives in a continuing vicious circle. Stress generates further stress.

Unless some way is found to break the cycle, the executive life may become increasingly unattractive. We already see some signs of this attitude developing among recent college graduates. The longer range adverse effects of such a situation for large organizations—public and private—are fairly obvious. The famed American spirit of enterprise may be on the downgrade.

ULTIMATE EFFECTS

8.11 We can only speculate on the ultimate effects of this trend: demise of the large-scale organization, decrease in the rate of acceleration of technological improvement, return to a slower pace of living, etc. Some readers will be quick to ask what is wrong with such a prospect; others may view such a prognostication as nothing more than the idle dreams of either a doomsday sayer or mischief maker. Take your choice.

SUMMARY

8.12 Our discussion of the effects of stress was intended to be more suggestive than exhaustive or comprehensive. It could hardly be otherwise, given the present state of knowledge, but we believe it is sufficient for our purposes.

In chapter 3, we identified a number of effects of stress at the microlevel of resolution: inflammation, increased flow of hormones, and other elements of the General Adaptation Syndrome (G.A.S.). In Part II, in addition to discussing the several categories of the causes of stress, we identified numerous immediate effects at a slightly higher level of resolution—the specific diseases of adaptation, mental and physical. In this chapter, we moved to a still higher level of resolution, first identifying what we have characterized as the mediate effects of stress: physical and mental illness, accidents, deaths, lowered effectiveness and efficiency, executive turnover and nonturnover. Finally, we suggested some lines along which our readers may speculate for themselves about the longer range and ultimate effects of stress. In the next chapter, we develop some estimates of the dollar costs of this phenomenon.

Chapter 9
The Costs of Executive Stress

9.0 This chapter develops a tentative model for assessing the costs of executive stress, identifies some of the more significant variables of such a model, analyzes the available data related to those variables, and postulates a rough range of estimated costs generated by the model.

So far as these writers have determined, this attempt to develop a model for assessing the costs of executive stress is a pioneering effort. Although many models have been proposed or developed for explaining the causes and effects of stress in terms of its physiological, psychological, or pathological manifestations in the individual, the extant literature does not reveal reports of any work in the formulation of models for assessing the costs of executive stress to the individual, to employing organizations, or to a national economy.

In systems analysis, the traditional approach to identifying costs is to categorize them into two classifications: tangible and intangible. Within the framework of this approach, those costs classified as tangible are usually merely the ones that the analyst finds easy to measure. In the published literature on executive stress (or even on human stress in general), one finds little in the way of references to costs and that little is usually in terms of intangible costs. One of the reasons for this dearth of information on the costs of stress may be the scantiness of available data for any such analyses.

There are, however, some data available and there are some clues and guidelines from other sources which suggest an approach to certain preliminary assessments. These clues and guidelines come primarily from the following fields of knowledge: (1) human resource accounting (see, e.g., Caplan and Landekich, 1974), (2) health econom-

128

ics (see, e.g., Rice, 1966), and (3) management (see, e.g., Drucker, 1974, chapters 15–23; and Quick, 1972, chapter 1).

Of course, given the necessary resources—time, money, organizational authority, etc.—a talented researcher could probably design an optimum, on-line, real-time, dynamic simulation model for identifying the adverse effects and assessing the consequent costs of executive stress in an organization. Absent these resources, one must settle for somewhat less. How much less is the first problem to be addressed in this chapter.

OF MODELS: IDEAL AND PRACTICAL

9.1 In Chapter 2, we considered the thesis that humans relate to "reality" through mental models—representations in the brain of objects and events in the outside world. We use a variety of types of models of varying degrees of abstraction in our efforts to cope with or control our environment. Such models may range from simple graphic sketches to highly elaborate, three-dimensional, operating machines; from simple verbal descriptions to highly complex mathematical formulae; from simple logical diagrams to highly abstruse philosophical expositions. Despite the wide range of models available to us, we are unlikely to find any one of them ideal for any particular purpose. Instead, they will vary in degrees of adequacy from completely useless (or even counterproductive) to optimum.

The success of an executive depends in large part on the appropriateness of his or her models and his or her ability to apply them properly. Thus, the real test of the value of any given model is not its degree of approach to the ideal, but, rather, its effectiveness in serving the purpose for which it is being used.

Real world models, as we previously recognized, are not "ideal." In assessing the cost of executive stress, the model we must settle for at this time is only an approximation and far from ideal.

A TENTATIVE MODEL

9.2 Chapter 8, above, identified some of the more significant mediate effects of stress—mental and physical illness, accidents, deaths, lowered efficiency, personnel turnover, and nonturnover. Our tentative model aims at relating these identified effects of executive stress to specific cost factors and providing some means of assessing such costs on an individual, organizational, or national basis.

SCOPE OF THE SYSTEM

9.3 We begin construction of our model by defining the scope of the system to be modeled. This study focuses generally on executives employed in large, bureaucratic, profit-making organizations in the Western World. For a variety of reasons, the system modeled in this chapter will differ in certain respects from that primary focus. Aside from the technological difficulties of constructing a model with the broader focus, the controlling reason for deviating from our primary focus is the lack of availability of data for that particular universe. We do, however, have some data pertaining to the class "executives in the United States." The projected model in this chapter, therefore, is limited in scope to executives employed in the United States. We define the term *executive,* for this purpose, in a later section of this chapter (see 9.17).

PERFORMANCE MEASURES

9.4 The second step in construction of our model is the specification of performance measures—what output we expect our model to produce based on the available input. The desired output was suggested at the beginning of this chapter: some estimate of the extent and related costs of executive stress. We discuss the available inputs below in section 9.13. As will be seen, there are significant constraints on our inputs. Despite this fact, however, by constructing our model for assessing the costs of executive stress, and by plugging in the statistical figures which are available we should be able to arrive at some rough estimates of the costs of executive stress. As in all pioneer model building exercises, adequate representation of "reality" is rarely accomplished during the first trial. Our model, of necessity, requires some cybernetic feedback for its further development, and at this stage much of this feedback is unavailable for the model discussed herein.

TYPE OF MODEL

9.5 Only in an authoritarian regime or a Utopian state would it be possible to exercise sufficient control over the components of the system to construct a dynamic model simulating the operation of the system being studied here. Even then, the model would be subject to certain limitations inherent in the study of black box systems. In fact, even the models for measuring the physiological and psychological manifestations of stress in individuals are subject to such limitations; the analyst is rarely permitted any insight into the inner structure or processes of the system under analysis, except on a postmortem basis. These difficulties tend to increase in at least a geometrical progression as systems consisting of more than one individual come under analysis.

Having ruled out the possibility of constructing a dynamic model for assessing the costs of executive stress, we are reduced to the necessity of accepting a static model. Further, the model developed herein, because of the nature of the system being modeled and the available data, is necessarily restricted to a type which can use a statistical form of input.

Under the circumstances, the most appropriate model would appear to be one which identifies the principal relationships among the several components (specified below) and allows for the processing of relevant statistical input.

Our tentative model, then, will assume the modest form of a graphic diagram supplemented by statistical tables serving as input. In skeletal form it will appear as sketched in Figure 9.1.

The primary variables in our model are the mediate effects of executive stress which constitute the subject matter of Chapter 8, above. The secondary variables in our model are the related cost factors, developed below. Together, these factors and their related statistics will generate the desired output: an assessment of the costs of executive stress.

As the discussion proceeds, the development of the cost factors and input of the related statistics will enable us to flesh out our skeletal model.

COMPONENTS OF THE MODEL

9.6 The essential components of our tentative model, then, are:

1. Causes of executive stress (see Part II).
2. Mediate effects of executive stress—primary variables—(see chapter 8).
3. Specified cost factors—secondary variables (developed below).
4. Statistics relevant to the cost factors (input).

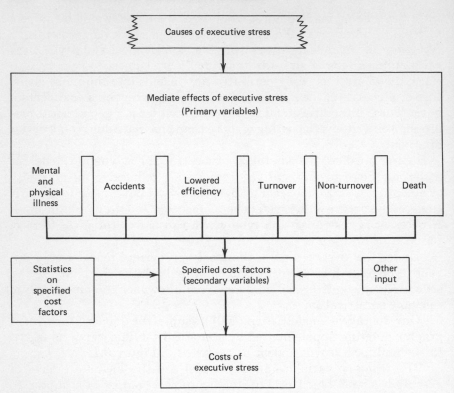

Figure 9.1   Skeletal form of tentative model for assessing costs of executive stress.

5.   Other input.

6.   Estimated costs of executive stress (output).

7.   Interrelationships among the above listed components.

The specified cost factors (secondary variables) will consist of those indicators, or symptoms, of the effects of executive stress which manifest themselves, directly, or indirectly, in the accounting, personnel, or production records of the organizations affected.

The relevant statistics (input) will consist of information on the incidence and (when available) the related dollar costs of the above mentioned specified cost factors as they pertain to executives working in large bureaucratic organizations in the United States, and related statistics on the costs of morbidity and mortality.

Other input will consist of miscellaneous other facts related to the effects of stress, selected expert opinions on the effects of stress and the related cost factors.

LEVEL OF RESOLUTION

9.7 Again because of the limitations on the availability of data, the model developed herein will be at a rather high level of resolution, namely national; that is, the model will utilize United States national statistics.

VALIDITY TEST

9.8 While the model developed herein is based on a generally accepted methodology (see: Rice, 1966; Myers and Flowers, 1974), certain factors prevent, at least at this time, a validity test being performed. The primary preventive factor is the "lumpiness" of the statistics. This defect may be remedied over time as the statistical gathering process is improved. At the present time it constitutes one of the pockets of our ignorance.

SUMMARY—A TENTATIVE MODEL

9.9 In summary, the resources are simply not available for construction of a model which would constitute even an approach to the ideal. Other constraints on our model building effort include: the black box nature of the systems under study (human beings and social organizations); the limitations of available knowledge about the operations of such systems and, more particularly, about the nature, incidence, and effects of stress on those systems; the paucity of statistical data about the extent of undue stress and its effects on the individuals and the organizations of which they are members; and the difficulties (discussed below) in fitting such data as is available to our model.

Recognizing these limitations and constraints on our model building efforts, we propose to settle at this time for a graphic diagram (Figure 9.1) indicating the basis or general relationships among the causes, effects, cost factors, and related statistics of executive stress.

Given all the difficulties and unavoidable constraints involved in constructing our tentative model, we still consider the effort eminently worthwhile. It appears to be worthwhile for at least three reasons. First, it is a major hypothesis of this study that executive stress constitutes a serious challenge to modern management and even partial answers to some of the underlying questions will be likely to represent a contribution toward improved management performance and theory. Second, even though, as we have seen in chapter 2 and in the discussion of models, above, no model will ever enable us to capture the whole of reality in any given situation, still the use of an appropriate model provides us with an effective means of dealing with that reality. Third, study of some of the relevant questions through the use of models and systems theory may not only produce some partial answers or better, but may, even more importantly, point the way to, and stimulate, needed further research, and in time, allow the development of an improved model.

SELECTED COST FACTORS

9.10 Some of the principal mediate effects of executive stress (our primary variables) were identified in chapter 8. In summary, they were:

1. Physical and mental illnesses.
2. Accidents.
3. Lowered efficiency.
4. Turnover.
5. Nonturnover.
6. Deaths.

These effects of executive stress are not, in themselves, directly measurable in terms of costs. Each of them, however, results in, and can be related to, certain specifiable items of individual and organizational expense. These expense items constitute the selected cost factors (secondary variables) in our model. We offer as a first, tentative identification of these cost factors the following list

1. Work loss: hours and days of absence from work.
2. Restricted activity: less work performed during regular business hours because of medical restrictions.

3. Medical and hospital expenses: direct payments to medical practitioners, hospitals, and others for health services.

4. Lifetime earnings: which provide a basis for estimating losses due to premature deaths.

5. Insurance premiums: payments to insurance carriers for health insurance, life insurance, workmen's compensation, etc.

6. Tort claims: payments to claimants stemming from litigation and the legal expenses involved in such litigation.

7. Decreased productivity: decreased output of individuals and organizations.

Quite obviously these are not the only costs of the effects of executive stress. They are, however, the costs for which data appear to be at least potentially available from conventional, present-day accounting records. Even with this limited list of selected cost factors, however, we shall find that certain relevant statistics are lacking. In sections 9.16 through 9.23, below, we shall present the available statistics. In sections 9.24 through 9.30, we shall discuss certain other costs.

The principal interrelationships between the mediate effects of executive stress (primary variables) and these selected cost factors (secondary variables) are, for the most part self-evident, or become so with only a casual inspection, but the full complexity of the interrelationships can only be suggested, not adequately portrayed, in a two-dimensional diagram. The accompanying second stage sketch (Figure 9.2) of our tentative model at once suggests the complexity of these interrelationships and illustrates the difficulty in adequately portraying them.

Despite the inherent limitations of our tentative model, however, the cost factors specified above do provide a mechanism for the input of some of the relevant statistics.

Unfortunately, we must now face up to these other constraints: 1) relevant statistics are not available for all of the cost factors listed above: 2) the statistics which are available are not always in a form which lends itself to direct application to these cost factors (see section 9.11, below); 3) not every one of the cost factors is susceptible to complete and direct measurement in terms of dollars. The nature of these limitations will become evident as we proceed, but by way of example at this point, we may cite the following: 1) while statistics are available for days lost from work, the more insidious form of economic loss which we have termed decreased productivity is more difficult to measure and is not reported in any of the available statistics; 2) while direct

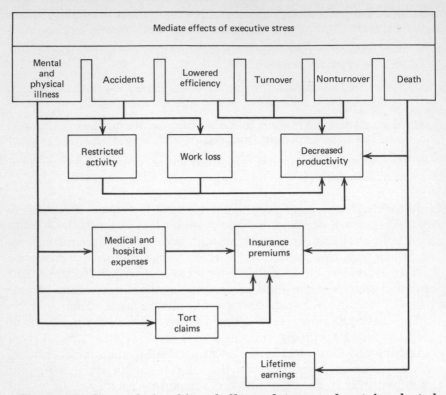

Figure 9.2   Interrelationships of effects of stress and certain selected cost factors.

payments to doctors and hospitals may be readily measured and reported, the effect of increased use of such services on health insurance and workmen's compensation premiums, although readily recognizable as being real and significant, is neither directly measurable nor reported; 3) some costs are completely intangible (e.g., personal suffering and the stressful effects of a stressed executive on his or her associates); 4) some costs, while they may be real and significant, are not identifiable (e.g., the effects on other organizations or the national economy of the behavior of stressed executives).

Actually, item 7), above, identifies only the tip of an iceberg; decreased productivity arises from multiple causes, takes many forms, and has multiple effects. It may result in part from work loss or restricted activity, but it may also result from a variety of other factors, such as decreased effectiveness or efficiency without work loss or restricted activity. We discuss some of these factors later in sections 9.24 through 9.30. Further, there may be decreased productivity of other members of an organization because of the work loss, restricted activity, or decreased productivity of one or more executives (see 9.28). Finally, productivity (and, therefore, decreased productivity) is measurable, if at all, in only gross terms—for an organization, or a large unit thereof—but rarely, if ever, for an individual executive. What we are suggesting here is that there are unmeasured, and perhaps unmeasurable, but significant losses from decreased productivity and that a major portion of such losses may be appropriately attributable to the effects of stress.

In sum, the cost factors may involve one or more of the following types of costs:

1. Tangible costs
    a. Directly measurable.
    b. Indirectly measurable.

2. Intangible costs.

3. Unidentifiable costs.

The nature of the costs in each of these categories will become clearer as the relevant statistics are presented in subsequent sections of this chapter. In the meantime, the accompanying diagram (Figure 9.3) may aid in visualization of the identifiable interrelationships and of the gaps in our knowledge.

FITTING AVAILABLE DATA

9.11 As previously mentioned, our efforts at constructing even the modest model we have proposed above for assessing the costs of executive stress will be subject to severe limitations in the availability of data specifically oriented to our needs. Even with these constraints, however, it will be possible to arrive at some preliminary figures that will enable us to formulate some rough estimates of the costs of executive stress. A description of the sources and types of data, and an indication of some of the difficulties involved follows.

Cost factors	Tangible Costs		Intangible costs	Unidentifiable costs
	Directly measurable	Indirectly measurable		
Restricted activity	Of stressed executive; *Not available*	*Not available*	Of stressed executive; *Not available*	Of others?; *Not available*
Work loss	Of stressed executive; *Partly available*	*Not available*	Of his associates; *Not available*	Of others?; *Not available*
Medical and hospital expenses	Of stressed executive; *Partly available*	Of his associates; *Partly available*	*Not available*	Of others?; *Not available*
Insurance premiums	For stressed executive; *Partly available*	For his associates; *Partly available*	*Not available*	For others?; *Not available*
Tort claims	Of stressed executive and his family; legal expenses; *Not available*	Time of other executives spent on such cases; *Not available*	Effects of such cases and settlements on other members of the organization; *Not available*	Effects on others?; *Not available*
Decreased productivity	Of stressed executive; *Not available*	*Not available*	Of his associates; *Not available*	Of others?; *Not available*

Figure 9.3   Cost factors and types of costs, with indication of availability of data.

SOURCES OF DATA

9.12 Most of the data used in the tentative model have been obtained from *The U. S. Factbook for 1975: The American Almanac,* (Factbook, 1975) which is a commercial re-publication of *The Statistical Abstract of the United States.* Other sources of data are explicitly identified in the footnotes.

Since *The U.S. Factbook for 1975* deals with figures released by The Bureau of the Census and since those figures are in highly summarized form, the statistics plugged into the model are necessarily "lumpy"—that is, they are aggregates which do not conform exactly to the categories used in our analysis. This, of course, allows for simplified computation but prevents validity testing, as mentioned above.

TYPES OF DATA AVAILABLE

9.13 The types of data available consist of the following:

1. Employment classifications and statistics.

2. Executive compensation statistics.

3. Work loss and restricted activity days statistics.

4. Hospital usage and costs statistics.

5. Mortality statistics.

6. Workmen's compensation statistics.

7. Industrial and commercial failures statistics.

These basic data provide some input variables for our model for estimating the costs of executive stress.

It is obvious from the above listing that the data available do not directly correspond to the cost factors (secondary variables) we have identified. For some factors some data is available and directly applicable but not complete; for others the data is only indirectly applicable; and for some no data is currently available. Nevertheless, we shall present such statistics as are directly relevant or may be related to our cost factors. We shall present such other types of information as may be available for other cost factors.

DIFFICULTIES WITH AVAILABLE DATA

9.14 One of the principal difficulties in dealing with the data is in estimating at a national level, or in tabulating at the individual patient level, the relationship between morbidity or mortality and that of executive stress.

As indicated in chapter 8, however, there are clearly demonstrated adverse effects of undue stress in human beings and a definite association of stress with some of the leading causes of death. On this basis, there appears to be adequate justification for the use of available morbidity and mortality statistics as applied to our model in this chapter.

A second major difficulty has to do with a lack of coincidence between the definition of *executive* used in this study and the definitions of categories used in The Bureau of Census employment statistics. Because of this lack of coincidence, some compromises are necessary. Since The Bureau of the Census does not use the term *executive* as a label for any particular employment category, it will be necessary to select those employment categories which most nearly coincide with the common understanding of the term.

There are also some minor difficulties with the data that have been used in our tentative model for assessing the costs of executive stress. For example, while mean income figures would be more suitable, The Statistical Abstract of the United States, published by the Bureau of the Census contains only median income figures. Consequently, and to the extent the models dealing with executive compensation are accurately formulated, the costs, based on lost earnings, are understated.

Other, more specific, difficulties exist, and will be identified at the point of presentation.

SUMMARY—FITTING AVAILABLE DATA

9.15 The currently available data, while adequate for model construction for assessing the costs of executive stress on an order of magnitude basis are by no means optimal. Having available the raw detailed data on the number of executives, executive earnings, and whether an illness was caused by stress or merely predisposed the patient to the illness, etc., would allow for more accurate figures; however, it would vastly complicate the computation process.

The next section, therefore, presents the data which is available. If better data can be obtained in the future then so much the better for assessing the costs of executive stress.

RELEVANT STATISTICS ON SELECTED COSTS OF EXECUTIVE STRESS

9.16 This section presents the available statistics on:

1. Number and compensation of executives.

2.   Work loss and restricted activity days of executives.

3.   Hospitalization expenses of executives.

4.   Executive mortality.

5.   Workmen's Compensation costs.

6.   Industrial and commercial failures.

The first category listed above provides the basic information required for computing costs related to all of the cost factors in our model.

The second category provides part of the data required for computing costs related to two of our cost factors: Work Loss and Restricted Activity.

The third category provides part of the data required for computing the costs related to the cost factor: Medical and Hospital expenses.

The statistics on executive mortality, the fourth category, are only indirectly related to three of our cost factors (Decreased Productivity, Insurance Premiums, Tort Claims), but provide a basis for computing certain other costs to the national economy, namely losses in lifetime earnings due to premature death.

The fifth category, Workmen's Compensation costs, provides part of the information for computing costs related to the cost factor: Insurance Premiums.

The final category, Industrial and Commercial failures, provides data indirectly related to the cost factor: Decreased Productivity.

There are no statistics available relating directly to the cost factors: Decreased Productivity and Tort Claims.

DEFINITION OF EXECUTIVE FOR STATISTICAL PURPOSES

9.17 An analyst studying an organization would probably have little difficulty in determining who is and who is not an executive in that organization. The problem of determining who is an executive on a national level tends to be more fuzzy. The Bureau of the Census does not list an executive category, and if it did it would probably not conform to the definition used in this study. In general, however, the following analysis aims at focusing on those census categories which most likely include those knowledge workers who are primarily responsible for contributing ideas for improving economic performance and for ensuring effective and economic performance of an organization.

The Bureau of the Census provides for categories and sub-categories of occupation types. (Factbook, 1975). The categories are:

1. Professional, technical, and kindred workers
2. Managers and administrators, except farm
3. Sales workers
4. Clerical and kindred workers
5. Craftsmen and kindred workers
6. Operatives, except transport
7. Transport equipment operatives
8. Laborers, except farm
9. Farmers and farm managers
10. Farm laborers and farm foremen
11. Service workers, except private household
12. Private household workers.

For purposes of this statistical analysis the following have been arbitrarily selected to constitute the executive class:

1. Professional, technical and kindred workers
2. Managers and administrators, except farm
3. Sales workers (all male-certain female).

The Bureau of the Census female "sales workers" category includes the following sub-categories (which do not correspond to the male sub-categories).
Sales workers:

1. Demonstrators, hucksters and peddlers
2. Insurance, real estate agents and brokers
3. Sales clerks, retail trade
4. Salesmen, retail trade.

The entire sales workers category comprises 2,247,000 persons. Of these, 64,000 are in the demonstrator, hucksters, and peddlers sub-category. These were summarily rejected as unrelated. The categories

(3) sales clerks, retail trade and (4) salesmen, retail trade were also excluded, retaining in the female group only the insurance, real estate agents and brokers sub-category. The rationale was as follows: (1) In this analysis it is preferable to·understate the case rather than overstate it. This will become evident upon examination of the calculation of the costs. (2) The excluded categories tend to have much lower salary figures, suggesting either part time employment or low level skill requirements or both. Neither part time work nor low level skill requirements lend themselves to presentation of the case. (3) It is generally accepted that some of these female workers move in and out of the job market with a high degree of regularity, for example, during the Christmas season. (4) Therefore, ónly one category, that is, insurance, real estate brokers, etc. was retained.

EXECUTIVES: NUMBER AND COMPENSATION

9.18 Table 9.1 shows total employment and median income by category for the entire executive population. The total executive population in the United States is 21,545,000, comprised of 15,681,000 males and 5,864,000 females. Table 9.2 shows the percentage distribution of executives by sex.

Table 9.3 calculates the average compensation for male and female executives and for all executives combined.

TABLE 9.1
EXECUTIVE EMPLOYMENT AND INCOME, BY SEX AND
JOB CATEGORY (1970)

	Total employment (thousands)		Median income	
	Male	Female	Male	Female
Professional, technical, and kindred	6,917	4,644	$10,735	$6,034
Managers and administrators	5,386	1,077	11,277	5,495
Sales	3,378	143*	8,451	4,835
Total executive employment	15,681	5,864		

*Includes only insurance saleswomen, real estate agents and brokers, as explained in the text.
Source: *The U.S. Factbook for 1975: The American Almanac,* New York: Grosset & Dunlap, 1974, pp. 352–355.

TABLE 9.2
PERCENTAGE DISTRIBUTION OF EXECUTIVES (1970) BY SEX

	%
Men	73
Women	27
Total	100

Source: *The U.S. Factbook for 1975: The American Almanac,* New York: Grosset & Dunlap, 1974, pp. 352–354.

TABLE 9.3
AVERAGE EXECUTIVE COMPENSATION

	Total employment (thousands)	Compensation (median earnings)	Employment compensation (thousands)
Male			
Professional, technical, and kindred	6,917	$10,735	$74,253,995
Managers, administrators	5,386	11,277	60,737,922
Sales	3,378	8,451	28,547,478
Total male	15,681		$163,539,395
Female			
Professional, technical, and kindred	4,644	$6,034	$28,021,896
Managers, administrators	1,077	5,495	5,918,115
Sales	143	4,835	691,405
Total female	5,864		$34,631,416
Total	21,545		$198,170,811
Weighted average salary	$ 9,198		
Average salary men	10,429		
Average salary women	5,905		

Source: *The U.S. Factbook for 1975: The American Almanac,* New York: Grosset & Dunlap, 1974, pp. 352–355.

WORK LOSS

9.19 The available statistics provide data on absences from work. They do not, however, provide any data on the reduced amount of work performed by executives who report for duty, but are unable to perform at their normal level because of illness or because they are suffering in one form or another from stress. Further, unfortunately, the statistics provide us with averages for only the entire population, not for individual employment groups; consequently, our only recourse is to apply these average population statistics to the executive population without modification. Table 9.4 shows the number of days of disability by type (work loss, restricted activity, and bed disability) and by sex.

Using the data from Table 9.3 and 9.4, we are in a position to calculate part of the cost of executive work loss in terms of salary compensation. Table 9.5 shows the calculation. The cost, in terms of salary is over four billion dollars.

Peter Blythe states that authoritative medical opinion in the United States and Britain estimates that up to 70 per cent of all patients currently being treated by doctors in general practice are suffering from conditions which have their origins in unrelieved stress. (Blythe, 1973.)

Assuming the validity of this estimate of the relationship of stress to work loss days, the four billion dollar figure would be reduced to a 70% level, leaving as an upper limit 2.861 billion dollars attributable to stress origins. This figure is merely the direct cost to organizations for work loss days of executives due to the adverse effects of stress. There are other related costs.

We may also estimate the cost of executive work loss days in terms of the Gross National Product (GNP). Table 9.6 calculates the indi-

TABLE 9.4
DAYS OF DISABILITY, BY TYPE AND SEX OF PATIENT (1970)

	Days/Person	
	Male	*Female*
Work loss	5.0	5.9
Restricted activity	13.2	15.8
Bed disability	5.2	6.9

Source: *The U.S. Factbook for 1975: The American Almanac,* New York: Grosset & Dunlap, 1974, p. 84.

TABLE 9.5
COST OF EXECUTIVE WORK LOSS DAYS (1970)

Male
  Average work loss days rate   5.0
  Average (median) annual salary male
    executive $10,429
    daily rate: ann. salary/250 days $ 41.72
  Total individual salary cost (lost days ×
    daily rate) $ 208.60
  Male executive population × Total
    individual salary cost (15,681,000) ×
    ($208.60)   3,271,056,000

Female
  Average work loss days rate   5.9
  Average (median) annual salary female
    executive $ 5,905
    daily rate: ann. salary/250 days $ 23.62
  Total individual salary cost (lost days ×
    daily rate) $ 139.36
  Female executive population × total
    individual salary cost (5,864,000) ×
    ($139.36)   817,195,000

Total cost executive work loss days (in
  salary) $4,088,251,000

TABLE 9.6
DAILY GROSS NATIONAL PRODUCT (GNP) EQUALLY DISTRIBUTED ACROSS THE NATION'S TOTAL EMPLOYMENT (1970)

GNP	$977.1 Billion
Total employment	78,627 Thousand
Individual contribution	$ 12,427.
Daily individual contribution	$ 49.71

Source: *The U.S. Factbook for 1975: The American Almanac,* New York: Grosset & Dunlap, 1974, p. 84.

146

TABLE 9.7
COST OF EXECUTIVE WORK LOSS DAYS TO GNP (1970)

Male		
Average work loss days	5.0	
Average daily contribution to GNP	$ 49.71	
Loss of GNP per year per executive	$248.55	
Male executive population x loss of GNP per year per executive		
(15,681,000) × ($248.55)		$3,897,512,550
Female		
Average work loss days	5.9	
Average daily contribution to GNP	$ 49.71	
Loss of GNP per year per executive	$293.29	
Female executive population × loss of GNP per year per executive		
(5,864,000) × ($293.29)		$1,719,852,560
Total		$5,617,365,110

vidual contribution by dividing the GNP by the total work force. This number assumes that every worker makes an equal contribution to GNP—which may provide us with an understatement for executives. Applying the executive work loss days figures in Table 9.4 to the figures developed for GNP in Table 9.6 permits the computation of the cost of executive work loss days in terms of the GNP in Table 9.7. The resulting figure of 5.617 billion dollars may then be reduced by 30%)as suggested above on the basis of Blythe's report) to yield 3.932 billion dollars as an upper limit to the cost to the nation because of executive work loss days.

As may be seen from the figures in Tables 9.5 and 9.7, any action to reduce the adverse effects of stress for executives could result in a significant reduction of work loss days with a resultant savings to both the involved organizations and the nation.

HOSPITALIZATION EXPENSES

9.20 Not only is there a cost associated with being away from work but there are medical and hospital costs to consider in some instances. Table 9.8 shows the hospital use statistics for the na-

TABLE 9.8
HOSPITAL USE (1970)

	General and special hospitals	Psychiatric hospitals	Tuberculosis hospitals
Admissions per 1000 population	152	3.3	.02
Total days in hospital per 1000 population	1440	862	22
Average length of stay	9.5	261*	122
Cost per day†	$58.59	$16.63	$53.10
Outpatient visits per 1000 population	869		

*Our estimate.
†Average total (all types of hospitals): $53.95
Source: *The U.S. Factbook for 1975: The American Almanac,* New York: Grosset & Dunlap, 1974, p. 80.

TABLE 9.9
COST OF EXECUTIVE HOSPITALIZATION (1970)

General and Special Hospitals
Executive admissions	3,274,840	
Average stay (in days)	9.5	
Average cost per day	$ 58.59	
Executive admissions × stay × cost per day		
(3,274,840) × (9.5) × ($58.59)		$ 18,227,923

Psychiatric Hospitals
Executive admissions	71,098	
Average stay (in days)	261	
Average cost per day	$ 16.63	
Executive admissions × stay × cost per day		
(71,098) × (261) × ($16.63)		$308,595,892

Tuberculosis Hospitals
Executive admissions	4,309	
Average stay (in days)	122	
Average cost per day	$ 53.10	
Executive admissions × stay × cost per day		
(4309) × (122) × ($53.10)		$ 27,914,563

Total cost of executive hospitalization	$354,738,378

TABLE 9.10
COST OF EXECUTIVE OUTPATIENT CARE (1970)

Executive population × Outpatients visits per 1000 population (21,545,000 × 869)	18,722,605
Assuming an average charge of $10.00 per visit	$187,226,050

tion. Using these figures, and assuming that the executive population conforms to the national average, the cost of executive hospitalization may be computed. Table 9.9 shows the results of this computation; at the 70% level (again, acccording to Blythe's suggestion) this amounts to 248 million dollars a year.

The analysis may be continued for outpatient care. Table 9.10 calculates the number of outpatient visits that could be expected from executives. In the absence of more definite information, a very conservative estimate of $10 per outpatient visit is applied. The resulting costs at the 70% level amount to an additional 131 million dollars paid to hospitals for outpatient visits.

Statistics are not available for other types of medical and hospital expenses of executives suffering from stress.

EXECUTIVE MORTALITY COSTS

9.21 In addition to causing illness, stress can also result in death. One popular saw tells the harried executive "Death is nature's way of telling you to slow down."

That admonition has even more pertinence for the organization; the death of an executive, particularly a premature death, is a way of telling the organization to slow down and pause to examine if any organizational practices may be contributing to stress-related death.

Table 9.11 shows the estimated executive mortality by sex, age group, and the ten leading causes of death in the U.S. This table was derived by multiplying the U.S. average death rate per 100,000 population (in two categories: 25–44 years of age and 45–64 years of age, in both male and female classifications) by the executive population.

Unfortunately the available statistics do not report the differences between the executive population and the non-executive population. If the figures were provided the severity of the problem could quickly be

TABLE 9.11
ESTIMATED EXECUTIVE MORTALITY, BY SEX AND CAUSE (1970)

Age	Heart	Cancer	Stroke	Accident	Pneumonia	Homicide	Suicide	Diabetes	Cirrhosis of Liver	Emphysema	Total
Male											
25–44	8,985	5,316	1,270	12,623	1,098	3,920	3,277	690	2,320	141	39,640
45–64	101,142	51,418	9,001	13,752	5,081	2,336	4,704	3,591	9,346	4,077	204,448
Total	110,127	56,734	10,271	26,375	6,179	6,256	7,981	4,281	11,666	4,218	244,088
Female											
25–44	1,143	2,363	487	1,220	264	346	598	182	510	29	7,142
45–64	12,813	14,900	2,586	1,783	921	182	703	1,402	1,654	352	37,296
Total	13,956	17,263	3,073	3,003	1,185	528	1,301	1,584	2,164	381	44,438
Total Executive Mortality	124,083	73,997	13,344	29,378	7,364	6,784	9,282	5,865	13,830	4,599	288,526

Estimated, using figures obtained from: *The U.S. Factbook for 1975: The American Almanac*, New York: Grosset & Dunlap, 1974. See p. 64.

determined. The death rate for the overall population group at the ages examined is 1.34 percent.

Table 9.12 calculates the total lifetime earnings of executives at various ages to age 65. The figure used for a starting salary is $9,198 (the weighted average of all executives, male and female). This is compounded at the rate of 6% to arrive at total lifetime earnings. (This is as suggested by Table 582, Percent Increase in Average Salaries for Selected Occupations in Private Industry 1968 to 1973. *The U. S. Factbook for 1975,* op. cit., p. 361.) These total lifetime earnings are then computed for present value, once again using 6%.

$$\text{PVLE} = \frac{\sum_{t=0}^{n} \$9198(1.06)^{n}}{(1.06)^{n}}$$

This table shows that in 1970, a 40 year old executive would have a total lifetime earnings on the job (retirement at age 65) of $544,115. The present value of those earnings assuming a discount rate of 6% is $119,601.

Using the figures computed in Tables 9.11 and 9.12 we can compute an expected value of the total losses (expressed in terms of executive earnings) due to premature executive deaths. The construction of Table 9.13 assumes death at the mid-point range, (i.e., for the 25–44 age group, the mid-point selected was 35 years of age). The mortality

TABLE 9.12
PRESENT VALUE OF EXECUTIVE LIFETIME EARNINGS (PVLE),* BY AGE (1970)

Age Now	Total Lifetime Earnings	PVLE
30	$1,095,665	$134,482
35	780,000	128,118
40	544,115	119,601
45	367,849	108,204
50	236,133	92,952
55	137,706	72,541
60	64,158	45,228

*Estimated at current average (median) salary increasing at 6% annually to age 65, and then discounted at 6%.

The rate of 6% for both salary increases and discounting present value of money appears reasonable for the year 1970, even though not at the time of writing. The reader may substitute any currently appropriate figures and rates without distorting the model.

TABLE 9.13
TOTAL EXECUTIVE MORTALITY LOSSES

Estimated present value of lifetime earnings discounted at 6% and age—1970

Age (mid-point of range)	Mortality Rate	P. V. Lifetime Earnings	Total PVLE
35	46,782	$128,118	$ 5,993,616,276
55	241,744	$ 72,541	$17,536,351,504
Total PVLE			$23,529,967,770

rate is multiplied by the present value of lifetime earnings to arrive a a total PVLE for each age group. The total PVLE for the two groups is 23.529 billion dollars. At the 70% level (mentioned above) this amounts to over 16 billion dollars for 1970.

WORKMEN'S COMPENSATION

9.22 Workers have been employed throughout all written history, but the rights of an injured worker throughout most of this time have been non-existent or at best vague. Even when it was clear that the employer had a liability, the worker generally had a difficult time pressing a claim.

Germany was the first to adopt a workmen's compensation law in 1884: the United Kingdom followed in 1897, and a number of American states followed shortly thereafter. The system is now almost universal in the advanced industrialized countries and very widespread in developing countries. (Quinn, 1972.)

The intent of workmen's compensation statutes is to provide a remedy for occupational injury or occupational disease arising from the worker's employment. In the past there have been rather strict interpretations of the statutes.

The more obvious of the occupational injuries include lacerations and bone fractures. More subtle and perhaps more destructive are the occupational diseases of which pneumoconioses (any disease of the lung caused by inhalation of dust) are the most common of the incapacitating. Of more recent interest are the effects of vinyl chloride.

The effects of stress, however, are more evident in the emotional and intellectual responses of individuals to the conditions of work.

Lesser cites a specific case which provides some insight into the liability of organizations for such conditions: in *McMillan v. Western Pacific Railroad Company* (357 P 2d 449), the California Supreme Court held the employer liable for a nervous breakdown sustained by a train dispatcher because of allegedly emotional stresses and tensions which he experienced in operating the central traffic control system of the railroad while 'people were shouting at him over loud speakers.' The Court held that the remedial and humanitarian purposes of the compensation law should not be thwarted by restricting the term 'injuries' to mean only bodily (organic) injuries. (Lesser, 1967.)

Lesser cites a number of other cases, the general thrust of which is that the effects of job oriented stress are now being interpreted in broad terms by the American judicial system.

Sometimes, indeed, employees are sufficiently disturbed to take action with disastrous consequences for the organization as a whole:

... A case study concerning a paper bag manufacturing plant will serve to illustrate the potentially high costs to workers and employers of job environments that adversely affect mental health. The workers in the plant described were, in general, poorly educated, low-skilled machine operators:

Management was suspicious of its employees, feeling that 'they are always trying to get away with something.' The factory floor was noisy, dingy, hot in summer, cold in winter. Rules were plentiful and strictly enforced. Suspicion and open dislike of management for workers and workers for management was evident. Two years ago, a factory worker died of a heart attack while working at his job. As the news got around the plant, several women employees became ill and fainted. A few weeks later, a noxious odor leaked into the plant through sewage pipes and a few employees were overcome and had to leave work. Although the odor was quickly eliminated, employees began complaining of dizziness, nausea, malaise, headaches, and other problems. A team from the Public Health Service was called in, but no toxic agents could be discovered, and medical doctors could find nothing physically wrong with any of the workers after thorough examinations and laboratory tests. A representative of the National Institute of Occupational Safety and Health was then called in, and concluded from the evidence that it was a case of industrial hysteria, a physical reaction to the psychological stresses of the job. He offered suggestions for remedying the situation, but no action was taken. A year later, the plant was burned to the ground. Arson was suspected.

What is particularly significant about this admittedly extreme example is that only a small investment might have offset the dire consequences of management's inaction. By using available job redesign techniques for reducing anxiety in the plant, the workers could have been spared mental and physical anguish, and both they and the company could have avoided the extreme costs.

Unfortunately, these job redesign techniques . . . have not been used on a wide scale They require tailoring to meet specific problems, but their potential value has been demonstrated. But before these techniques can be put into practice, we must make a commitment to improving the mental health of workers as a good in itself and accept the desirability of reducing medical costs though preventive measures in the workplace. (U.S., Dept. of Health, Education, and Welfare, 1973, p. 90−91.)

Every state in the Union now requires employers to provide workmen's compensation benefits to their employees. Most companies obtain workmen's compensation insurance to pay these benefits, the premium costs for workmen's compensation insurance are calculated on the basis of the workmen's compensation benefits paid. Table 9.14 shows these costs for three selected years and the percentage increase. As may be seen in the table, the annual costs to organizations in 1972 was less than the benefits paid; therefore, in ensuing years the costs will rise to cover this deficit. Quite obviously, failure to take account of the direct and indirect effects of stress will serve to increase such costs.

INDUSTRIAL AND COMMERCIAL FAILURES

9.23   While the general trend of productivity in the United States has been on the increase for the last one hundred years, there are significant deviations in individual enterprises and industries. We discuss the effect of stress on productivity later in this chapter (9.24); here we cite some statistics which have at least an indirect bearing on the subject. The number and rate of business failures provide some, however tenuous, indication of productivity in individual enterprises. While failures may occur for other reasons (e.g., insufficient capitalization, inappropriate marketing, etc.), inadequate productivity is certainly one factor to take into consideration. But inadequate productivity, in turn, may have a variety of causes, only one of which is ineffective management. Unfortunately, there are no statistics available to indicate the role of ineffective management in business failures. We can only speculate about the degree to which it is responsible. The costs of business failures, however, are of such a magnitude that even if ineffective management is the cause in only a small percentage of instances, there is still a basis for concern.

In its fiftieth anniversary issue, *Forbes* magazine (9-15-67) analyzed the changes over a fifty-year period in the standings of the top one hundred companies in the United States. During that period, 189 company names appeared in that list, indicating, to some degree at

TABLE 9.14
WORKMEN'S COMPENSATION STATISTICS (1965, 1970, AND 1972)

	1965 (millions)	1970 (millions)	% Increase	1972 (millions)	% Increase
Workers covered (estimated)	51	59	16	62	5
Benefits paid during year	$1814	$3011	66	$4023	34
Annual costs to organization	2042	3492	71	4014	15

Source: *The U.S. Factbook for 1975: The American Almanac,* New York: Grosset & Dunlap, 1974, p. 84.

least, and even after allowing for mergers, the rate of failure among the leading business organizations. *Forbes* attributed success and failure alike to the quality of management.

Among lesser companies, of course, the failure rate is still greater. Table 9.15, shows the number of new business concerns and business failures in 1970; Table 9.16 shows the distribution by type of business and size of liability. Table 9.17, shows the same type of information for the four-year period 1970–1973. Business analysts seem to agree that business failures may be generally regarded as symptomatic primarily of the quality of the internal management of the involved organizations. We can only speculate about the degree to which ineffective performance by management in such instances is stress-induced, but intuitive judgment would lead us to believe that it is no small proportion, the dollar costs are significant. Table 9.17 also shows what the national losses would be if only one out of every five business failures is attributed to stress.

TABLE 9.15
NEW BUSINESS CONCERNS AND BUSINESS FAILURES (1970)

	Number
New business incorporations	284,000
Business failures	10,748
Current liabilities	$1,887.8 million

Source: *The U.S. Factbook for 1975: The American Almanac,* New York: Grosset & Dunlap, 1974, pp. 476, 492, and 818.

TABLE 9.16
INDUSTRIAL AND COMMERCIAL FAILURES (1970)

	Size of Liability	
Industry	Under $100,000	$100,000 and Over
Mining and manufacturing	1069	966
Wholesale trade	650	334
Retail	3984	666
Construction	1229	458
Commercial services	1087	305
Total	8019	2729

Source: *The U.S. Factbook for 1975: The American Almanac,* New York: Grosset & Dunlap, 1974, Table No. 814, p. 493.

TABLE 9.17
ESTIMATED NATIONAL LOSSES DUE TO BUSINESS FAILURE

Year	Total No. of Firms That Failed	Over $100,000 Liability	Average Liability	20% Total Liability
1970	10,748	2729	$176,000	$ 96,060,800
1971	10,326	2581*	186,000	96,013,200
1972	9,566	2526	209,000	105,586,800
1973	9,345	2718	246,000	133,725,600

*Estimated.
Source: Adapted from *The U.S. Factbook for 1975: The American Almanac,* New York: Grosset & Dunlap, 1974, Tables 812 and 814, pp. 492–493.

OTHER COSTS OF STRESS

9.24   The foregoing statistics on certain selected costs of executive stress are admittedly incomplete. We have presented only limited data on work loss, and extremely limited data on, and only indirectly related to, decreased productivity. Our estimates of hospitalization expenses should be supplemented by the costs (probably of equal or greater magnitude) of medical services, medications, and related services and supplies. We have discussed only one element (workmen's compensation) of the cost factor of insurance premiums, which should be supplemented by other insurance costs: health, life, casualty, etc. We have not yet discussed the factor of tort claims. We have barely mentioned the indirectly measurable costs related to these factors and the intangible costs. Further, there may be numerous costs which we have not, or cannot yet, identify. In addition to all of these costs, there are certain other costs which, although we cannot yet measure for one reason or another, we can directly or indirectly attribute to certain of the mediate effects of executive stress. In the following sections we discuss some of these items: (1) the previously mentioned cost factor of tort claims, (2) the costs of turnover, (3) the costs of nonturnover, and (4) the costs of poor human relations—in the organization, in the family, and in society in general.

TORT CLAIMS

9.25 One source of cost of increasing significance is that of tort claims for stress-related disabilities and deaths. The primary significance of these court cases for this study is the increasing degree of recognition by the courts of the role of stress in creating or triggering compensable disabilities or death.

The law tends to move slowly, sometimes the changes in law seem almost imperceptible. This process of evolution, rather than revolution, in law tends to provide the stabilizing factor in our relations with each other. This stability, while necessary for business and society, may also provide the top management of organizations with a false sense of security. The executive may believe that understanding of the law as it stood some years ago makes one competent to understand the law today.

For example, it is generally considered that management has the right to make work assignments for its employees. To a certain extent that is correct thinking, but there are exceptions, particularly where stress is involved. The case of Mr. Dilworth Thomas Rogers is an interesting example. Rogers had been a research chemist for a large petroleum company for thirty years when he was forced to retire at the age of sixty. He died of cancer several years later. In the suit, Mrs. Rogers and her daughter (a coplaintiff) charged that Rogers, after nearly thirty years service had been assigned to menial tasks when he refused to resign, that he had been discriminated against because of age, and that, as a result, he had suffered severe emotional distress. The jury awarded the plaintiffs $780,000. The case is one of a number indicating a trend toward more limitation on the discretionary authority of employers, particularly when the arbitrary exercise of that authority produces stress in the employee. (See: *The Atlanta Constitution,* p. 1, col. 5, 2-7-75.)

A further implication of such cases is that employees, particularly those under undue stress, or those who feel they are being harassed or discriminated against will begin to build their cases for subsequent civil suits while still working for their employers. Under these circumstances, the employers may actually be paying their employees to prepare cases against them.

One may readily conclude that the opportunity for great financial loss or for high costs associated with executive stress is increasing in the legal arena.

TURNOVER

9.26   Harry Truman once said, "If you can't stand the heat, get out of the kitchen." Many executives are literally following this advice. Exactly how much executive turnover is taking place is difficult to estimate. However, according to Dean Peskin, high executive turnover is a fact of corporate life. (Peskin, 1973.) Further, as Peskin suggests, executives are tending increasingly to identify with the profession or occupation of executive or manager, per se, rather than with a specific employing organization. Thus, they have become one of the most mobile occupation groups in the nation.

The prevailing view among social scientists is that people work because they have needs that work can satisfy. When these satisfactions are not present they think about leaving. When they leave, there are inevitably related costs to the employing organization, costs which would not be incurred absent the turnover.

Although most employing organizations do not know what their turnover really costs, and although there appear to be no reliable statistics on the costs of turnover for any employment category, much less for executives, we may secure some qualitative idea of such costs from a mere enumeration of some of the direct and indirect costs which are obviously related to personnel changes at the executive level (Table 9.18). This is not to suggest, of course, that each and every instance of personnel turnover at the executive level is accompanied by each and every one of the items of cost listed in this table. It is to suggest, however, that each and every one of these costs is incurred in one or another instance of executive turnover and that each instance of executive turnover involves an unspecified number of these itemized costs.

Table 9.18
THE COSTS OF TURNOVER*

I. Tangible Costs

A. Recruiting and Employment Expenses
  1. Advertising associated with recruiting.
  2. Executive search fees.
  3. Employment agency fees.
  4. Selection: prescreening, interviewing, medical examinations, testing, reference checking.
  5. Travel and living expenses for candidates.
  6. Travel and living expenses for recruiters.
  7. Printed materials that aid in recruiting process. For example, forms, booklets.
  8. Wages and salaries of those employed in recruitment, employment, and placement activities.
  9. Apportioned wages and salaries of those who assist in recruiting, employment, and placement activities.
  10. Apportioned salaries of those involved in interviewing and decisionmaking.
  11. Allocation of normal office stationery and supplies.
  12. Direct and indirect items supplied to new hires: identification cards, photographs, and so forth.
  13. Allocation of organizational overhead expenses.
  14. Relocation expenses.
  15. Temporary living expenses during relocation.
  16. Temporary travel expenses to and from residence until relocated.
  17. Mortgage arrangements with financial institutions.
  18. Moving expenses.
  19. Lost time of employee while engaged in moving.

B. Breaking-in costs
  1. New employee programs (indoctrination programs, orientations, briefings and tours).
  2. Initial training schools.
  3. Travel and living expenses involved with off-site training.
  4. On-the-job training.
  5. Materials and equipment for on-the-job training which include waste because of lack of proficiency.
  6. Supervision for on-the-job training.
  7. Wages and salaries of those who track learning curve statistics and other trainee measurements.
  8. Material development for on-the-job training.
  9. Special tools or "gear" supplied to new employees.
  10. Tuition and reimbursement for education expenses outside the organization.

C. Separation Expense
  1. Lost production until replacement is productive.
  2. Idle machine capacity because an employee has left.
  3. Wages and salaries and other allocated expenses of those working on termination activities.
  4. Severance pay.

159

Table 9.18 *(cont'd.)*
THE COSTS OF TURNOVER*

I. Tangible Costs

D.   Short-timer costs
  1.   Reduced productivity for employee.
  2.   Reduced productivity of fellow workers.
  3.   Employee absence due to job hunting, indifference, and so forth.
  4.   On-the-job job hunting: time, resume writing, telephone calls, company resources used.

E.   Social Security tax payments (front-end loaded).

F.   Unemployment insurance contributions (front-end loaded).

II. Intangible Costs

A.   Demoralizing effect on employees, affecting productivity.

B.   Time for employee to become effective. (Some executives say that it takes six months.)

C.   Intentional sabotage by a disgruntled employee (may remain unknown to the organization).

D.   Employees (especially executives) leaving with company secrets, that is, new product plans or patents, marketing strategies, technological processes that innovate production, or customer and prospect lists.

*Many items in this list were suggested by Peskin (1973, p. 72); however, we have supplemented the list, particularly to include those items that carry the heaviest expense.)

NON-TURNOVER

9.27   Although the specific data are not available at this point, the identification and analysis of the costs of turnover, would be rather straightforward in any given organization. Estimating the costs of non-turnover are much more difficult.

As indicated in chapter 8, some executives who are extremely dissatisfied stay on, but their commitment has gone; in effect, they become executive dropouts. They go through the motions of performing, perhaps even vigorously, even though their performance is at, or very near, minimal levels. For obvious reasons, data on the costs to the individuals and their organizations of such situations are even less accessible, much less available, than the elusive data on the costs of turnover. While the costs associated with such phenomena are difficult to identify and estimate, they are nevertheless real and they signifi-

cantly affect the bottom line performance on the profit and loss statement. The effect is double-edged, in addition to the direct quantitative
effect on profit and loss, there is the serious qualitative effect on the
calibre of management—the most dynamic, progressive executives
leave for better opportunities, the less effective executives stay on,
resulting in a continuing and self-reinforcing deterioration of the general level of management, which in turn serves to further deleteriously
affect the profit and loss statement.

Auren Uris devotes eleven chapters of one of his books to describing
the situations in which executives find themselves (Uris, 1972). He
finds a high degree of degradation and dehumanization in the modern
organization. He also finds companies at the other extreme, very large
corporations which are very paternalistic and provide a benevolent,
protective, and secure working environment so that the employees
become contented and lose their vigor and sharpness: and vigor and
sharpness are the very qualities which employing organizations need
most in their employees.

POOR HUMAN RELATIONS

9.28 Thus, both the autocratic and the paternalistic styles of
management tend to be stress-producing. In fact, poor
human relations of any type are stress-producing and are the most
fruitful source of the psychological causes of stress. Perhaps less clear
is the role of stress in the development of poor human relations in the
first place, but, as we saw in chapter 5, stress tends to beget stress; not
only is there a vicious cycle within the self-system, but stress is contagious. One stressed individual in an organization can serve as a
potential stressor for many others with whom interaction occurs. This
is especially true of those in an executive capacity. All those members
of the organization who must deal with the stressed executive suffer
some of the same adverse effects, and poor human relations permeates
the organization. The costs are intangible and incalculable.

POOR FAMILY RELATIONSHIPS

9.29 The stressed executive, of course, does not and cannot leave
work-induced stress at the office. The adverse effects of
undue stress go home with the executive and almost invariably infect
the family relationships. If the resultant stressful conditions do not

disrupt the family altogether through separation or divorce, they take their toll in other ways—physical and mental illness, accidents, suicide, and other forms of death. Further, the stress of the parent is visited upon the children, who pass it on in turn. Again, the costs are both intangible and incalculable.

POOR SOCIAL RELATIONSHIPS

9.30 Just as the stressed executive does not and cannot leave work-induced stress at the office, so the executive's family members do not and cannot leave their stress at home. They, in turn, infect others and when they interact with other stressed individuals, the adverse effects are multiplied. Thus, stress tends to ramify through society as a whole, with untold costs for generations to come.

SUMMARY

9.31 The foregoing analysis identifies some of the principal costs of the effects of undue stress on the individual executive; the costs are both direct and indirect, both tangible and intangible, and they bear, without effective discrimination on the individual, the employing organization, and the family, as well as the society of which they are part. While the above listing of costs is imposing, it is not intended to be either comprehensive or exhaustive. Only a controlled interdisciplinary study bringing to bear the combined resources of physiology, medicine, psychology, psychiatry, sociology, economics, political science, and other disciplines could begin to approach a comprehensive analysis of the total costs to the individual, the organization, and society.

Despite the limitations, however, the above listing indicates that the problem of undue stress is a significant one requiring further and closer attention by the top management of every large organization. Ignoring for the moment those costs to which we have been unable to assign specific dollar figures, and looking only at those selected cost factors for which specific cost estimates were made, the total is imposing by any current standards.

Let us recognize, however, that the estimates are subject to challenge and may not be acceptable to some readers as directly related to stress. We need not, of course, offer any defense of the census figures on whch the cost estimates are based. But our acceptance of Peter Blythe's suggestion (based on his survey of medical authorities) that up to 70% of all patients currently being treated by doctors in general practice are suffering from conditions which have their origins in unrelieved stress may offer pause to some readers. Let us assume, therefore, that the 70% figure overstates the actual situation by 100%; in other words, let us assume that only 35% of all patients currently being treated by doctors in general practice are suffering from conditions which have their origins in unrelieved stress. Table 9.19 lists the figures previously computed at the 70% level and reduces them to the 35% level. In constructing this table, the cost of executive work loss days was entered using the salary computation rather than the larger figure which was used to compute the cost in terms of GNP.

Even at the 35% level, however, and for only a few of the selected cost factors, the cost of executive stress is calculated to be almost $10 billion. On the basis of these calculations, the national cost of executive stress in 1970, is topped by the revenue of only three industrial corporations in that year. Costs of that order of magnitude would represent a significant problem, one worthy of attention in any nation, even the most highly industrialized. Furthermore, we need to recognize the necessity for adding to these figures the presently incalculable costs of such items as health and life insurance premiums, medical expenses, turnover; non-turnover, tort claims, decreased productivity, and impaired human relationships at the family, organization, and national levels. If we could mobilize the data on these other cost factors, the total would probably be raised by several orders of magnitude.

TABLE 9.19
COSTS OF EXECUTIVE STRESS, COMPUTED AT 70% AND 35% OF TOTAL COSTS OF MORBIDITY AND MORTALITY

	70% Level	35% Level
Cost of executive work loss days (salary)	$ 2,861,775,700	$1,430,887,850
Cost of executive hospitalization	248,316,864	124,158,432
Cost of executive outpatient care	131,058,235	65,529,117
Cost of executive mortality	16,470,977,439	8,235,488,720
Total	$19,712,128,238	$9,856,064,119

Chapter 10

Implications of the Costs of Stress

10.0 The two preceding chapters point up the enormity of the effects and dollar costs of stress, measurable or not at this stage, but there are other costs and effects—for the individual, the organization, and society. These other costs and effects are only implied in the above discussion; in fact, not all of them can even be identified. Some of them, at least, are, nevertheless, highly significant. Even when they can be identified, there is no known way, at present, by which they can be incorporated in our model for assessing the costs of stress. Our treatment of the subject would, however, be less than adequate if we failed even to mention such other costs and effects. Accordingly, even though no in-depth treatment is possible, we identify below some of the implications of the costs and effects of undue executive stress.

FOR THE INDIVIDUAL

10.1 The physiological and psychological costs of undue stress, in terms of physical and mental well-being as well as length of life span, are fairly obvious and have been discussed in Part II. Not mentioned there, yet inevitably affected, is the quality of life of over-stressed individuals—the effect of undue stress on their "pursuit of happiness." Less apparent is the effect on their philosophy, their cosmology, their outlook on life—and the consequent indirect effects of such philosophy on their interactions with other individuals, the organization, and society. Undue stress will also affect their attitudes and temperaments and thereby the fundamental nature of their very existence, their behavior, and their interrelationships with other individuals and organizations. The ramifying effects are obvious and legion.

FOR THE ORGANIZATION

10.2 Executives are, of course, members of many organizations, beginning with the primary group—the family—on up to the nation and society in general. Any event or situation which affects them, inevitably affects their interrelationships with every other person in every organization of which they are members. Thus, the individual executive must be recognized not only as a stress-receiving, but also as a stress-producing, system. Undue stress serves as positive feedback in any system, tending to further exacerbate the situation and eventually driving the system out of control. The nature of the effect is the same regardless of the hierarchical level of the system; the differences are in degree only.

FOR SOCIETY

10.3 A world of stressful individuals interacting in a variety of systems at various hierarchical levels in such a way as to continually increase the level of stress in each individual probably seems too dire a prospect to contemplate. Yet the implications of the present situation are clear unless some effort is made at some level to reduce the stressful inputs.

SUMMARY

10.4 We have now developed our tentative model to the limit of present capability; we have identified the existing limitations and constraints; we have collected and analyzed the available statistics; and we have identified the gaps in our knowledge. The results of our analysis appear in Figure 10.1.

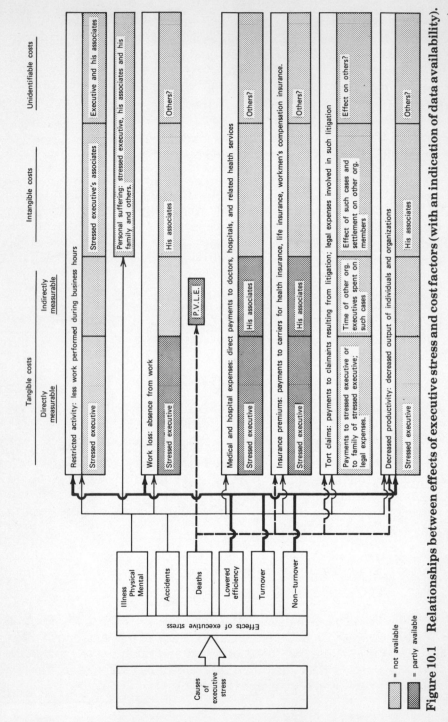

Figure 10.1   Relationships between effects of executive stress and cost factors (with an indication of data availability).

Because such little work has been done in assessing the costs of executive stress, and because any frontier models are necessarily tentative until they are subjected to scientific scrutiny and testing, the model we propose is more suggestive than indicative of the costs and effects of stress. Given the existing limitations, and subject to further testing, however, the projected model appears to be reliable and valid, at least in terms of the order of magnitude. Even this rough measure reveals the significance of the problem. Furthermore, if our estimate of its significance proves to be generally acceptable, then it may be worthwhile to fine-tune the model and make provision for collecting or gaining access to the necessary additional information that is not currently in the public domain. Finally, it may even be worthwhile for large organizations to begin to gather, and to share, data on the costs of executive stress. Currently, most organizations tend to keep such information confidential, if it is available at all.

The potentialities of such a more nearly complete model of the costs and effects of executive stress are almost limitless and to a management theorist very exciting. From a broad entrepreneurial point of view, the costs of executive stress now represent real and significant vulnerabilities within the economic system—vulnerabilities which could, with the aid of adequate knowledge, be converted into entrepreneurial opportunities. Shifting personnel resources from low productivity to higher levels of productivity without increased cost—in fact, with real probabilities of long-range, significant decreases in costs through elimination of stress-related costs—offers prospects of hitherto unvisualized economic improvement. Such improvement would indirectly benefit consumers as well, since the customer never really pays for costs (or waste), but only for utility.

From an even broader point of view, the possibilities of delimiting the adverse effects of undue stress offer even greater advantages—opportunities, not only for improving economic performance, but for improving the health and social well-being of one of our most important vocational groups, our managers and executives, as well as the individuals and organizations with whom they interrelate.

PART IV
THE MANAGEMENT OF
STRESS

As with the causes of stress, there is not, to the best of our knowledge, currently available any systematic treatment of the remedies for stress, much less any proposals for a systemic approach to the management of stress. In chapter 13, we propose to sketch out the framework for such an approach—a systems approach to managing stress. First, however, we review in chapter 11, some of the more prominently mentioned measures for the alleviation of stress; we call them coping mechanisms. For the most part, the coping mechanisms are techniques for relieving accumulated stress or for offsetting some of its adverse effects. The application of these techniques is analogous to the ad hoc approach to management—applying grease to the squeaking wheel. In chapter 12, we discuss some of the more generalized measures which may be taken for the prevention, diversion, or control of stress. Such measures represent an advance over the ad hoc approach, but in themselves are still inadequate for the effective management of stress.

Any program for the effective management of stress must take into consideration both the inevitability of stress and its dual nature—eustress and distress. Recognizing its inevitability, the executive should seek, not to eliminate it, because such effort would be futile, but to manage it so as to maximize its benefits and minimize its deleterious effects. Recognizing its dual nature, executives should learn to seek out methods for utilizing their eustress to improve their creativity and productivity, while minimizing their distress so as to reduce personal suffering. Chapter 13 outlines a systems approach for managing stress to achieve these results. The approach we suggest is relatively simple, but not easy. It will require a basic change in the life style of an executive, but the cost-benefit ratio is far more favorable than any that the executive will ever encounter in his or her business dealings.

In addition to the systems approach for the individual management of one's own stress levels, we also identify some responsibilities of the employing organization and of society in general for the improvement of the life styles of their members through the management of stress.

Chapter 11
Coping Mechanisms

11.0 We should understand from the outset that there is no panacea for stress. (See: Selye, 1974.) The reader who has come this far in our discussion of the causes and effects of stress will appreciate its highly individual nature; one person's stress is another person's zest, and vice versa.

In the light of this basic fact, the existence of a general treatment, or even a general pattern of treatment, of stress is not to be expected. Instead, one might expect to find in the literature on stress a wide variety of proposed coping mechanisms and purported cures and, in fact, that is exactly what we do find. What we do not find is any systematic analysis or discussion of such proposals. We propose to take a first step in that direction.

First, however, let us dispose of a number of nontechniques, of contraindicated coping mechanisms. Many executives, looking for quick relief from the adverse effects of stress, and impatient of any necessarily time-consuming analytical or systematic approach to the solution of their problems, will frequently, and illogically, resort to the use of almost any means which offers promise of alleviation of the immediate symptoms. The same executive who would disdainfully dismiss any such approach to the solution of an organizational problem, will unthinkingly accept with alacrity any expedient which provides even temporary relief, and without regard for the long range consequences to mental or physical well-being. Such an executive will zealously guard the integrity and future security of the organization, while neglecting or abusing his or her own self-system, failing to recognize the mutual interdependence of the two. Incapable of accepting, or unwilling to believe, that personal distress is other than momentary or at most ephemeral, the executive seeks relief in palliatives, which, in turn, become habit-forming and thereby serve as additional sources of stress in a vicious cycle. Among the most popular of such palliatives are alcohol, tobacco, tranquilizers, sedatives, and certain mind-altering drugs.

Although usually considered to be a stimulant, alcohol is actually a depressant. While it may seem to relieve fatigue and provide energy, alcohol actually merely lowers certain cerebral inhibitions and thereby provides the illusion of relief from stress, but at the cost of slowing the thinking processes and neural reflexes, and impairing judgment. Initially, alcohol inhibits hypothalamic activity (countering the action of the G.A.S. (see 3.3)); continued ingestion, however, begins to dull the senses and leads eventually to unconsciousness. Long term use leads to addiction (alcoholism) with attendant hallucinations and frequently to the mental disorder of delirium tremens. Alcoholism also results in certain nutritional deficiencies because alcohol provides sufficient calories to keep the imbiber from becoming hungry, but the calories are empty, the alcoholic fails to receive needed vitamins, minerals, and other essential nutrients. The deficiency diseases affect the brain, the nerves, and the liver. There is even some evidence that heavy drinkers are more susceptible to cancer of the mouth than moderate drinkers or teetotalers. In addition to leading to the loss of mental and physical health, alcoholism also frequently results in loss of friends, family, and job, and thereby to financial ruin.

Alcohol, when prescribed by a physician, may be useful in the treatment of certain diseases and physical conditions, but should not be given indiscriminately as a treatment in other instances, certainly not as a first-aid treatment—it may be harmful or even fatal in cases of heatstroke or snakebite. The moderate use of alcohol for occasional relaxation, although still somewhat controversial, probably is not unduly harmful; at least, there seems to be little, if any, evidence that it has any long term adverse effects. Many physicians and other health authorities maintain that wine, in moderate amounts at mealtime, may aid digestion for some individuals. Yet even the occasional use of alcohol results in some impairment of judgment and coordination.

Smoking and other uses of tobacco occasionally and in small amounts similarly provide an immediate stimulating effect upon mental and bodily powers, but continued use or use of larger amounts have a depressant effect. The narcotic effect of tobacco gives a false sense of relief from stress and frequently leads to addiction. The adverse effects are numerous and significant. Continued and excessive smoking, especially of cigarettes, leads to palpitation and irregularity of the heart; occasional giddy spells; sudden attacks of faintness; liability to fatigue on slight exertion; dyspepsia and peptic ulcers; dimness of vision and impairment of ability to see colors; chronic sore throat and coughing; cancer of the tongue, mouth, throat, lungs, and bladder; and cardiovascular diseases.

Tranquilizers provided such a remarkable degree of success in the treatment of certain psychotic disorders that a number of physicians, especially in the 1950's and 1960's, began to prescribe them more freely for the relief of stress and some of its related disorders. Tranquilizers tend to induce a mental state of calm, peace, and serenity, free from worry, anxiety, and psychomotor agitation, and without clouding consciousness. Although alcohol, tobacco, and the barbiturates might be included in this category, the term commonly applies to only certain drugs: for example, chlorpromazine, reserpine, meprobromate, benactyzine, and diazepam (Valium). Unfortunately, the freedom with which such drugs were dispensed led to serious abuses— some patients securing prescriptions by telephone without seeing a physician, much less undergoing a physical examination and diagnosis; some individuals using another's prescriptions or procuring the drugs without a prescription; black market sales, etc. Indiscriminate users found, however, that the drugs produced such adverse side effects as: toxic delirium, jaundice, skin eruptions, asthmatic attacks, and significant changes in blood chemistry.

A number of commonly prescribed sedatives (chiefly the barbiturates and bromides), while serving beneficial uses in a limited number of instances and under the direction of a physician, have equally severe adverse effects when used inappropriately. Sedatives may be prescribed for insomnia, headaches and other types of pain, stomach disorders, migraine, emotional disturbances, and other adverse effects of stress, with beneficial results, but they are toxic and may produce unwanted side effects similar to those mentioned above for tranquilizers. The so-called "pep pills" (such as benzedrine and caffeine) have much more limited beneficial effects, but at least as serious adverse effects. Pain relievers of all kinds are habit forming and should be used only under the direction of a physician.

The more powerful narcotics—cocaine, heroin, LSD, marijuana, and morphine, etc.—are even more dangerous when not administered under the care and direction of a physician. The relief from stress that they seem to provide is purely illusory. Although some meditation techniques may include the use of one or more of these mind-altering drugs, other techniques are much more likely to be effective in the long run and will not entail the risks involved in the use of such drugs.

All of the above mentioned nontechniques have one characteristic in common: they are all typical of the ad hoc approach to management;

they are suggested by out-moded single-cause habits of thinking; they completely avoid the systems implications of executive stress. At best, such measures constitute mere temporary palliatives; they serve only to alleviate some of the symptoms of undue stress; they interfere with any logical approach to a systematic treatment program. They are basically unsound, invalid, and unwarranted.

There are, however, a number of more legitimate coping mechanisms aimed at reducing an individual's vulnerability to stress, correcting certain kinds of maladaptive behavior, or improving the stressed individual's way of dealing with the vagaries of life.

In this chapter we shall identify those treatments and techniques which seem to be most significant in terms of the attention they have received from serious students of the subject. Our discussion of each coping mechanism will be limited to an exposition of its general nature and its intended effects. In addition, we shall provide citations to some of the most prominent references, for the guidance of the reader interested in pursuing any given coping mechanism in further detail.

After setting out this array of available coping mechanisms, we shall examine how they relate, individually and collectively, to the causes of executive stress as discussed in Part II. This analysis of the proposed coping mechanisms should help to prepare us for the discussion in chapter 13 of a systems approach to the management of stress, indicating the opportunities open to the executive and the corporation for dealing with this highly significant and extremely expensive phenomenon of modern business life.

Before embarking on this review, however, we should remind the reader of the point which has been made before that stress is essential to life and the only way to eliminate all stress is to eliminate life itself. Our aim then is not to eliminate stress, but to learn how to manage it so as to enjoy the benefits of eustress, to reduce or eliminate undue stress, and to alleviate the deleterious effects of such undue stress as cannot be avoided. Whether any of the coping mechanisms described below, or any other given technique or strategy serves a useful purpose depends on the context, the individual's vulnerability, and the specific stressors. For this reason, our mention in this discussion of any particular coping mechanism must not be taken as an endorsement of its indiscriminate application as a cure or treatment of stress, but merely as an indication that an executive might reasonably consider its applicability to his or her particular situation. We shall indicate the possible and potential effects of each coping mechanism we mention and, in chapter 13, we shall suggest how some of them might be fitted into a more systematic approach to the management of the individual's stress levels.

To facilitate our exposition and evaluation of these coping mechanisms we have established our own categorization. The proponents of any given technique may not agree with our assignment of it to one of our categories, and any one of the techniques might properly be classified in more than one category, but the classification will serve our immediate purposes.

We shall divide the proposed coping mechanisms into six categories: biofeedback techniques, meditation and relaxation techniques, body (physical) therapies, exercise techniques, dietary regimens, and psychological therapies.

BIOFEEDBACK

11.1 According to Buryl Payne there are over 2000 feedback systems in the human body. (Payne, 1972.) It is this feedback that allows normal and proper functioning of the body. When one of these feedback mechanisms fails to operate properly the result is faulty functioning of one or more parts of the self-system; for example, in such conditions as *intention tremor* or *Parkinsonianism*. (See Wiener, 1950, p. 224.) But these faulty feedback mechanisms are not restricted to intention tremor and Parkinson's disease. They may involve blood pressure, heart rate, and even the involuntary raising of hairs on the body or the involuntary dilation of the pupils in the eye.

For a long time medical scientists had assumed that the body functions that are normally controlled by the autonomic nervous system could not be brought under conscious control—breathing being the exception. However, the scientists did not know quite what to think about individuals like yogis, who seemed to possess phenomenal control over their internal processes. For a long time, the general belief was that people who could walk on live coals, have themselves buried alive, or stop their hearts were beyond the realm of science, but science, and especially the field of medicine, is now paying more attention to these phenomena. This is due, in large part, to the increasing knowledge of, and interest in, biofeedback.

Basically, biofeedback is simply a process of monitoring one or more physiological functions of the human body with some type of instrumentation and translating the recorded activity into audio or visual signals (negative feedback) which are transmitted directly to the individual whose functions are being monitored. The theory is that the individual may, by observing these signals, learn to exercise some degree of control over the particular function being monitored. Just as in the mastery of any other motor skill—typing, riding a bicycle, etc.—the individual makes use of the continuous flow of sensory feedback signals to modify his or her continuing performance. Experiments have demonstrated that through this process one may learn to control such processes (hitherto considered involuntary or autonomic, and beyond direct conscious control) as: (1) temperature of specific parts of the body (hands, feet, forehead, etc.); (2) certain brain waves (particularly Alpha); (3) pulse rate; (4) blood pressure, etc.

Biofeedback instruments exist for many body processes; among the more popular are the feedback thermometer, the electroencephalograph (EEG), and the heart rate monitor. More extensive types of equipment exist, but these are generally limited to use in clinical laboratories and will not be discussed here. A brief description of the various pieces of equipment presently available and their respective uses follows.

THE FEEDBACK THERMOMETER

11.2 Some individuals who suffer from migraine headaches have had some success in reducing or eliminating the pain by the use of the feedback thermometer. (Jones, 1973, p. 150; Diamond, 1977.) The technique requires that finger bands be attached to the fingers. The patient then attempts to increase the temperature in his or her hands. This increases blood flow to the extremities. In increasing temperature and blood flow to the hands and feet, vasodilation in the head decreases and the pain subsides.

THE ELECTROMYOGRAPH

11.3 The electromyograph (EMG) measures muscular tension. Some individuals have found it useful for relief of tension headaches. (Jones, 1973, p. 149.) Tension headaches are brought on by, or result from, chronic muscle contraction. An EMG monitor attached over the frontalis (forehead muscle) provides the patient with a feedback on the state of forehead relaxation. As the frontalis becomes more relaxed, the tension headache tends to disappear.

The EMG is also reported to be useful as a therapeutic device for relief of the following condition: subvocalizing, paralysis, anxiety, inability to relax, depression, and other mental disorders. (Karlins and Andrews, 1972, p. 48.)

THE DERMOGRAPH

11.4 The dermograph (or psychogalvanometer) monitors the electrical conductance of the skin, sometimes called galvanic skin response (GSR). Generally, this measurement is made on the palmar surface of the hands or the fingertips.

The slightest bodily stimulus results in an alteration of the resistance of the skin to electrical conductance. Even those stimuli which do not arouse responses at the conscious level have this effect. The dermograph detects this phenomenon and produces a perceptible signal as a result. Unlike other biofeedback instruments, however, the dermograph produces information, not primarily about the particular tissue (the skin) being monitored, but about the activity of the central nervous system. In this instance, the skin is simply a conduit of the flow of information. In this manner, we can detect variations in the intensity of the emotional and mental responses to stimuli at the conscious, subconscious, or unconscious level of being. By monitoring such responses, the subject learns to control them and, thus, to control his stress reactions.

THE ELECTROENCEPHALOGRAPH

11.5 Probably no other type of biofeedback has caught the public's attention like that of brain wave monitoring, particularly alpha brain waves. As we saw in chapter 5, the brain is the focal point of the nervous system through which there is a continual flow of electrical energy in the form of reference signals, input signals, and output signals. Some of this energy is dissipated into the environment and it is this dissipation that allows it to be measured by placing electrodes on various parts of the head.

The major brain wave patterns and the associated feelings for most people are about as follows:

Brain Wave Pattern	Hertz	Associated Feeling
Alpha	8 to 13	Relaxation
Beta	14 to 30	Arousal
Delta	0.5 to 3.5	Deep sleep
Theta	4 to 7	Dreaming or deep relaxation

The above categorization requires some tempering; there are significant variations in the frequency and amplitude of alpha waves. Some subjects in the alpha pattern also report different feelings including: at ease, neutral, sluggish, powerful, elated, illusion, dreamlike. (Brown, 1974, p. 314.) As a result of these variations, we find considerable disagreement among brain researchers about the meaning and function of alpha waves.

Despite this disagreement and lack of full understanding of alpha waves, there appears to be a consensus on certain findings, and the little that can be said about alpha is important. It is particularly important for the executive under stress. During mental effort, frustration, or visual activity, alpha tends to be replaced by beta. Alpha appears when the eyes are closed, during relaxation, with the rest that naturally occurs after mental tasks, and during drowsiness. Thus, it is the relaxation aspect of alpha that is important; in fact, some scientists believe that alpha relaxation could be substituted for pharmaceutical tranquilizers. The voluntary generation of alpha waves does often seem to promote a sense of internal rest and quietness that has been found to be useful in coping with problems related to anxiety and stress. Some corporations are now incorporating biofeedback generation of alpha waves as part of their training programs for business executives. Psychotherapists and conselors are also using such techniques, to an increasing degree. Manufacturers of biofeedback equipment also claim similar benefits in the treatment of insomnia, learning difficulties, and hypnagogic states.

Brown states tthat some of her subjects reported such results as transcendental thinking, and contemplative, mysterious, uncertain, and reflective moods. (Brown, 1974, p. 360) Another writer reports that the alpha-theta threshold is a point where the individual is highly susceptible to suggestion or autosuggestion. (Stearn, 1976, p. 70)

MEDITATION AND RELAXATION

11.6 We use the term meditation here in a general sense to cover various types of meditative contemplation, including, specifically, Transcendental Meditation, the Relaxation Response developed by Herbert Benson, as well as other similar techniques.

The term meditation is usually applied to any state of sustained reflection upon a word (mantra), prayer, subject, or object (mandala). When the reflection is on an object (mandala) such as a candle flame, a simple circle, or a crucifix, the eyes are open, otherwise the eyes are generally closed. Meditation is not the same as daydreaming. Some forms of meditation require that the individual silently count breaths—*one* on inhale, *two* on exhale—until ten has been reached, whereupon the sequence begins again at one. If a distracting thought interferes with the count, the meditator begins again at one on the next inhale. Other forms of meditation require internal silence.

One example of the silent repetition of a word or mantra is the now popular Jesus prayer which, according to William Johnston, originated with the Hesychasts, a sect of contemplative monks in the early Greek Church. Presently the practice is similar to transcendental meditation in that the meditator silently repeats a mantra or sacred word, in this case the word *Jesus*. (Johnston, 1974, p. 17.)

Meditation is generally performed in the normal sitting position (specifically with the back straight), although some Eastern forms of meditation require that the practitioner take a specific posture, such as sitting with crossed legs (the lotus position). Meditation teachers generally recommend that the practice begin in a quiet room with subdued lighting, although more experienced practitioners are able to meditate even in brightly lighted, noisy rooms. However, this environment is not recommended for best results.

The "whirling dervishes," a Sufi sect who spin in a circle while constantly repeating a single word or phrase, constitute one exception to the rule about sitting in a quiet contemplation. The whirling dervishes are able to go into a trance or experience ecstatic phenomena as a result of their repetitions and spinning. (Ornstein, 1972, p. 116-117.) The Sufis are also well known for their teaching stories, which provide subjects or problems to meditate upon. Idries Shah, who recounts many of the Sufi teaching stories, suggests that they cannot be appreciated beyond a certain point except within the real teaching situation, which requires the physical presence of a Sufi teacher. (Shah, 1971, p. xxiii; see also Shah 1968 for examples of the teaching stories.)

Another form of teaching story (or problem) is the *koan,* also from the Eastern traditions. A well known example of a koan is, "What is the sound of one hand clapping?" The meditator is generally given the koan by a teacher or superior monk and is asked to meditate upon it. Robert Ornstein provides us with the rationale of the koan, he suggests that the koan is not to be taken as a problem to be worked through, but as a useful technique, demanding focus of attention over a long period of time. The koan is a constant and compelling focus of awareness, which will eventually allow intuitive enlightenment to be gained. (Ornstein, 1972, p. 111.)

Another exception to the sitting rule is Tai Chi Chuang, which originated in China, and involves a rhythmic motion. The movement is slow, graceful, and fluid; it is based on the coordination of the mind and the body. In Tai Chi, as it is called for short, the object is to discipline the mind into a concentrated quietness through meditation. Tai Chi, however, is usually offered first as a form of exercise, and secondly as a martial art. As a form of exercise, Tai Chi reputedly provides relaxation and relief from body aches and pains, but even in the performance of the exercise, the practitioner is supposed to empty his or her mind of thought and allow it to be wholly concerned with, and aware of, each movement of the body. (Maisel, 1972.) This relaxation of both body and mind, and quieting of the nervous system, is supposed to provide a definite relief from stress. (Shiffrin 1976, p. 118.)

There are many other varieties of meditation; in fact, the variety is probably endless. Most of the techniques come to us from the East, where every Yogi has his yoga and few of them agree. Some techniques, however, originated in the Western world, and almost every culture and religion has its own garden variety of meditation.

Regardless of the variations, there are certain underlying similarities: (1) adoption of a passive attitude of quiet repose, with a reduction of physical and mental activity to a minimum, and preferably in a tranquil environment; (2) the repetitive use of some sort of mental device, a focusing of the mind or thoughts on a singularity—in the Hindu varieties, a *mantra* (word or thought), or a *mandala* (physical object), with elimination of all distracting thoughts, ideas, feelings, and emotions; and (3) attainment of an altered state of consciousness in which the mind is completely free of all thought and worldly feelings, in which the self is liberated from the bonds of the physical body as well as the mind.

The initial object of concentration is usually meaningless in itself and irrelevant to the process of meditation, although some techniques make the selection of the mantra or mandala a highly ritualistic and mystical ceremony. The sole purpose of the mantra or mandala, or course, is simply to serve as a device for clearing the mind of all other thoughts; the intense concentration clears the mind of all distractions and tends to facilitate the inducement of the altered state of consciousness.

The achievement of the altered state of consciousness—variously described as mystical, enhanced awareness, deeper consciousness, etc.—represents an ideal to be strived for, but to be obtained only by the most serious meditators and only after long practice.

Much of the current popularity of the meditation techniques may be attributed to efforts at simplification by some teachers from the East. One of the early leaders of this movement was Maharishi Mahesh Yogi, who introduced the practice of Transcendental Meditation to the Western world in 1959.

TRANSCENDENTAL MEDITATION

11.7 Transcendental Meditation (TM) is being practiced by more than a million people and about half of those are Americans, according to a 1975 estimate by a Transcendental Meditation instructor.

Some idea of the degree of interest in TM may be derived from the fact that it has acquired its large enrollment in spite of the fact that each student must pay a fee of $125 just to learn the technique. Douglas Shah estimates that the revenue to the TM organization in 1974 was $18 million. (Shah, 1975, p. 97.)

The popularly available literature on TM from the organization does not include instructions on how to perform it. Instruction is given only in the privacy of a room with a TM instructor and the meditation trainee. Trainees sign a contract that states that they will not reveal certain aspects of the training ritual. However, the popular press provides many articles describing the details of preparing for the training ritual.

Despite the TM claim to be totally secular, there have been some objections on religious grounds and some demands that as a Hindu ritual and theology, it will have to remain off public school grounds.

To offset such criticisms, the TM organization provides copies of letters from clergymen who not only endorse TM but state that it does not conflict with their religion. In fact, some say that one's faith should be enhanced, rather than diminished, by the use of Transcendental Meditation.

The American Management Association recently distributed a free copy of a book on TM as part of its membership services. (Kory, 1976.)

Stress reduction is perhaps the most emphasized benefit claimed for TM, and it is this aspect that interests us. Even its detractors agree that there are a number of benefits that derive from TM. Some of these benefits, however, may be difficult to substantiate. For example, one benefit frequently claimed by practitioners has been improved performance at work or in school, together with a greater degree of inner stability and general calm. The calm feeling and inner stability would, of course, serve as an antidote to stress. Some writers substantiate these reports. Robert Wallace and Herbert Benson in physiological tests found that experienced meditators approached and crossed the alpha-theta brain wave threshold, a significant indicator of relaxation and a feeling of calmness. (Wallace, and Benson, 1972.)

Benson, after further investigation, concluded that other techniques also elicit this relaxation response to psychologic changes. He found, for example, that TM tended to decrease oxygen consumption, respiratory rate, heart rate, and blood pressure, while increasing the alpha waves, but both Zen and Yoga produce similar results. Other techniques in this category (e.g., autogenic training, progressive relaxation, hypnosis with suggested deep relaxation, and sentic cycles) produced some but not all of these results. (Benson, 1975, p. 70–71.) Sentic cycles is an active meditative method in which the meditator focuses upon certain emotions like joy or grief; it allows the meditator to get in touch with his innermost feelings while producing a feeling of peace. (Clymes, 1977.)

There are several hypotheses to account for the effect of TM on the alpha waves, but not much in the way of supporting clinical research. There is, however, adequate research support for the claimed effects on blood pressure, heart rate, metabolic rate, and oxygen consumption. There is also clinical evidence, in the form of tests of spontaneous skin resistance responses, indicating greater stability in the autonomic nervous system on the part of subjects practicing TM, and even after meditation. This is indicative of a greater resistance to environmental stress, psychosomatic disease, and behavioral instability, as well as greater efficiency in the normal performance of the nervous system. However, as indicated above, similar results may be achieved by other means with somewhat less mysticism. One such technique is Benson's Relaxation Response.

THE RELAXATION RESPONSE

11.8 As a result of his studies on the physiological aspects of meditation, Benson was impressed with the fact that practicing transcendental meditators being tested under laboratory conditions had a drop in blood pressure levels, but he noted that those who discontinued TM soon lost the benefits of decreased blood pressure. After much research, he found that TM was not the only technique to elicit what he now calls the "Rexlation Response," it is merely one of many.

The biggest difference between TM and Benson's more general approach appears to be that Benson is giving away free the same type of information and advice for which the TM organization charges $125.

Here is what Benson recommends: a passive attitude, a quiet environment, a comfortable position, and a mental device such as the word "one," but many other single syllable words will serve as well. Then the individual should close his or her eyes, relax all muscles and breathe through the nose. During inspiration and expiration, the individual should silently repeat the chosen word. This process should continue for 20 minutes, then, when completed, the individual should sit quietly for a few minutes, first with eyes closed and then with eyes open. (Benson, 1975.)

ANTHROCENTRIC MEDITATION

11.9 The success of the TM school and the ensuing controversy over the relative merits of TM versus Benson's Relaxation Response technique have spurred other practitioners to develop and propagate other varieties of this highly simplified form of meditation. Anthrocentric Meditation (AM) is one such effort. AM maybe learned by reading a book and it teaches the essential points covered by TM instructors. (Nicholas, 1975.) It differs from Benson's Relaxation Response in that it provides lists of mantras, some of which are English words, others are nonsense words which are apparently intended to replace the Sanskrit words given as mantras in TM. The reader is encouraged to experiment with various words and find one that is satisfying.

AM texts propose to teach the reader the entire course in four days. However, the first lesson provides the reader with enough information to actually meditate. The rest of the information is mostly amplification of the basic principles.

AUTOGENIC TRAINING

11.10 Autogenic Training (AT) is a technique that is better known in Europe than in the United States; it was developed by Johannes H. Schultz, M.D., in Germany in 1920. It is a method of autosuggestion or self-hypnosis. (Rosa, 1976.) The importance of the instructor is emphasized in the literature of AT; apparently the exchange of thoughts and experiences is viewed as very important in the process. There are basic and advanced training sessions in AT.

AT may be practiced in either the supine or sitting position. (The instructions for sitting are quite specific.) The eyes are closed whichever position is assumed. The next step in the procedure is relaxation—"concentrative self-relaxation." (Lindemann, 1973.) This process is highly repetitive and starts with the favored arm (right handers start with the right arm.) The subject, silently and with deep concentration, repeats the training formula: "My right arm is very heavy." This training formula is silently repeated (but not articulated) about six times. This is followed by: "I am completely calm." Then six more repetitions of: "My right arm is very heavy." The process continues for eighteen repetitions of the favored arm. Next it is repeated for each of the other extremities.

When this process has been mastered, the second step is to induce warmness. This is accomplished by six repetitions inducing heaviness followed by "I am completely calm," followed by eighteen repetitions of "My right arm is warm," with the appropriate calming statement after each six repetitions. Again the process is directed to all four extremities.

Heaviness induces muscle relaxation; warmth induces blood vessel dilation which increases blood flow; and, the calming statement induces general relaxation throughout the body, the antithesis of stress.

Next comes generalization, i.e., inducing the feeling of heaviness and warmth throughout the trunk of the body, but preferably not the head and neck. There are no formulae for the trunk, which is why it is called generalization; the student is on his or her own to produce the desired sensation. However, there is an additional training formula for the abdomen which is part of the basic training. (step 5, below).

The third step is the heart regulation step, and the training formula is: "My heart beats calmly and strongly."

The fourth step, which is interchangeable with the third step, is control over breathing. The training formula is: "My breathing is very calm."

The fifth step directs attention to the abdomen and the solar plexus. One of two training formulae apply: "Abdomen (or solar plexus) flowing warm." Exactly why the abdomen step follows the heart and breathing steps, after generalization is brought about, is not explained in the literature; however, it would probably be best to address the abdomen as step five since there is such a heavy emphasis on following the procedures.

The sixth, and final step, in the basic training is the head exercise. The training formula is: "Forehead is pleasantly cool."

In the above set of six steps only the extremities receive the eighteen repetitions, and that is the first time the heaviness and warmth exercises are performed: thereafter, six repetitions are recommended.

Presumably this is designed to get the subject used to the auto-suggestion process.

There is one additional process that requires special attention: coming out of autogenic training; it is called canceling or returning. Since the practioner is in a deep state of relaxation, a procedure to bring him or her back to normal is required, otherwise feelings of heaviness may persist for hours after the exercise. Canceling requires the firming of the arms (or firsts), stretching of the arms, a deep breath followed by the opening of the eyes.

Autogenic training is generally performed under supervision of a medical specialist, frequently a physician. Since it is a training technique, there is an emphasis on note taking by the trainees. Notes allow the trainers to review the individual's progress and spot any conditions that require improvement, or approaches that require additional training.

Lindemann recommends certain specific training formulae for the solution of medical problems. (The reader is reminded that most of the people practicing AT reside in Europe.) Some of the medical problems addressed are: stress and heart disease, asthma, skin problems, susceptibility to colds, and female complaints.

Elmer and Alyce Green, of the Menninger Clinic, starting in 1965, did research on Autogenic Training. (Green, 1973.) The research began with 33 housewives who were given Autogenic Training and allowed to practice for 2 weeks. At the beginning and end of their training they were measured for physiological variables such as brain waves, heart rate, skin potential, skin resistance, breathing rate, blood flow in the fingers, and temperature on both sides of both hands. The research indicated that Autogenic Training worked. In further research, AT was combined with biofeedback and showed improvement results based on the physiological measurements; that is, biofeedback combined with AT improved the subjects' performance. The Greens called this new approach Autogenic Feedback Training. They believe that this technique holds a lot of promise for stress relief; for example, Autogenic Feedback Training demonstrates to the individual that Autogenic Training works for him or her. (Green, Green, and Winters, 1976.)

PROGRESSIVE RELAXATION

11.11   Progressive Relaxation is the technique developed by Edmund Jacobson. Tension, according to Jacobson, manifests itself by the shortening of muscle fibers; he recommended that the method of progressive relaxation should be employed for prophylaxis as well as for treatment. (Jacobson, 1976.)

Jacobson, in his medical practice, uses a process he calls Electroneuromyometry which means the measurement of neuromuscular states. (Jacobson, 1970.) He has designed his own clinical laboratory equipment, because he thinks commercial electromyographs are inadequate for his purposes. He includes in his equipment a computer, pen recorders, an oscilloscope, a fluoroscope, X-ray machine, plus other standard medical equipment.

Jacobson insists that patients take responsibility for their condition and for their own progress. According to Jacobson, patients must learn not only control over their condition but they must observe both subjective and objective proof of progress performance. The objective proof comes from pen recordings and pictures taken of the oscilloscope display.

In Progressive Relaxation therapy, Jacobson is generally against the use of suggestion because he feels that this would tend to interfere with an anxious person's ability to relax. He does not favor autosuggestion either. The tension relaxation process is divided into two major approaches: lying and sitting. For each of the major approaches there are seven practices: (1) arm practice, (2) leg practice, (3) trunk practice, (4) neck practice, (5) eye region practice, (6) visualization practice, and (7) speech region practice.

The first practice alone requires fourteen one hour periods for relaxation of the arms. The amount of time involved is, thus, rather lengthy. Despite the lengthiness of the procedure, however, Jacobson claims a great deal of success in curing a variety of anxiety ailments.

A more popular (rather than medical) treatment of Progressive Relaxation may be found in *You Must Relax*. (Jacobson, 1934.)

SELF-DIRECTED RELAXATION

11.12 Self-Directed Relaxation was developed by David Harold Fink. (Fink, 1943.) It involves a series of silent directions to various parts of the body to relax and let go. The directions are given serially over a period of ten weeks to the arms, chest, back, legs, neck, face, scalp, eyeballs, and speech muscles, in that order. The subject wears loose clothing or none at all, assumes a supine position, in a quiet, darkened room, with one pillow under the neck, another under the knees, and one under each arm. Relaxation starts by slightly dropping the lower jaw, allowing the tongue to rest gently against the lower teeth, and gently closing the eyelids. The subject then starts giving the silent commands: "Arms let go. Let go more. Let go more, more, more." The subject practices this drill for about an hour a day for a week or two, then extends the practice to the other body parts in the order named above, but on a cumulative basis—arms and chest; then arms, chest, and back, etc. Full benefits may be obtained only by understanding the rationale for the exercises, as explained by Fink.

Fink also suggests that the technique may be applied while sitting or standing, and in fact, for maximum benefits, should be applied for a few minutes at a time frequently during each day. He recognizes, however, that, as we have indicated in chapters 4 and 5, muscle tension is not a simple state or condition, but the result of an emotional process involving many interrelated internal activities of the self-system stemming from the stress response and reinforcing themselves in a positive feedback cycle. That response, as we have seen often persists long after the stimulus is removed. Although a hot bath, followed by a good massage may provide temporary relief from the distress of tense muscles, the real remedy requires a more fundamental approach, an attack on the basic causes. Relaxation, even when practiced several times a day must be supplemented by some method of avoiding or dissipating the emotional behavior patterns that tend to create the muscle tension in the first place. With a more systematic approach to the problem, however, relaxation may aid in the relief of sleeplessness, fatigue, postural defects, fear, anger, anxiety, and some of the diseases of adaptation (ulcers, hypertension, etc.).

BREATHING

11.13 Controlled breathing is an ancient practice and can be traced back to the origins of Indian Yoga and Chinese Taoism. Many of the practices involved with relaxation also emphasize the importance of controlled breathing, although the actual directions on breathing technique vary.

In Hatha Yoga controlled breathing is a major part of the exercises. Instead of the slow, silent breathing of zen, Yoga requires deep breathing. Deep breathing oxygenates the blood stream and as a result the cells of the body are revitalized. Claims are made that deep breathing strengthens the heart, builds up recuperative powers, slows down the aging process, clears the lung of congestion, and increases the stamina of the lungs. (Carr, 1974.)

Breathing is also reputed to reveal your inner state. If you are in good health, happy and in control of yourself, your breathing will be deep. If you are nervous, however, your breathing will be rapid and shallow, and if you are anxious you will gasp and catch your breath. Irregular breathing indicates irritability. (Kohler, 1973.)

Some inventive individuals, utilizing the eclectic method, have developed innovative packages for stress reduction. These packages frequently combine a variety of coping mechanisms. Bruno Geba, for one, developed a package which emphasizes breathing, called GEBA (Gestalt Body Awareness). (Geba, 1973.) (One cannot help but notice the similarity between the last name of the author and the acronym of the package.)

There are three major aspects of GEBA: supportive practices, energy explorations, and sonance explorations. Geba recommends that at least two people participate, if possible, for the best results. Supportive practices are done by the inactive partner and include observation, dialogue (for instruction, sharing, or note taking), massage, physical arrangements (e.g., fixing pillows), holding hands, and other comforting actions. Some of the supportive practices remind one of the Gestalt program at Esalen. Energy explorations involve deep relaxation of the body and production of the "energy state" which is somewhere between being awake and asleep. In order to produce the energy state, Autogenic Training type phrases are used. Sonance explorations involve the sensing of body and emotional feelings. According to Geba, if you are sonant, you sound good, you breathe well. During the sonance explorations, both nose and mouth breathing are performed. During mouth breathing, the active partner will be making sighing sounds—sonance.

GEBA involves many other features which may be found in other techniques.

Whatever technique an individual might select, deep breathing, even if it is only ten to twenty breaths, can be accomplished almost anywhere, so that if one cannot engage in a favorite coping mechanism one can always refresh with a very short break of deep breathing exercises.

SUMMARY: MEDITATION AND RELAXATION

11.14 Meditation can produce a calming effect on the individual and this will, at least, have a short term beneficial effect.

Probably the most important aspects of the approaches that have been discussed are their applicability to learning theory. The common thread running through these approaches is that the individual can *learn* certain techniques which will enable one to manage, or at least to cope with, the stresses in one's life.

BODY THERAPY

11.15 In the discussion of posture in chapter 4, we saw that poor posture may result from arrested or incomplete learning, which, in turn, could be traced to an anxiety complex. In this section, we will examine four therapies—Bioenergetics, Structural Integration, Awareness through Movement, and Structural Patterning—all aimed at correction of the bodily symptoms of stress.

BIOENERGETICS

11.16 Bioenergetics is a neo-Reichian school of psychoanalysis. It combines traditional psychoanalysis with body therapy. Reich, it will be recalled, got in trouble with the U. S. Government for sales of his orgone accumulator. Bioenergetics is essentially Reichian therapy without the orgone hypothesis. (Kovel, 1976.)

In the following description we concentrate on the body aspects of bioenergetics, we omit any discussion of the psychoanalytic aspects of bioenergetic therapy because they tend to follow traditional Freudian lines of thought which need no exposition here.

One of the fundamental concepts in bioenergetics is "grounding." Grounding of an electrical circuit is used as an analogy to describe the concept; it is one of two basic processes of the body: charging up and discharging down. These two processes are normally in balance. The upper part of the body is mainly concerned with charging up—intake of energy (food, oxygen, sensory stimulation.) The lower part of the body is mainly concerned with the discharge process—through movement or sexual activity—the experience of pleasure. (Lowen, 1972.)

Lowen describes a set of bioenergetic grounding exercises (actually *positions* would be a better word because of the connotations of activity brought to mind with the term *exercise*). One of the positions utilized to develop grounding is to stand with the bare feet six inches apart with weight placed between the balls and heels of the feet. The body should be straight with hands hanging loose at the sides. Next the knees are bent but weight is maintained on the feet as described above. This position should be maintained for two minutes if possible. The purpose of this position is to bring the patient back in touch with his legs and feet.

Another grounding exercise starts with the feet placed eight inches apart with the toes pointed slightly inward. The patient then bends over with the knees flexed and touches the floor with his finger tips. Then the patient attempts to straighten the knees until a vibration occurs. The legs should never stiffen nor should the knees be fully extended. Both of these exercises, according to Lowen, will improve circulation to the hands and feet, and will deepen breathing. There are a number of other grounding exercises, of course, but these two will suffice as examples.

A second purpose of the grounding exercises is to diagnose the condition of the patient. Grounding exercises tend to produce signs that the therapist can interpret. Generally speaking, the patient is clothed in such a way as to make these signs more apparent (e.g., leotards or briefs are frequently used).

In addition to the grounding exercises, other exercises are used in the course of therapy. These exercises are called active to distinguish them from the positions described above, for example, lying on a bed and kicking or punching a bed with fists (women use a tennis racket). This allows patients to discharge their anger, the theory being that every patient has something to be angry about.

In bioenergetic therapy about half of the time is spent on body work, the other half of the time on traditional psychoanalytic therapy. This split distinguishes it from structural integration.

STRUCTURAL INTEGRATION

11.17   Structural Integration is commonly known as Rolfing, after Ida Rolf, who developed this form of therapy. Structural Integration is designed to evoke a series of systematic changes in the body as a whole. Through these systematic changes, the body is supposed to become more balanced, better aligned, and integrated, and, therefore, in a better position to function optimally. (Hamman, 1972.)

Ida Rolf sees absence of stress as the balance of the body within the field of gravity; stress is imbalance, visible as the inappropriate position of body components in space. (Rolf, 1973).

Structural integration aims to align the body in the gravitational field. A great deal of emphasis is placed on physical body structure and gravity in the Structural Integration literature. Unless the physical structure of the body is properly aligned in relation to gravity there is the danger that this force may function entropically, disordering and breaking down the body. (Sobel, 1973.)

A basic of premise of structural integration is that man is a plastic structure and capable of dramatic reorganization and change. Certified Rolfers (individuals trained at the Rolf Institute in Colorado) set about to change the physical structure of their patients.

In Structural Integration the body is seen as a stack of blocks (such as children's building blocks) in a three dimensional space. The blocks correspond to the head, the thorax, the pelvis, and the legs. The process of living and interacting with the environment tends to move these blocks out of perfect alignment. These departures from perfect alignment are seen as deviations which produce compensatory adjustments and strains on other parts of the body. (The systems theory concept of high interconnectivity of subsystems has specific application to this line of thought.)

Structural Integration is essentially a technique of applying mechanical energy to manipulate connective tissues, reorganize muscle relationships, and balance the body according to a presumed anatomical norm. This process takes place in a series of ten one-hour sessions which are aimed at sequentially unwinding and freeing the muscles, "decompensating previous compensations," and integrating the total structure. Rolfers attempt to treat the body as a whole, with emphasis on integrating and relating the segments, rather than on treating localized symptoms or complaints. (Sobel, 1973.)

This type of manipulation should not be confused with chiropractic or osteopathic adjustments. When the Certified Rolfer manipulates he will use his fingers, hands, or elbows to press upon the musculature of the body. The process is reputed to be extremely painful. In many cases the full weight of the Rolfer is used to evoke the desired change. There may be considerable emotional and physical pain involved. The pain is most acute where joints are released.

The theory behind the manipulation is that the musculature of the body contains emotional memories of psychic traumas that caused the body's disintegration. This is consistent with Powers' view that memory is stored throughout the body (See: Section 5.2.) The Rolfer aims to release these memories and as a result the tensions in the rest of the body disappear spontaneously.

The world of business is being attracted to Rolfing. One company which had its executive staff Rolfed found that the groups who had the treatments carried out their business assignments with a great deal more energy and enthusiasm and approached their business responsibilities with a completely different outlook. Since then the program was extended to the wives (and children with problems) of the company executives.

After Rolfing takes place, the spontaneous integration of the body is supposed to continue for at least a year as a result of better alignment and balance.

AWARENESS THROUGH MOVEMENT

11.18 After writing his book *Body & Mature Behavior,* (1949) Moshe Feldenkrais did some individual therapy on a part time basis before launching into his Awareness Through Movement program in Israel. Awareness Through Movement is a series of deliberate, slow, and mild exercises based on a reversed pattern. A reversed pattern breaks the habitual motion of muscles in the normal gravitational field. Some of the exercises are even delicate. The reversed pattern is designed to break up the habituated pattern of muscles operating under gravitational force. Gravity is minimized by lying on the floor. The exercises emphasize *sensing,* designed to promote awareness of the body and its movements.

Westinghouse Learning Corporation is now marketing Feldenkrais material on Awareness Through Movement programs in book form and magnetic tape cassettes.

STRUCTURAL PATTERNING

11.19 This technique is closely associated with the Rolfing movement. It was developed by Judith Aston after taking Rolfing training. All Patterners must, at the minimum, audit the Structural Integration class before attending Structural Patterning courses. There is nothing written on the subject of Structural Patterning, but it is a basic core of exercises in deep breathing and in posture improvement: sitting, standing, walking, etc. Beyond the basic core, Patterning extends into the individual's daily activities such as exercise to insure that proper posture is being maintained.

EXERCISE

11.20 Although every technique discussed in this chapter is subject to controversy, exercise seems to be one of the more controversial. Some authorities believe exercise is a way of reducing stress, others disagree. (See, for example, Englebardt, 1974; Stein-crohn, 1960, 1968, 1973; Prinzmetal and Winter, 1965.)

Dr. Peter Steinchron, for example, is an anti-exercise advocate; he suggests that the rocking chair or hammock will do you more good on weekends than enforced exertion that is anathema to you.

Some doctors say that the reward for jogging is a heart attack or death. (See: Friedman and Rosenman, 1974.) While light exercise seems to be of no particular advantage, men with life-long vigorous exercise habits proved to have heart disease at the rate of one-third of other men. (Scheimann, 1974, p. 17.) It is very important for everyone who is about to go on a *vigorous* exercise program that they consult their physician—this is not a trivial warning.

One popular form of exercise that some physicians warn against is isometrics. Isometric exercises are described and advocated in *The NFL Guide to Physical Fitness* (Pickens, 1965), which defines the term as simply pushing, pulling, or lifting against an immovable object—by exerting maximum force for a few seconds. The 'object' can be part of your own body or something stationary such as a metal bar, a wall or doorway. The Guide admits that while isometrics may help one to develop great strength and some body tone, calisthenics is the only means of developing endurance.

Some studies show that isometrics appear to be much more likely than dynamic exercise to produce rhythm disturbances in people who have coronary heart disease. (Miller, Galton, and Brunner, 1972.)

The best exercises are running, swimming, cycling, and walking, but certainly for anyone over forty, only with the advice of a physician.

Morehouse, after experimenting in the laboratory with biomonitoring equipment, developed an exercise plan tied to age and pulse rate. (Morehouse and Gross, 1975.) Throughout the exercise program the participant pauses to take his or her pulse and adjust the level of activities accordingly. This program was adapted by NASA for astronauts. Morehouse and Gross warn, however, you should not start such a program if you have: pains in the chest, dizziness or faintness, gastrointestinal upset, difficulty in breathing, or flu-like symptoms. They also recommend consultation with a personal physician if any of the folowing conditions are present: high blood pressure, heavy smoking, high cholesterol, total lack of exercise, history of heart disease in the immediate family, tension, or obesity.

Morehouse and Gross further say that a person under severe emotional stress should not exercise that day, but what they do not allow for, apparently, is the executive who, because of his or her job, is under constant, severe emotional stress.

One of the few really scientific approaches to the prescription of an exercise program is that developed by Dr. Kenneth H. Cooper, and officially adopted by the United States Air Force, the United States Navy, and the Royal Canadian Air Force. Dr. Cooper calls his exercise program *Aerobics*, because it is based on the measurement of oxygen consumption. The program is designed so that you may test yourself, decide how much exercise you need, select your own individual plan of exercise, and measure your week-to-week progress on a point scale. The types of exercise recommended do not include any complicated calisthenics, but such normal activities as walking, running, cycling, swimming, and a few group sports. Readily admitting the continued extent of our ignorance of the subject and the need for a great deal of additional research on the subject of exercise in general, Dr. Cooper offers his program as a safe and reasonable approach that has produced demonstrated favorable results in large numbers of participants.

By now the fundamental disagreement on the subject should be clear. Some exercises are good and some are bad, but which are which depends not only on the physical and psychological condition of the individual but also on which expert or advocate you consult. There appears to be disagreement about every aspect of exercise, including whether you should indulge in it at all. There is, however, sufficient evidence to indicate that vigorous exercise for someone in good physical condition does tend to reduce tension and facilitate turning off the emergency response resulting from stress. Each executive, then, will have to make his or her own determination—although he or she would probably be wise to consult a physician in any circumstance.

DIET

11.21 We have seen that exercise is controversial, but nutrition control appears to be even more controversial. Vitamins, refined sugar, refined wheat flour, white rice, and almost everything else you eat is involved in the controversy, as well as the additives, pesticides, and pollutants found in our foods.

We know from our discussions in chapters 3 and 5 that stress and disease both put additional nutritional demands on the body. Since the metabolism rate is always increased as part of the General Adaptation Syndrome, the nutritional needs invariably increase at the onset of stress and remain high. If these increased nutritional requirements are timely met, little harm is done; if not, however, the adverse effect may be severe or even fatal.

Unfortunately, much of the results of scientific research on the foods we eat seem to be creating public anxiety, rather than providing any solution. Thus, stress is increased, rather than decreased. The continuing controversy simply adds confusion to the anxiety.

The editors of *Consumer Reports* for a long time have taken the position that all you need is a balanced and varied diet with proper proportions of the four basic food groups: milk, meat, vegetables and fruits, and breads and cereals. They cite government documents available to the public and then conclude that no one needs a detailed knowledge of nutrition to eat properly. The simple selection of the proper number of servings from each of the four protective food groups solves the whole problem.

H. L. Newbold, a nutritional psychiatrist, strongly disagrees with this position. (Newbold, 1975.) He terms a fallacy the belief that the American diet is "normal, well-balanced, and nutrionally adequate." He indicts among other foods: refined wheat flour, refined sugar, and white rice. He thinks the term "refined" should be replaced by "stripped" in terms of wheat flour because twenty-three essential nutrients are taken out; when flour is enriched only six of the cheapest nutrients are put back in. He charges that refined sugar does not simply fail to provide nutrients: it actually robs your system of nutrients vitally needed elsewhere. As for white rice, we apparently save the wrong thing, it is the husk that has most of the vitamins and nutrients.

Of course, people are biochemically different; some individuals are allergic to certain foods, large people have different requirements from small, active people are different from lethargic people. For these reasons Newbold thinks that the idea of average nutritional needs is irrational, but few, if any experts would recommend that every person ingest the same (average) diet every day.

In the opposite corner, Erwin DiCyan, citing American eating habits, recommends an intake of the U.S. RDA (U. S. Recommended Daily Allowance) which the Food and Drug Administration adopted on the basis of the recommendation of the Food and Nutrition Board of the National Academy of Sciences, National Research Council. He believes adherence to such standards to be sufficient to prevent deficiency for the average person in good health. (DiCyan, 1972.) DiCyan also emphasizes the need for an adequate amount of water in the diet, which is needed not only to flush the system but also as a medium for biochemical energy conversion.

Almost standard advice from cardiologists to their patients is go on a low cholesterol diet, but there is still much conflict on the possibility of preventing or modifying the course of coronary heart disease by a low-cholesterol diet.

Mark Altschule, writing in *Executive Health* (1976), reviews ten cholesterol studies that were performed to find out whether low cholesterol diets change the incidence of deadly heart attacks. The results of these studies indicate there is no difference. He also indicates that atherosclerosis is due more to high blood pressure and poisons such as carbon monoxide, than to diet.

This information has not received a great deal of publicity—if it did, it would probably create a great deal of anxiety and stress for those who have been on these diets.

The executive already under stress does not need to add to that stress by worrying about diet, but, as we have seen, diet determines, to some degree, how one will respond and recover from stress. One can prepare oneself for stress through proper diet, but where does one turn in the face of such controversy. The answer is not clear; even though the individual is biochemically unique, answers tend to come in terms of averages. Your doctor has probably never had a course in nutrition. Even worse, nutritionists are diametrically opposed on many of the issues.

PSYCHOLOGICAL THERAPIES

11.22 According to some psychological theories, an executive, even without training in psychology, can quickly gain insights into his or her own feelings and behavior and the behavior of others; with this insight, one may be able to cope with and perhaps cure major stresses in one's life.

We discuss below four techniques of psychological therapy: Transactional Analysis, Rational-Emotive Therapy, Reality Therapy and Assertive Therapy, each of which is claimed by its advocates to aid in reducing stress on the individual executive, his or her subordinates, peers, superiors, family, and others with whom the executive deals in the course of business.

The approach we take here is to select those schools of thought that: (1) are reasonable, rather than highly imaginative, in their approach; (2) can be described simply; and (3) are easily relatable to executive stress research.

TRANSACTIONAL ANALYSIS

11.23 One school of thought that meets the above mentioned criteria is Transactional Analysis, a system of group therapy. (See: Berne, 1963.) The main contributor and originator of this particular type of therapy was Dr. Eric Berne, author of the best-seller, *Games People Play.* (Berne, 1964.) The technique was further developed by Dr. Thomas A. Harris, and explained in his *I'm OK– You're OK: A Practical Guide to Transactional Analysis.* (Harris, 1967.) Here we can give only a brief summary of what is involved; for those who are further interested, we recommend the two books mentioned above.

According to the practitioners of Transactional Analysis (TA), the fundamental unit of social action is a "stroke." Stroking, in TA, is the psychological equivalent of physical caressing; it implies recognition. The exchange of strokes is a *transaction.* A friendly greeting is a simple stroke. Most of our social exchanges are so structured that they border on rituals, governed by certain unspoken rules. The rules generally remain latent until an infraction occurs; this gives rise to a symbolic, verbal, or legal cry of "Foul." Berne calls these rituals *games,* hence the title of his book. The rituals, or games, provide a means for the regulation of our emotions.

TA is based on the hypothesis that each individual has three inherent psychological ego states. These ego states are not merely roles that are being played, they are psychological realities. The three ego states are: (1) exteropsychic, which resembles that of a parental figure; (1) neopsychic, which is autonomously directed toward a more nearly objective appraisal of reality; and (3) the archaeopsychic, which is dominated by feelings and perspctives fixated in early childhood. The three are more popularly known as Parent, Adult, and Child, respectively.

The Parent state is characterized by a large collection of recordings assimilated, for the most part, during the first five years of life, and consisting primarily of certain unquestioned fundamental rules of behavior taught us by our parents or other authority figures. The Parent state is an essential and useful element of life; the recorded rules constitute the mores and generally accepted patterns of habit and behavior response to most of the social events in our culture. The Parent state obviates a lot of unnecessary thinking and decision making in a number of social situations; its existence means, essentially, that we have been programmed to respond in socially acceptable ways.

The Child state is characterized by a collection of recorded feelings, assimilated during the same early years of life. These recordings are principally of internal events, the responses of the child to what he or she sees and hears during those early years. Since the little person (as Harris prefers to call the child as distinguished from the Child state) has not yet acquired a vocabulary, most of these recordings are emotional responses—reflections of the child's inherent dependence, weakness, ineptness, and clumsiness.

In contrast, the Adult state is characterized by the mature, discriminatory approach to social transactions. It is aimed primarily at determining the information value of stimuli, processing and filing the results of such analyses, and responding to stimuli on the basis of informed judgements rather than on a preprogrammed basis.

Each individual integrates these three states in one of an unlimited variety of proportions. The Adult state may draw upon both Parent and Child states for data, in addition to its own internalized data bank. Each individual makes decisions and probability estimates with one of the three states having a dominant influence. The proportions are not static; they may change from time to time and are subject to conscious influence.

Communication between individuals may occur successfully when transactions are complementary—Adult to Adult, Child to Parent, Parent to Child, etc. When crossed transactions occur, communication fails. Crossed transactions occur when the conversation starts with the speaker in one state, but the response is made as if he or she were in another state; for example, a question may be posed on an Adult to Adult basis, but the response is made on a Parent to Child, or Child to Parent basis. The possibilities, of course, are numerous, and the results often disastrous—activation of agonistic behavior mechanisms as in any stressful situation.

The communication, of course, need not be entirely, or even partly, verbal. Nonverbal communication on a crossed-transaction basis may be equally stressful.

Dr. Harris, building on this basic theory, traced the effects of the early childhood recordings to the establishment of the life positions as we have previously discussed (see: 5.12).

To the extent that we fail to achieve and maintain the "I'M OK—YOU'RE OK" life position, we are allowing some of our early childhood recordings (Parent or Child) to impair our Adult state. No one, of course, can completely avoid such influences all of the time, but many of us manage to minimize them and to keep to a minimum the number of instances in which we deviate from the "I'M OK—YOU'RE OK" position. When, however, the Adult state is impaired to the extent that it interferes with normal functioning, when we find ourselves frequently failing in our communications because of crossed transactions, when we find ourselves in one of the other three life positions more often that in the "I'M OK—YOU'RE OK" position, we are at the stage where we should consider the need for treatment. Whether that treatment should be in the form of the group therapy of Transactional Analysis or some other form is a question to which we cannot provide an answer. Possibly, however, the reader in need may find some guidelines in this and the next two chapters for discovering his or her own answer.

For the purpose of coping with executive stress, TA is one technique which executives in need of assistance should at least consider as holding some promise of success in aiding them to:

1. Perform their own self analysis (see: Mok, 1975.)

2. Improve their interpersonal relations.

3. Eliminate, or reduce in number the games that they ordinarily become involved in.

4. Direct behavior and feelings so that they maintain the I'M OK, YOU'RE OK position, with only very rare deviations.

5. Identify the life script that they have assumed and lead them to a script-free life.

The executive who wishes to seek out a group or learn more about the group therapy technique may call or write to:

The International Transactional Analysis Association
3155 College Avenue
Berkeley, California 94705

Berne suggests that a game is an ongoing series of complementary ulterior transactions progressing to a well-defined, predictable outcome. Games are played so that each party ends up collecting negative strokes (bad feelings) as a payoff. These bad feelingsare accumulated as "trading stamps" which can later be redeemed for a tantrum, a drinking spree, a divorce, suicide, or explosive guilt-free rage.

According to Theodore Novey, game playing (in the Eric Berne sense) is likely to be much more frequent in those organizations in which the predominant management style involves a higher incidence of critical PARENT states or NOT-OK CHILD positions on the part of key executives (Novey, 1973.) Novey developed a synthesized model of organizational behavior which he used as a basis for identifying various forms of organization with the life positions of effective and ineffective managers.

Both Novey and Jut Meininger (Meininger, 1973) discuss the perils of game playing in organizations and provide advice on reducing or eliminating it. By reducing the amount of organizational game playing, executives can direct their own and others' efforts to more productive behavior. In this way, they will be less stressed, will feel better, and can reduce the stress levels of others in the organization. Reduction of game playing in the organization will also facilitate efforts by the executive and others to maintain the "I'm OK—You're OK" life position, to stay in the Adult ego state when it is appropriate, and to convert to a script-free life.

Steiner performed a structural analysis of scripts and found that they fit into one of three categories: lovelessness, mindlessness, or joylessness. (Steiner, 1974.) The no-love script means that the individual will be unsuccessful in developing loving relationships and, in tragic forms, ends up with extreme depression or suicide. In the tragic form of the mindlessness script, the individual goes crazy. The no-joy script, in its tragic forms, ends in drug addiction or alcoholism.

According to Steiner, the cure for a lovelessness script is to organize a circle of friends in which relationships are developed. In addition, the person with this type of script must learn how to give, receive, reject, and ask for strokes. For mindlessness, Steiner believes a group such as a Transactional Analysis group is an effective way to begin change. For joylessness, Steiner recommends deep breathing and bioenergetics as two possible solutions, because this individual needs to get back in touch with his or her body.

Berne provides a forty question checklist for those interested in learning about their own degree of freedom from scripts. If you can answer *Yes* to all of the forty questions, you are script-free. (Berne, 1972, p. 437-439.)

Executives who can attain these three aims: (1) eliminating games, (2) eliminating scripts, and (3) taking the I'm OK—You're OK position, will enhance their freedom to act and educe their stress levels.

RATIONAL-EMOTIVE THERAPY

11.24   Rational-emotive therapy was developed by Albert Ellis, and expounded by Ellis and Robert Harper. (Ellis and Harper, 1975.) They take the position that some of us allow certain powerful, irrational, and illogical ideas to interfere with our leading an anxiety-free, unhostile life. They provide a list of ten of those irrational ideas which serve as the basis for Rational-emotive therapy. For example, one item on the above mentioned list suggests (irrationally) that people and things should turn out better than they do and that you must view it as awful and horrible if you do not find good solutions to life's grim realities. But the fact is, of course, that there is no reason things should turn out better than they do. Maxie Maultsby, who is a RET therapist(although he calls his technique Rational Behavior Training) says, that *everything is exactly the way it should be.* (Goodman and Maultsby, 1974, p. 34.) His thinking is that going back into antiquity the prerequisites for any given reality have been fulfilled in order for any given reality to exist.

To the complaint that people should not behave the way they do, RET responds that words like should, ought, must, and their negative equivalents are confused with people's desires. In RET the preferable way to phrase a grim reality is to say, "I would have liked it to turn out differently."

If other people behave other than the way you like, it does not adversely affect you unless you think it does. RET holds that nobody can make you do anything you do not want to do. That includes feeling bad—no one can make you feel anything. Only you can make yourself feel depressed or happy, or experience any other emotion. (Lazarus and Fay, 1975, p. 20-22.)

RET, it would appear, gives us some insight into many facets of executive stress. How much stress is due to irrational ideas of what *should* be? How much stress is caused by irrational expectations of other people's behavior?

One way for executives to find out is to monitor their inner dialogue (Goodman and Maultsby call this "self-talk.") Behavior and emotions do not just happen in the brain, they have thought content, and frequently take the form of conversations. Once this dialogue is written down on paper it can be analyzed for its irrational content, but Goodman and Maultsy say that when patients are first going through the process of learning to isolate and articulate their irrational self-talk is when they are in the most need of professional guidance, or at least experienced help from ex-patients.

For a relatively healthy, even though stressed, executive, guidance in identifying self-talk is probably not necessary—although at first such analysis may be difficult—but gaining some insight into what one is saying to oneself may be worthwhile.

Another method of therapy, based on RET's inner dialogue concept, is called Anxiety Management Training. (See: Frank C. Richardson, 1976, p. 103-115.)

REALITY THERAPY

11.25 Reality Therapy was developed by William Glasser. The basic tenet of Reality Therapy is that individuals must accept responsibility for their own actions and behavior. Reality Therapy does not accept the concept of mental illness, nor does it accept the theory that current behavior is a result of the past. There is a strong emphasis on morality. (Glasser, 1965.)

The main reason for including Reality Therapy here is that it alone among the current types of psychotherapy takes special cognizance of certain changes that are taking place in our society. Glasser asserts that while the institutions of our society still operate as if goal took precedence over role, the fact is that role, or identity, is now so important that it must be achieved before we set out to find a goal. This position is consistent with the theory of Graves and others that an evolution in the levels of psychological existence is taking place. (See 5.13.) For the modern executive the significance of Glasser's theory lies in its relevance to his interpersonal relations, especially his relationships with younger personnel who are seeking identity (a role) rather than the traditional goals of our society.

Unlike traditional forms of therapy, patients engaged in reality therapy are encourged to discuss current events, not the past. By pointing out the difference between responsible and irresponsible behavior, the therapist attempts to get patients to understand how they are currently acting. Irresponsible behavior is not excused by the therapist on the grounds of negative emotions, e.g. anger, feeling, rejected or upset, etc.

ASSERTIVE THERAPY

11.26 Assertive Therapy is known under a variety of names, such as: assertiveness training, and assertive behavior. It identifies three basic types of behavior: non-assertive, assertive, and aggressive. Aggressive behavior is seen as a behavior that results in a "put down" of another person. Non-assertive behavior results when individuals are denying themselves or are inhibited from expressing their feelings, maybe because of politeness. Assertive behavior is seen as that behavior which results from choice and results in individuals feeling good about themselves. (Alberti and Emmons, 1974 a and b, 1975; Smith, 1975.)

There are two reasons an executive might be interested in assertive therapy. The first reason is that one can expect people to become assertive and refuse to be manipulated. Unfortunately, not only are they being trained to assert themselves, but the finishing touch on most of their assertive statements tends towards the obnoxious. This type of behavior, in itself, may be extremely stressful for the executive, since the assertive remarks may be manipulative in themselves. However, with knowledge that this kind of therapy and training is taking place, and with knowledge of how people are trained to respond, executives can become assertive in their own right without becoming manipulative in return. To a certain extent this strategem is like fighting fire with fire, but if executives are to face the realities of the modern day world, they would be advised to know what kind of psychological training is being given to large numbers of people.

Assertive therapy attempts to get people to focus on interpersonal relationships and goals. Patients are encouraged to observe their own behavior and especially keep track of the number of times they have been assertive. Written homework is stressed in order to keep track of progress. Behavior modification techniques are used such as imagining situations which produce anxiety or aggressive behavior, then the patient imagines ways of handling the imagined situation in an assertive way. The patient is then encouraged to practice assertive behavior in similar real-life situations.

SUMMARY: PSYCHOLOGICAL THERAPIES

11.27   Of the four techniques described above, two— Transactional Analysis and Rational-Emotive Therapy—would seem to be the most worthwhile for the executive to examine first. Any of these techniques, however, may provide some insight into the way people feel and behave and the reasons therefor. Sharp executives may believe they already have an adequate intuitive grasp of the psychology of interpersonal relations; even so, it might be helpful to supplement this intuition with the more recent findings from psychological research. There is nothing magic, of course, about these four techniques—the executive may find other theories or techniques more interesting. For information leading to improved self-understanding and stress reduction, the field of psychology offers innumerable possibilities.

RELATIONSHIPS OF COPING MECHANISMS TO CAUSES OF STRESS

11.28   The foregoing discussion identifies the principal mechanisms proposed in the literature for coping with stress. As indicated, there are a wide variety of other techniques, most of which are simply variations or modifications of those discussed above. Some are highly touted as cure-alls, others make more modest claims. Almost all, however, claim some benefits in the way of providing general relief from the symptoms of stress.

Upon further analysis of each of the proposed coping mechanisms, however, one finds that the technique is usually more specific in its application, being directed at the alleviation or elimination of one or more of the physiological or psychological causes of stress which we identified in Part II. None are specifically directed at any of the environmental causes of stress and probably for good reason, as we shall see below.

In the following discussion, the identified benefits are those claimed by the advocates of each of the several coping mechanisms. (See sections 11.1 through 11.26, above, for the references to the literature claiming the specific benefits.) Scientific demonstration of such benefits is, in general, not readily available, hence we can only leave to each individual the task of determining for himself or herself the value of each of these coping mechanisms. Some degree of experimentation appears to be both safe and worthwhile when combined with the broader systemic approach suggested in chapter 13.

COPING MECHANISMS AND THE PHYSIOLOGICAL CAUSES OF STRESS

11.29 Comparing the list of physiological causes of stress discussed in chapter 4 with the techniques described in this chapter, we find no coping mechanisms specifically directed to the causes we have identified as genetic characteristics and congenital problems. We find four types of techniques aimed at the correction of disturbed biological rhythms: biofeedback, meditation and relaxation, body therapy, and exercise. Only one technique is directed to the correction of sleeplessness: biofeedback. For the correction of dietary deficiencies we find a plethora of recommendations, almost all of which are highly controversial, involving, as they do, either greater reliance on, or the complete elimination of, one or more of the generally accepted articles of the standard American diet.

At least four techniques make some claims, more or less modest, for relief or cure of one or more diseases: biofeedback (migraine, hypertension), meditation and relaxation (hypertension), exercise (heart and lung ailments), diet (migraine and a variety of disease conditions). Body therapy and exercise routines are directed at the correction of improper posture and the diseases and conditions resulting therefrom. Four of the listed techniques aim at the alleviation of muscular tension

TABLE 11.1
RELATIONSHIPS OF COPING MECHANISMS TO PHYSIOLOGICAL CAUSES OF STRESS

Physiological Causes of Stress	Coping Mechanisms					
	Biofeedback	Meditation and Relaxation	Body Therapy	Exercise	Diet	Psychological Therapies
Genetic characteristics						
Congenital problems						
Biological rhythms	X	X	X	X		
Sleeplessness	X					
Diet deficiencies					X	
Disease	X (Migraine)	X		X (Heart, Lung)	X	
Improper posture	X	X	X	X		
Fatigue	X	X	X	X		
Muscular tension		X	X	X		
Diseases of adaptation					X	

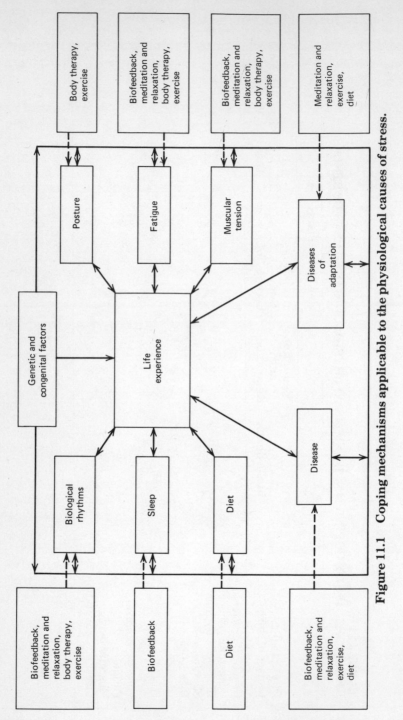

Figure 11.1 Coping mechanisms applicable to the physiological causes of stress.

and fatigue: biofeedback, meditation and relaxation, body therapy, and exercise. Only two of these techniques seem to be aimed at the diseases of adaptation: meditation and relaxation, and exercise.

The situation is summed up in Table 11.1. It shows at a glance the limited applicability of the proposed coping mechanisms. As may be readily observed only 11 of the sixty cells are occupied. This, of course, is not, in itself, necessarily an indication of inadequacy, but it may serve to point up the needs for further research and the need for development of additional techniques. Figure 11.1 shows how the several coping mechanisms relate to our model of the physiological causes of stress.

COPING MECHANISMS AND THE PSYCHOLOGICAL CAUSES OF STRESS

11.30 Comparing the list of psychological causes of stress discussed in chapter 5 with the techniques described above, we find only the four psychological therapies with any general applicability. In addition, biofeedback, meditation-relaxation, and body therapy claim some benefits in the relief of anxiety; meditation and relaxation techniques also apply to frustration. The situation is summed up in Table 11.2. Here again the coverage is limited, with only 17 of the 78 cells occupied, and similar conclusions may be drawn. Figure 11.2 shows how the several coping mechanisms relate to our model of the psychological causes of stress. Each of the coping mechanisms produces both perceived and nonperceived events, both internal and external.

In addition, biofeedback influences both perceptions and feelings and emotions; meditation and relaxation techniques influence perceptions, feelings and emotions, and perception of situations; body therapy influences feelings and emotions; and the several psychological therapies affect perceptions, feelings and emotions, perception of situations, life experience, life decisions, and behavior. Of course, all the mentioned therapies indirectly influence behavior through their effects on the other elements of the self-system.

COPING MECHANISMS AND THE ENVIRONMENTAL CAUSES OF STRESS

11.31 Because all of the proposed coping mechanisms are directed at the internal operations of the human body— physical or mental—they naturally have no direct applicability to the

TABLE 11.2
RELATIONSHIPS OF COPING MECHANISMS TO PSYCHOLOGICAL CAUSES OF STRESS

Psychological Causes of Stress	Coping Mechanisms					
	Biofeedback	Meditation and Relaxation	Body Therapy	Exercise	Diet	Psychological Therapies
Feelings and Emotions						
Anxiety	X	X	X			X
Guilt and Worry						X
Fear						X
Anger						X
Jealousy						X
Loss and Bereavement						X
Situations						
Threat						X
"Near Miss"						X
Frustration		X				X
Conflict						X
Life Experience						X
Life Positions						X
Life Scripts						X

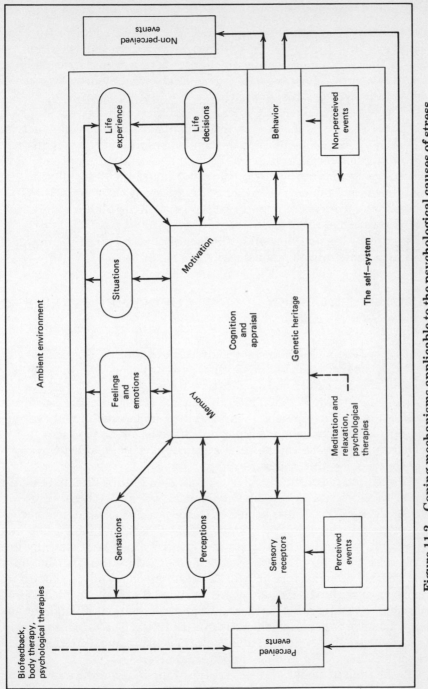

Figure 11.2 Coping mechanisms applicable to the psychological causes of stress.

209

control of external stressors. Instead, they aim to improve the individual's ability to cope with, at least certain, external stressors. In view of the fact that, as we saw in chapter 6, any event in the ambient environment (and even some in the distant environment) may serve as a potential stressor, this approach is not entirely illogical.

Of course, supplementing these efforts there are the, by now, well established health and safety programs for the prevention of industrial and occupational accidents and the control or elimination of industrial and occupational hazards. In addition, there are the relatively new national programs aimed at the control of environmental pollution and other hazards. Both of these types of programs are directed toward the protection of workers in general or the general population, not necessarily toward the stress-prone executive.

Figure 11.3 shows how all of these activities relate to our model of the environmental causes of stress.

SUMMARY: RELATIONSHIPS OF COPING MECHANISMS TO CAUSES OF STRESS

11.32 The McLean model discussed in chapter 7 (Figure 7.1) will serve as the basis for relating the various coping mechanisms to the causes of executive stress.

McLean indicated that for symptoms.of stress to exist, the three circles representing stressors, vulnerability, and context must overlap. Coping mechanisms obviously do not directly affect stressors in the environment, but the coping mechaisms obviously do affect the stressors that exist within the self-system.

A modification of the model is presented in Figure 11.4. In addition to the three circles in the McLean model, we show three groups of coping mechanisms. These groups are separated somewhat arbitrarily, but with some thought. For example, biofeedback, and meditation and relaxation techniques have been grouped together because they are more alike in terms of effect than the other techniques that have inputs to the same factors in the McLean model. The psychological theories, as may be seen, affect all parts of the McLean model and, therefore, are separated from the other techniques although no attempt is made to separate them from each other. The remaining techniques are grouped together, although they each have different effects on both vulnerability and on the internal stressors.

In the revised model, we see that the group of techniques consisting of biofeedback, and meditation and relaxation techniques affects both

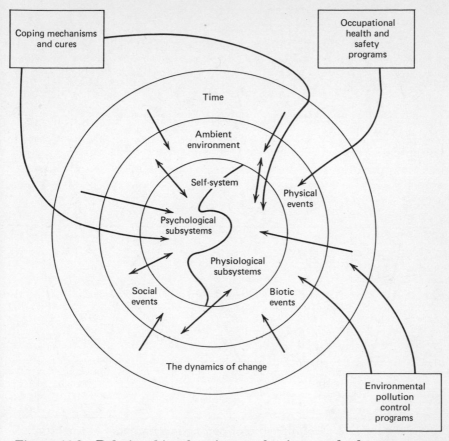

**Figure 11.3   Relationship of coping mechanisms and other programs
to the environmental causes of stress.**

the vulnerability and the internal stressors. For example, these techniques can produce a calming of the individual and a lowering of the
blood pressure. The calming response tends to alleviate existing stress
and therefore decreases the vulnerability of the individual. The lowering of the blood pressure tends to prevent secondary reactions which
might result from that condition.

The group that includes body therapy, breathing, diet, and exercise
also affects the vulnerability and the internal stressors. For example,
proper diet aids in preventing both mental and physical disease
(stresses) and decreases the vulnerability.

Finally, the psychological therapies influence all parts of the Mc-

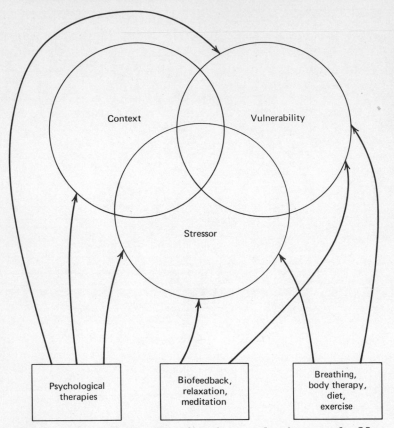

Figure 11.4   Relationship of coping mechanisms to the Mc-Lean model.

Lean model. First they can influence the context: for example, we have seen that RET advises against the use of words like *should, ought* and *must*. When the use of these words is eliminated from the vocabulary, individuals tend not to upset themselves with other people's behavior. By changing the context of interpersonal relations, the vulnerability to these same situations changes. Finally, by eliminating use of these words, our cognition and appraisal may change so that stress precipitators that might have once existed in the system are now eliminated.

This model should be viewed as an initial step in developing a systematic framework for relating the coping mechanisms to the causes of stress. The next step in developing a more complex model would require a combinatorial approach at a finer level of detail. There appears to be little or no investigative work underway to determine what happens to an individual who practices a particular combination such as Transcendental Meditation, Rational Emotive Therapy, and an optimum diet, or any other combination of the techniques we have discussed. Interest, to date, appears to lie mostly in exploring a single technique. The only exception is the limited research being done on Autogenic Feedback Training.

SUMMARY

11.33 Obviously, at this particular stage of the state of the art, it is not possible to recommend a comprehensive stress reduction program based on the arsenal of coping mechanisms presently available. Furthermore, executives differ in personality, in job, in family situation, so that a program designed for one executive would not be appropriate for another; and our knowledge of these differences and how to deal with them is as yet inadequate.

Interested executives with a felt need and an experimental bent might select one or more of these techniques for a trial period to determine its value for them, personally. If so we recommend that they first become thoroughly acquainted with the details of the technique as well as its claimed benefits and possible drawbacks, and, secondly, discuss the matter with their physicians if there are any possible adverse effects on physical or mental health.

Chapter 12
Reducing Stress Levels

12.0 The coping mechanisms discussed in the previous chapter were directed primarily at providing relief from the adverse effects of stress and only secondarily at preventing undue stress. As we saw (11.29—11.33), each of the coping mechanisms had limited applicability and related to only a few of the wide variety of causes of stress. In this chapter, we discuss some more general means of dealing with stress. First we discuss some preventive measures, some means of avoiding undue stress. Next we discuss some diversion techniques, ways of spreading the effects of stress so as to avoid too great a degree of stress on any one or few elements of the self-system. Finally, we take up certain control measures, ways of regulating the levels of stress. In each instance, we relate the measures or techniques to the three factors involved in the stress situation: stressors, context, and vulnerability. (See: chapter 7.) As we shall see, the basic principles of defense against the adverse effects of stress are essentially the same at every level—individual cells and tissues, physiological subsystems, the self-system, or even social organizations. (See: Selye, 1974, p. 17.)

PREVENTIVE MEASURES

12.1 Because no single one of the three factors (stressors, context, vulnerability) is susceptible to complete control by the individual, there is no way in which you can completely prevent the impact of stress on your own self-system. There are, however, certain preventive measures one can take to reduce one's exposure and vulnerability to stress. You can take steps to reduce your exposure to certain stressors and to certain contexts which you know in advance may subject

214

you to undue stress. You may also take certain measures to reduce your vulnerability and increase your resistance to those forms of stress which you know produce adverse effects for you. This approach suggests the advisability of a self analysis to: (1) identify the specific stressors and types of contexts which constitute the greatest contributors to stress; and (2) determine one's own physical and psychological strengths and weaknesses so as to identify one's specific vulnerabilities.

The results of such a self analysis will suggest the specific preventive measures which are needed. In this discussion, obviously, we cannot possibly treat all of the potentially useful preventive measures for any one individual, much less for everyone. We limit ourselves to a few illustrative examples which will indicate the general approach.

AVOIDING CERTAIN STRESSORS

12.2 By examining in detail your daily pattern of living in relation to the categories of physiological, psychological, and environmental causes of stress we discussed in Part II, you may easily identify the specific stressors which occasion you the most difficulty. You may then take appropriate action to reduce your exposure to such stressors. For example, you may refrain from ingesting foods and other substances which are allergenic for you; you may seek to avoid other individuals who consistently exhibit agonistic behavior towards you; you may refrain from indulging in the use of known stressors (for example, narcotics and other palliatives) which add to your stress instead of relieving it.

There is even the possibility that the colors of your immediate environment may tend to increase your level of stress; repainting the walls of your office or den in one of the softer pastels (green or yellow) may eliminate a stressful context of which you have not been conscious.

AVOIDING STRESSFUL CONTEXTS

12.3 In a similar manner, you may identify the specific contexts or types of contexts which you find most stressful and seek to avoid such situations or, at least, reduce your exposure to them. Depending upon the circumstances, this may involve changes in your family, social, or business life, ranging from minor to drastic. Only you can determine whether the potential benefits will outweigh the disadvantages of a change in job, family relationships, or pattern of social activities. The decision may require a type of cost-benefit analysis, with, perhaps, somewhat less precision in the calculations, but with, perhaps, greater consequences for your personal well-being than a similar type of business decision. For example, if you happen to find that committee or staff meetings are particularly stressful events for you, you may find avoiding them relatively easy—pleading press of other work, other engagements, sending an alternate, etc.—or, on the contrary, you may find that the only way to avoid such meetings is to get another job, perhaps even with a lower salary. The question in such an instance is whether the stress of such situations poses sufficient danger to your long range health or life expectancy as to warrant the financial sacrifice which might be involved. Obviously, only you can make such a decision.

REDUCING VULNERABILITY

12.4 If your self analysis reveals specific vulnerabilities, you may take action to abate them and, of course, you may exercise a little more control over improvements in this arena than in the other two. For example, if you find that you perform better with more sleep, you can change your sleeping habits. Likewise, you control your own diet, your posture, your physical exercise regimen, and certain other biological rhythms. As we saw in chapter 5, you can control your own perceptions—including your perceptions of "Situations" (see 5.10), your perceptions of the contexts of events—and, thereby, your feelings and emotions, your life decisions, life experience, and total behavior patterns. (See: 5.9—5.13.)

Even a minor change in any one of these factors could convert what might have been a stressful event into a benign or beneficial one. For example, refusing to respond in kind to the agonistic behavior of another individual may completely defuse the situation and obviate the possibility of stressful effects for both. Such refusal may be made easier by simply adopting a different attitude toward yourself; there is some evidence to indicate that your attitude toward yourself tends to be reflected in your attitude toward others. Thus, an improved self-image, a higher level of tolerance for one's own peccabilities may increase one's willingness to tolerate such failings in others.

On a broader basis, with an improved understanding of the nature and causes of the stress response, you may adopt a different attitude

towards stress in general, seeking to turn it to constructive or beneficial ends. Thus, the decision whether to fight or flee may be made on
rational rather than emotional grounds, once you have gained control
over your attitudes. In a given instance, for example in the face of
agonistic behavior directed towards you by another person, you may
weigh the relative advantages of ignoring it, responding in kind, or
simply escaping. Your choice of response in such an event may then be
based on your assessment of the long range benefits of each of these
alternatives rather than an autonomic emotional reaction. You do not
need to be controlled by your phylogenetic tendencies. You have the
power to improve upon nature by suppressing certain inherited tendencies which may have had defensive values for our primitive ancestors, but which are not necessarily useful today. Although we may
need to seek the aid of a physician in regulating our responses to
certain physical stressors, in the forms of stress arising from interpersonal relations we can, and usually have to, be, as Selye suggests, our
own doctor. (See: Selye, 1974, p. 72.)

There is also some evidence to indicate that each of us may, to some
extent at least, regulate his stressful reaction to pain. Studies show
that extroverts tend to complain most loudly about pain, while intro-
verts will endure at least moderate amounts of pain in silence, even
though the tolerance levels are approximately the same. In other
words, the reaction is controllable. Further, many pains are
psychogenic in origin; they are brought on by emotional conflicts and
feelings of a need to suffer—masochistic tendencies. Pain is a perceptual experience and, since we control our own perceptions, we may at
least influence, if not fully control, its quality and intensity by the
meaning we ascribe to it.

Likewise, the number and severity of accidents we experience may
be attributed in part to our emotional state. Emotional conflicts may
find their physical expression in increased accident proneness, and in
the trauma of accidental injuries. The emotionally immature, or emotionally upset individual is likely to have more accidents than the
emotionally mature, stable individual. Again, to the extent that we
can control our emotions, we can at least influence our tendency to
avoid accidents.

Obviously, we have a great deal of freedom of choice in the measures we take for the relief of the adverse effects of the daily stresses
we encounter on the job or elsewhere. We may certainly choose not to
use such contraindicated nontechniques as smoking, or the ingestion of
alcohol or drugs, which simply increase our vulnerabilities. By avoiding such measures, we can at least obviate adding to our vulnerabilities.

DIVERSION TECHNIQUES

12.5 Selye suggests that when there is too much stress on one part of the body, diversion is necessary to relieve such stress by spreading it over other body parts. Diversion is any activity which changes the focus of attention away from the stress-producing stimuli. Diversions, however, must be selected with care; one person's diversion is another person's stress. A weekend of golf may be a diversion for the deskbound executive, but not for the professional golfer. Likewise, an extended fishing trip is not likely to be diversionary for an executive at a time when another corporation is trying, against his wishes, to gain control over his or her organization through a stock tender; instead, any such attempted diversion is likely to be counter-productive, it is more likely to exacerbate the stress by inducing feelings of anxiety.

Quite obviously, the opportunities for diversion are unlimited and the diversionary effort may be aimed at the stressors, the context, or one's own vulnerability, as suggested below.

DIVERTING STRESSORS

12.6 In some instances, one may seek to divert known stressors away from oneself. To resume an example cited above, facing an agonistic attack from someone, the individual may seek to divert the attack to a common but indefinite enemy, to a situation, or to an inanimate object; or one may seek to divert the agonistic behavior itself by humor, or agreement, or other pacific gestures.

Conversely, one may divert oneself away from a threatening stressor: one may simply ignore the agonistic behavior of another; one may shield oneself from stressful situations, or the perception of stressful events, or the physical insults of stress-producing objects and events (harmful radiation, excessive noise, extremes of temperature, inclement weather, flying missiles, etc.).

DIVERTING STRESSFUL CONTEXTS

12.7 Since any given context is, in part at least, a factor of one's perception, one may seek to change the context by re-examining and re-appraising one's perception of it. There is hardly any concatenation of human events which does not contain some element of humor; hardly any combination of ills which does not contain some benefits for someone. One does not necessarily become a Pollyanna merely by seeking out the lighter or brighter elements of a situation in order to relieve the stressful effects.

Nor need you limit your efforts to your own perception of a given context. With due exercise of tact and discretion, you may make positive efforts to influence others' perceptions and thereby actually change the context itself, not merely your own view of it. One simple but effective way of accomplishing this end is to convert an otherwise serious situation into a game situation. Arguments over probabilities may easily be converted into gambling games, or computer games, or both. There are, of course, many other possibilities.

While seeing the humor in a situation may divert its stressful effects from oneself, expressing the humor may aid others in achieving the same result; thereby changing the context for all so as to make it less stressful. Similarly, by following Ben Franklin's advice to adopt a questioning attitude instead of an attitude of rectitude or belligerency, one may frequently convert a stressful context into a nonstressful one.

Diversion may also be useful when one finds impossible, for the moment at least, the completion of a particular task or project. A great many artists and scientists have attested to the value of a complete change of pace or focus of attention when they have run into a blank wall—a long walk, a swim, a game requiring physical exertion, even starting on a new and entirely different task or project may provide the necessary relief. Such substitute activity—whether utilizing a different set of muscles or a different type of mental ability—not only provides a certain degree of satisfaction in itself, but, by refocusing conscious attention, obviates the tendency to worry about the frustrating obstacles to completion of the original task.

DIVERSION OF VULNERABILITY

12.8 Diverting stressors away from the self-system may not be feasible in some instances; instead, the easier course may be to divert the self-system (and its vulnerabilities) away from the threatening stressors. Therein lies the value of hobbies and other avocations, sports and other games, physical exercise for the desk-bound executive, reading or television for those engaged in more strenuous vocations; in short, any activity which involves a change of pace, the active employment of the muscles instead of the mind or vice versa, and a change in focus of the conscious attention. All such changes tend to produce eustress and reduce distress.

Contraindicated are any activities which, while producing changes of pace and focus, in themselves tend to produce other forms of distress; for example, overindulgence in eating or drinking may produce significant changes in pace and focus, but, in themselves, are stress-producing. Likewise, indulgence in narcotics simply produces a different form of distress. Of course, any of the beneficial diversionary activities, when indulged to excess, may also produce adverse effects: overexertion, too strenuous or too serious participation in sports, too much exposure to television. The key to success in diversion is variety, a balancing of different activities.

CONTROL MEASURES

12.9 Prevention and diversion are, of course, in themselves, types of control, but when such measures do not succeed in producing the desired results or when they prove to be infeasible, other methods of regulation may be indicated. When overstressed, you may, by analyzing your situation, discover that while you cannot avoid exposure to, or divert, certain stressors, you may be able to lessen their impact, or mitigate their effects by improving your own resistance.

CONTROLLING STRESSORS

12.10 Certain stressors are, at least theoretically, quite amenable to control; for example, the regulation of noise levels is technically feasible; likewise, temperature levels and rates of change indoors; also lighting conditions; physical discomforts can be diminished by various means; muscular strains can be reduced by use of tools, machines, and other labor-saving devices.

Certain psychological causes of stress may be decreased by various types of training to improve human relations in an organization, or in the family, thereby reducing the amount of agonistic behavior of members of the group. Individual members of a group who persist in engaging in purposeful aggression may be ostracized, thereby eliminating a common source of stress for other members of the group.

The individual's own diet, exercise regimen, posture, sleep, and other patterns of daily living are subject to direct control. To some extent, one may also regulate the amount of fatigue one endures from day to day. In a variety of ways, we may regulate the flow of stressors in our daily lives.

CONTROLLING STRESSFUL CONTEXTS

12.11 The types of training in human relations, mentioned above, while tending to reduce the amount of agonistic behavior of members of the group will also have the effect of changing the context for each. Each member of the group so trained will have a different perception of the interactions of the members of the group, a different perspective on the activities of the group as a whole. Thus, the members of the group will find that they have the power, individually and collectively, to control the context and thereby lessen the adverse effects of the unavoidable stresses involved in working together.

By other types of psychological training (see: 11.23 to 11.28), individuals may also alter their perceptions and perspectives, thus regulating the context of stressful situations for themselves.

CONTROLLING VULNERABILITY

12.12 Probably the most effective way of controlling your own vulnerability to stress is the age-old advice of maintaining a sound mind in a sound body: adopting a rational life-style, with adequate diet, exercise, rest,and recreation; with a mature mental and emotional outlook; with moderation in all activities and avoidance of excess in any. Few, if any, of us, of course, are capable of maintaining such an ideal type of existence for long periods of time, but the closer we approach such an ideal, the less likely we are to suffer from the adverse effects of stress and, therefore, the easier we shall find the effort.

We may also make life easier for ourselves by recognizing the inevitability of some adverse effects of stress and identifying in advance the appropriate measures of relief. For example, many find strenuous physical activity an effective cathartic for mounting anger and agonistic tendencies; others may discover the possibility of channeling the otherwise wasted energy of anxiety into productive or creative activities; strong emotions and feelings may frequently serve as stimuli to thinking and progress, rather than as avenues to depression; neurotic tendencies may often be controlled by cold logic; even the simple remedy of a couple of hours of extra sleep may prove highly therapeutic and all that is necessary to eliminate a budding tendency to worry, fear, guilt, or anxiety. Merely adopting an attitude of tolerance for pain may effectively serve to reduce the stressful effects of that universal stressor.

In fact, learning to manage one's own feelings, emotions, and attitudes is probably the single most effective way of controlling vulnerability to stress.

SUMMARY

12.13 The variety of ways of preventing, diverting, or controlling stress is probably as great as the variety of stressors, and such measures and techniques may be directed at any one or more of the three factors in the stress situation: stressors, context, vulnerability. Given such a variety, there is no way anyone can prescribe a specific set of measures or techniques for any one individual, but we can suggest a course of action. You may easily discover which measures or techniques are most effective for you by analyzing your own peculiar set of vulnerabilities; such an analysis should almost automatically prompt or suggest appropriate means of reducing stress levels. At the very least, an individual seeking ways of reducing his or her own stress levels should find in the general suggestions offered in this chapter some avenues for exploration and experimentation. For the relief of temporary or occasional undue stress, such measures should prove beneficial.

We must, at this point, however, reiterate a word of caution about the dangers of single-cause habits of thinking (see: 2.17). Every event has multiple causes and multiple effects. We cannot make a single change in any system, not even our own self-system. The executive particularly needs to keep in mind the systems effects and potential effects of every action. While you may find that particular measures or techniques ameliorate your condition by relieving or reducing the stresses of the moment, they will not provide a sound basis for long range management of your stress levels. Such a basis may be provided only by a systems approach. We outline such an approach to the management of stress in the next chapter.

Chapter 13
Managing Stress: A Systems Approach

13.0 The coping mechanisms and regulatory measures discussed in chapters 11 and 12 are, in a sense, the tactical means for dealing with stress; they may be implemented as needed for the short term relief of occasional, undue stress. They are inadequate, individually or in any combination, for the long term management of stress levels. If you are seriously interested in managing your own stress levels so as to enjoy the maximum benefits of eustress while reducing to a minimum the adverse effects of distress you need a more comprehensive approach, a long term strategy. In this chapter, we offer a guide or framework for developing such a strategy.

Our guide is based on the fundamental concepts of systems thinking as discussed in chapter 2. It takes recognition of the fact that the individual is a system (the self-system), operating within a hierarchy of systems (the universe) and, because every event has multiple causes and multiple effects, it is impossible to make a single change in any one of the systems in this hierarchy, even the self-system. Also, the self-system is a black box (see 2.18), so that no one, not even the self-system itself is able to observe all of the interactions which take place within that self-system. Furthermore, some combinations of changes may have a synergistic effect, being multiplicative rather than merely additive, not only in magnitude but in duration as well. For these reasons, we can never be quite certain about the results to be expected from any change that is made in, or affects, the self-system. The behavior of the self-system, however, is not completely unpredictable; we can express with some degree of confidence the effects of certain changes based on experience—our own experience or that of others. What we need to remember is that the self-system is highly dynamic, constantly changing, and eminently adaptive. These characteristics must be considered in the development of any strategy that is to be successful. Our guide provides for the consideration of these systems characteristics of the individual, and for the systems effects and implications of any proposed changes in the self-system. In other words, we recommend a systems approach to managing stress.

Our model for the discussion of a systems approach to managing stress takes the form of a large cube (Figure 13.1), divided first into three horizontal layers, then vertically into three columns, and vertically again at right angles to the first vertical division, the whole forming a cube containing twenty-seven, equal sized smaller cubes or compartments. Each of these compartments is then divided into three equal parts, which we shall call cells.

The three horizontal layers of our model cube represent three levels of responsibility: the lowest level represents the responsibility of the individual for managing his or her own stress levels; the middle level represents the responsibilities of an organization in the management of the stress levels of its members; the highest level represents the responsibilities of society in the management of the stress levels of its members. For the two higher levels, we are definitely not suggesting any type of Skinnerian control; we are merely asserting that an organization (particularly, an employing organization) and society (particularly, the government of a state or nation) do have certain inescap-

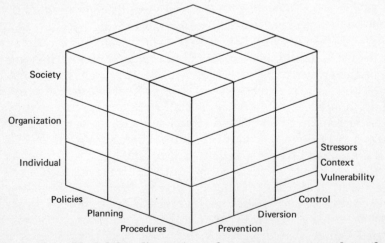

Figure 13.1   Model for discussion of a systems approach to the management of stress.

able responsibilities in the overall pattern of the process of managing the stress levels of their members. We elucidate this point below (13.6 and 13.7).

The three columns of the first vertical division of our cube model represent the three major management processes: policy making, planning, and the design of operating procedures. These processes, we suggest, should be carried out by each level of our model: individual, organization, and society. In the following sections of this chapter, we offer some ideas on the form and content of these processes as they apply to the responsibility for the management of stress at each of the three levels of our model.

The three columns of the second vertical division of our cube model represent the three principal ways of regulating stress levels: prevention, diversion, and control (see chapter 12). We have already discussed the specifics of some of these regulatory methods in chapters 11 and 12. Below, we suggest some further allocations of responsibility and a systematic approach to fulfilling those responsibilities.

The final division of each of the twenty-seven smaller cubes or compartments into three cells represents, in each instance, the three factors in the stress situation: stressors, context, and vulnerability. (See chapter 7, and Figure 7.1.) We suggest that all three of these factors should be taken into consideration in the policies, plans, and operating procedures of all three levels of responsibility for the prevention, diversion, and control of stress.

We do not propose to discuss in this chapter the substantive content of each of the eighty-one cells of our model; rather, we shall simply indicate an approach (the systems approach) to the fulfillment of the responsibilities of the three levels and offer some ideas on the form and content of the three management processes involved.

RESPONSIBILITY OF THE INDIVIDUAL

13.1 The problem of the executive is not primarily one of finding methods to relieve the adverse effects of undue stress; rather, it is one of understanding the fundamental nature of the stress response (see chapter 3) and of developing an approach to managing it so as to realize the greatest benefits and the least harm. An adequate understanding of stress begins with the recognition of its dual nature: its stimulating or therapeutic effects, and its debilitating or disabling effects. In the form of eustress it is a stimulus to action, creativity, and progress. Even as a reaction (in the form of the General adaptation

Syndrome) to the insults of environmental stressors, stress has a therapeutic effect and, in fact, a survival value. Only in the form of undue stress or distress does it entail the adverse effects of the diseases of adaptation and the psychogenic disorders. In chapters 3 through 10, we have tried to provide the essential information for an adequate understanding of this fundamental nature of stress. Now we turn to the problem of managing it.

As with the management of any other activity, the executive needs: (1) a policy—a set of goals and guiding principles; (2) a plan—a formal design for relating available means to the desired goals; and (3) an operating procedure—a detailed description of the actions to be taken and the methods to be applied or followed. We discuss each of these in turn below, but first we should mention certain preliminary steps that are essential to the success of this management effort. These steps take the form of a self-inventory.

The first of these preliminary steps is to have a thorough medical examination so as to identify one's physical strengths and weaknesses, one's physiological capacities and vulnerabilities. This examination should also provide an indication of any corrective measures which should be taken for the remedy of specific disorders, disabilities, or disease conditions.

A physical examination, however, provides only a partial inventory. The individual also needs an inventory of his or her psychological strengths and weaknesses. The way to acquiring this information, unfortunately, is less clearcut. There is no generally accepted psychological analog to the standard medical (physical) examination. In the public mind, at least, the services of a psychotherapist (psychiatric physician or psychoanalyst) are normally engaged only in the event of severe mental disorder or disturbance. Furthermore, the process is time-consuming, expensive, and uncertain as to results. The alternatives are only relatively better in these respects and may be contraindicated in some instances.

One such alternative is group therapy, which is usually less costly, but may be equally time-consuming, and either more or less effective in any given instance. There are a variety of schools of thought and techniques available, but no reliable basis for selecting one over another. One of the most recently developed techniques, which seems to offer a reasonable approach without the sometimes unreasonable claims for success, is Transactional Analysis (see 11.23).

Another alternative, although far less expensive than either individual or group therapy is probably far more difficult to pursue successfully and may be equally time-consuming. It is self-analysis. The interested reader may find some guidance for such endeavors in the works of Karen Horney (Horney, 1942) and in a number of more recent popular treatments of the subject (for example, Lindgren, 1953; Rubin and Rubin, 1975; and Jourard, 1971.)

Another essential step in this inventory-taking is the identification and listing of the specific internal and environmental stressors to which one finds oneself particularly susceptible and the nature of one's reaction to each such stressor. To the extent possible, the individual should attempt to distinguish between those stressors which produce phylogenetic reactions (over which one is less likely to be able to exercise any control) and those stressors which produce reactions acquired or learned in one's sociocultural development (over which one should be able to develop some degree of control.) Further, one should attempt to distinguish between those stressors which produce a desired reaction of stimulation to creativity and progress and those which produce distress.

The final step in the inventory is the individual's determination of his or her own optimum stress level—the level at which he or she derives the greatest stimulation to creativity or productivity without the undue adverse effects—the appropriate eustress-distress balance. At this level the individual will feel adequately motivated and sufficiently challenged by his or her chosen activities without feeling driven or overtaxed by undue stress. Most individuals feel a need for commitment to certain goals and a pride in the achievement of those goals. For most of us, at least some of those goals are realized in the vocation we choose. The achievement of such goals requires the expenditure of a certain amount of the adaptation energy with which we are genetically endowed. The continued expenditure and gradual exhaustion of the individual's reserve of adaptation energy constitutes the process of aging. (See 3.9.) Accordingly, the individual should provide for the appropriate budgeting of this energy in his or her stress management. This means maintaining the optimum stress level.

With such an inventory of physical and psychological states and of known stressors, the individual should be ready to develop his or her own policies, plans, and operating procedures for the management of his or her stress levels—which is, in effect, the management of his or her life.

INDIVIDUAL POLICY MAKING

13.2 Underlying every plan is a set of goals, which in turn, are based on a set of values. Both the goals and the values may be either explicit or implicit, but they are ineluctable; whether or not we are conscious of them, they are there, guiding our actions, our behavior, our lives. They may be rationally derived or the product of irrationality or neuroses; they may issue from mature deliberation or unthinking adoption of another's guidance, direction, or propaganda; they may emanate from any of multifarious motivations. The set of goals and values may be logical and internally consistent or illogical and internally conflicting. They may evidence emotional maturity and psychological soundness or deep-seated fears, guilt, and anxiety. Whatever their nature, they govern our lives consciously or subconsciously.

We suggest there are inherent benefits to the individual in making his or her own personal goals and values explicit; for one, the very process of explicitly stating and recording one's goals and values makes far easier the subsequent processes of planning and developing operating procedures. There are other benefits. Making one's goals and values explicit tends to facilitate future decision making, to obviate ambivalence and vacillations, to bolster self-assurance, and to increase one's feeling of control over one's own courses of action. It tends to eliminate feelings of helplessness and drifting; it gives a sense of power. It helps to give some purpose to one's life.

We do not propose to suggest any specific goals or values, they must come from the individual's own inner resources, shaped by one's heritage and sociocultural development. One person may find inspiration in the writings of the great thinkers, another in the guidance of favorite teachers, another in the lives of respected leaders, but in the end, the choice must be your own. Even in uncritically accepting the goals and values of someone else, you are, of course, unconsciously making a choice.

Your values determine for you what is right and what is wrong, what is good and what is bad, what should be done and what should not be done, what should be sought after and what should be avoided. They provide the basis for decision and action in all aspects of your life. They serve as the framework for the formulation of a set of goals.

Your goals determine your basic life direction. The set of goals should include your general long range aims for educational, vocational, and perhaps financial achievement, for family status, and for other important aspects of your life. Only if the goals are reasonable, realistic, authentic, and bona fide, not spurious or sham, will they serve as a sound basis for planning. No set of realistic goals, of course, can be static; stability may be desirable, but the executive must keep in mind the ubiquity and inevitability of change (see 2.16). Some degree of flexibility should be built into any set of goals, while preserving one's fundamental values. In giving explicit form to your goals, you should also keep in mind the role of perspective (see 2.1), so as to avoid self-delusion.

One's perspective—view of the world—constitutes a major element in one's personal philosophy or cosmology. It determines how one will relate to his environment—physical and social; it provides the basis for one's interpersonal relations. It is also a significant determinant of one's life style or life script (see 5.12).

One of the elements of life style is tempo, the pace of existence. If you, like the Red Queen in *Alice,* find that it takes all the running you can do just to keep in the same place, perhaps you had better re-examine your schedule of activities and your list of priorities. You will likely find some difficulty in determining the most appropriate tempo for every one of your activities, in modulating the tempo according to need and purpose, and in regulating the tempo from life passage to life passage (see 5.11), but any such effort will pay big dividends in the form of facilitating the management of your stress levels. Mumford suggests that we should keep time in life as we do in music. (Mumford, 1951.) The analogy has significant implications for the stress-ridden executive.

Another significant element in life style is balance. We should all do well to lay firm hold of poet John Hall's silken string of moderation, an ideal of the ancient Greeks and what Euripides called the noblest gift of heaven. The Greeks strongly urged moderation in all things, and the advice is still sound today. All work and no play does indeed make Jack a dull boy. Executives who seek to manage their own stress levels will find great aid in balancing their activities, in a frequent change of pace, in conscious utilization of the practice of diversion (see 12.8). They will find adequate time for each of a variety of activities: education, exercise, self-improvement, rest, and recreation—reading, sports, cultural activities, entertainment, and just plain loafing. Of all these, the most difficult for overstressed executives to practice is probably the last—loafing. They may not even know how to go about it; or they may be so keyed up that they are simply psychologically incapable of loafing. One does not need to spend a lot of time in loafing to secure the therapeutic benefits it can provide. Some authorities on stress recommend at least one full day of loafing per month. Loafing involves complete freedom from scheduled activities, from constructive thinking and effort of all kinds (whether work oriented or not), and from purposeful activities. Loafing is time spent in idleness. It is probably the most effective form of diversion available to the over-stressed executive.

Humor is also a very effective form of diversion. Unlike loafing, it does not require any specified allocation of time. It is also an effective means of emotional catharsis and a natural stress reducer. As previously indicated, humor is quite often an effective device for diverting agonistic behavior and for converting a stressful context into a neutral or benign one (see: 12.6 and 12.7). Although many executives will fail to appreciate this observation, the fact is that the modern large organization probably provides more material for humor than any other aspect of life. Finding the sources of such humor merely requires the adoption of the right perspective.

Executives, and especially those who tend to find this life a very serious affair, would find great value in developing a habit of consciously looking for the humor in every situation, particularly those which either promise or demonstrate stressful effects. We guarantee the practice will lower the executive's own stress levels, and will probably contribute to a lowering of the stress levels of others in the organization. Furthermore, humor is contagious; others will catch on; and there is a positive feedback effect. Of course, as in all activities, moderation is still the ideal, but the practice of humor need not detract one whit from the serious accomplishment of the organization's goals. In fact, it should facilitate such accomplishment by making everyone less stressed and therefore more effective and more efficient.

A well-developed sense of humor also contributes to the maintenance of an appropriate balance—of activities, of emotional behavior—and is effective as a regulator of changes of pace. In sum, it is a significant element in the life style of executives who desire to effectively manage their own stress levels.

Determining their own life style also requires executives to examine the nature of the groups with whom they associate. We have spoken of the importance of developing a mature attitude in our interpersonal relations—the I'M OK, YOU'RE OK position (see 11.23). Selye espouses a philosophy of "altruistic egotism", which, he suggests, has amply proved its value throughout the entire process of evolution from the simplest multicellular organism to man; it provides a basis for promoting the interests of society without curtailing the self-protective values of the individual. H. A. Overstreet suggests we may cultivate such an attitude more easily by associating with groups that promote emotional maturity. (Overstreet, 1949.) Overstreet's recommendations are directed primarily to our association with community organizations, but the same advice applies to all other organizations, including the primary employer. An organization which seeks to maintain a mature approach to all of its activities and interpersonal relations is likely to promote a mature attitude on the part of all its members, thereby reducing their stress levels. Conversely, individuals who aim to manage their own stress levels will carefully select the individuals (wife, boss, friends) and the groups and organizations with whom they associate so as to avoid the harmful effects of stress; they will try to confine their interpersonal relations to those whom they like and respect, or at least to those who do not directly cause them undue stress.

This discussion does not, of course, represent a comprehensive coverage of the elements of an individual's life style, but it should suffice to suggest the nature of the effort that is required for establishing a rational, script-free life style based on a realistic, mature philosophy. Only by making such an effort may executives give explicit form to their own set of values and their life goals. With such a statement they have a firm basis for developing their life plans.

INDIVIDUAL PLANNING

13.3 It is indeed passing strange that a generation of executives who have clearly recognized the vital importance of setting objectives and developing plans for the organizations they direct have at the same time completely failed to realize that such practices have equal validity for their own personal lives. Perhaps in midcareer or later a few begin to appreciate the need for personal planning, but few, even then, take corrective action. Those who do any planning at all tend to concentrate on financial and estate planning primarily for family protection. Few concern themselves with plans for the other aspects of their lives. Many executives have formulated some general ideas of what they want to do; they have some vague career objectives, but the written plan is a rarity.

The advantages of a personal life plan are analogous to the advantages of a plan for any organization. A written plan lends clarity, precision, a greater degree of certainty to goal achievement; it makes specific the means to be applied in achieving those goals. Besides removing vagueness, a plan tends to ensure commitment; it obviates aimless wambling and hopeless vacillation. It provides a basis for control, a set of standards against which one may measure progress. The very process of writing a plan forces to the surface for resolution any existing uncertainties or conflicts inherent in the goals and the allocation of resources.

The Maslowian statement of basic human needs provides a reasonable outline for an individual life plan and the supporting subplans.

(See: Maslow, 1970.) Relating your plan to your own personal expression of these basic human needs will enable you to ensure a greater degree of reality and practicality. The overall life plan will probably include at least the following subplans: educational, career, financial, family, geographical.

The life plan and each of the subplans should undertake to translate the individual's lifetime goals into specific objectives, each of which should be explicitly defined. The spelling out of these objectives and the statement of the resources to be applied to ensure their achievement constitute the principal content of each plan. The educational subplan should include provision for continuing as well as pre-career requirements. The career subplan specifies the types and level of vocational work, perhaps a specific type of job, or a specific organization; it may also include geographical specifications. The financial subplan covers such items as income levels, savings, investments, and insurance; it also includes provision for the financial support of each of the other subplans. The family subplan specifies the desired marital status; the number of children, if any; housing and related facilities; educational plans for the children; perhaps geographical specifications. The geographical subplan specifies the desired localities for work, residence, recreation, retirement, etc.

In addition to this basic content, each plan should include some type of metric against which one may periodically evaluate progress toward the stated objectives. This means that each objective must be quantifiable to some extent at least, and specific checkpoints should be provided at specific times.

Each plan should also, of course, include some provision for periodic review and revision; a good plan is dynamic, not static; it is a flexible guide, not a straitjacket. Flexibility in a plan involves provision for alternative courses of action in the event of identifiable, and, if possible, identified, contingencies, and for re-evaluation of the objectives and means in the event of unanticipated emergencies. One way of coping with contingencies is to list expectations in order of decreasing subjective probabilities. Alternative courses of action may then be developed for those expectations with high probabilities. For example, you might, at the time of planning, specify for yourself the conditions for accepting offers of employment (from other organizations, in other geographical locations, in a different line of work, etc.). You might then provide in your plan the alternative course of action for each such contingency. When and if you accept such an offer, your alternative becomes your primary plan and should be reviewed and revised in the light of the new circumstances.

The planner may have separate plans, or separate provisions in his or her plan, for the short range, intermediate, and long range future. Financial plans—particularly savings, insurance, and investment—lend themselves to this treatment very easily. For example, if a long range objective is to accumulate twenty thousand dollars in ten years, the intermediate range objective might be five thousand dollars in five years, and the short range five hundred dollars the first year, the assumption being that the amount of annual savings will increase as earnings increase. Additional short range and intermediate range plans may be developed as progress is made toward the long range objective.

Plans become increasingly more specific, the shorter the range. Long range plans may necessarily have to be expressed in more general terms. For example, an executive may have the long term objective of early retirement from his or her chosen vocation to allow for entry into a second career. The first career may be expected to provide the financial foundation for a second, perhaps more satisfying but less remunerative, career. Any such long range plans will necessarily be in general terms—with only order of magnitude time periods and financial objectives—to allow for the vagaries of constant change, including such items as inflation, physical and mental health, family situation, etc.

In the final analysis, planning is simply a device for ensuring greater clarity, definition, and explicitness in knowing what one is doing and where one is going; it tends to reduce some of the uncertainty from day to day existence. As we saw in chapter 5 (5.13), uncertainty (immobility) may lead to a variety of stress-inducing feelings and emotions (fear, guilt, worry, anxiety) and further complications. The reduction of uncertainty by the substitution of definitive plans for aimless activity tends to reduce the stress of decision-making and other purposeful behavior.

The availability of a plan also permits more effective and efficient use of time, energy, and other resources, thereby tending to reduce fatigue, muscle and nervous tension, interference with the normal biological rhythms, and the stress which normally results from these conditions. Thus, planning tends to obviate many of the potential sources of stress before it occurs. Further, in the process of developing a plan, the individual may eliminate at least some of those activities and contextual situations which can be identified in advance as stress-producing. From one's self analysis, one will know which are the more significant stressors and stressful contexts for oneself and then can plan to avoid them or take appropriate action to counteract them. From the standpoint of this discussion, this is the most important feature of the whole planning exercise—the opportunity to anticipate stress and avoid or offset it. This advantage alone makes the whole exercise worthwhile.

The complete set of plans comprising the individual's life plan should provide for the conservative use of available adaptation energy without serving as a source of distress to those with whom he or she associates or any others. To accomplish one's life goals—whether self-expression; achievement of power, fame, or fortune; or merely some degree of security—one must determine one's optimum stress levels and budget one's available adaptation energy accordingly. One must establish the general direction and rate of expenditure of such energy which will make effective use of one's talents and abilities without undue stress.

INDIVIDUAL OPERATING PROCEDURES

13.4 Likewise, in scheduling your day-to-day activities in accordance with your plans, you may avoid at least some of the specific activities and context which you know would be stress-producing. You will find yourself in a much better position to engage in the types of preventive, divertive, and control measures described in chapter 12; and for the unavoidable stresses, you may more effectively choose from among the specific coping mechanisms described in chapter 11.

Applying your knowledge of the causes of stress, you may adjust your own living habits; your methods of work; your interpersonal relations; your use of time, energy, and resources; and your mode of behavior in general; all so as to reduce your own stress levels as well as your tendencies to produce stress in others, which, of course, also serves to provide positive feedback to raise your own stress levels. You will learn to substitute rational choices for unreliable emotional reactions in your daily activities and dealings with others. Your understanding of the nature and operation of the stress response applied to your daily behavior will considerably facilitate choices which will lead to goal achievement and avoidance of failure and frustration—to eustress rather than distress. Recognizing that the stress response (G.A.S.) is essentially an instinctive reaction developed early in man's evolutionary history and, therefore, not necessarily suited to life in modern society, you will seek to control your adaptive responses and direct them into more constructive channels. You will capitalize your ability to make effective choices about your behavior and immediate environment so as to increase your eustress and decrease your distress. You will take full advantage of your inherent ability to select your own life style, make your own life decisions, and choose your own adaptive responses. This will, of course, require conscious (perhaps even painful) effort, but the dividends will be enormous.

SUMMARY: INDIVIDUAL RESPONSIBILITIES

13.5 The fulfillment of one's individual responsibilities for the management of executive stress must be based on a high degree of self-understanding as well as on an understanding of the fundamental nature of the stress response. With such knowledge, the individual may arrive at a reasonable and realistic set of goals based on a set of sound values; in sum, a set of guiding principles for a life free of unwanted stress. You may develop for yourself a formal, logical life plan which will enable you to maximize eustress and minimize distress, to take greater advantage of the stimulating and therapeutic effects of stress, and to avoid many of the adverse effects of undue stress. By thus reducing the uncertainties of the general direction of your life, you may more effectively and efficiently schedule your day-to-day activities and may apply more effective and efficient operating procedures, thereby further reducing your stress levels. In all of these activities you may consciously eliminate identifiable stressors and stressful contexts; you may consciously include appropriate measures for the prevention, diversion, or control of stress; and you may identify in advance and more successfully apply appropriate coping mechanisms for the relief of unavoidable stress. In effect, you may adopt a totally new life style, basing your behavior on conscious, rational choices which are creatively adaptive rather than simply reactive to the influences of your ambient environment. There is considerable evidence to indicate that flexibility and adaptability are personality characteristics which promote successful coping with stress. Thus, the ability to adopt a new life style will, in itself, represent a step forward in the successful management of stress.

This approach to the management of stress may seem formidable in prospect; it would probably involve, for most executives, the development of a whole new life style, but the benefits to be derived would certainly be worth the effort involved. As we saw in Part II, the costs of stress are incalculable even for a single individual. Avoiding such costs alone could be worth many times the effort called for by this approach, but as an added dividend there are available the indescribable benefits of eustress in the form of greater productivity, creativity, and general enjoyment of life.

RESPONSIBILITIES OF THE ORGANIZATION

13.6 The toll levied by individual stress on the executives and other employees of the modern, large organization provides a clear indication of the urgent need for attention to this problem and, rough as they are, our cost estimates will furnish at least a tentative basis for developing cost-benefit ratios for any corrective measures which might be initiated. We do not propose to spell out in detail the measures which should be taken by any given organization, since they must be tailored to the needs and resources of the particular organization. We shall, however, suggest a framework within which specific policies, plans, and procedures may be developed.

First, we again remind our readers of the impossibility of making a single change in any system; any change will have multiple effects and every effort should be made to anticipate the effects—good and bad—of any proposed change before it is instituted. Secondly, we urge the logic of the advice to know where you are—the present state of the system—before embarking on any significant changes. Thirdly, one final bit of general advice, the leaders of any organization should take full cognizance of the nature of the human systems with which they are dealing; each individual is a unique dynamic, teleological, cybernetic system, with his or her own set of values, goals, plans, motivations, and personal problems. Further, the individuals in the organization interact in an unlimited variety of ways, with both positive and negative feedback effects. All of these systems effects are highly significant for any proposed changes.

Given these prerequisites to change, the first modification we suggest is the incorporation in the policies of the organization of a positive intent to reduce the stress levels of all those who are suffering from undue stress. This should include a recognition of the fact that any such measures are highly likely to enhance the possibilities for achieving the other goals of the organization by increasing the effectiveness and efficiency of all members.

In accordance with such a policy change, the organization may include in its plans the provision of adequate means to achieve specific objectives consonant with the organization's goals. For example, the organization could provide for periodic physical and psychological examinations and personnel surveys to ascertain current stress levels, to identify specific stressors of significance, and stressful contexts. The organization could also provide personnel counseling aimed at identifying undue stress levels of individual members of the organization and advising on corrective measures. The organization might also decide to provide technical or financial assistance in the application of specific coping mechanisms or in the development of longer range capabilities for stress management. Included in such measures might be group therapy sessions, training in meditation techniques, training in interpersonnel relations, etc.

An organization with such a policy would want to develop and maintain a data base which would enable it to monitor the incidence of stress in the organization, its costs and other effects, and the costs of any corrective measures. Part II of this volume suggests some starting points for building such a base.

In addition to these measures, an organization would be well advised to re-examine its personnel policies, not only to identify possibilities for eliminating stressors and stressful contexts, but to identify opportunities for deriving greater benefits from eustress in terms of creativity, productivity, and progress.

The employing organization is in a position to take advantage of the fact that work is a necessity for most humans—as for all forms of life. In humans, the development of the brain has made possible the anticipation of future gains from work and, thereby, the development of motivation and commitment to a cause. The same factors, however, account for the cybernetic effects on productivity and creativity of undue stress. Thus, the basic human need for work constitutes both an opportunity and a challenge for the organization.

The infinite variety of differences in individual responses to, and tolerance of, stress likewise constitutes an opportunity and a challenge for the organization—to place individuals so as to allow them to realize their full potential with a minimum of distress to themselves and others. Those who thrive on stress will likely make the greatest contribution in executive positions; those with low levels of tolerance for stress, in more routine activities. Proper placement allows individuals to secure maximum satisfaction from their accomplishments, thus avoiding the distress resulting from frustration and worry.

In summary, the responsibilities of an organization in the management of stress levels include a total reexamination and revision of policies, plans, and procedures so as to enhance each individual member's own stress management efforts and to provide a general organizational climate which encourages the development of eustress while minimizing distress.

Recognizing that stress is a normal, and even desirable, response of the self-system to every sort of challenge—in work or play—while distress is neither desirable nor necessary, the organization may develop policies, plans, and operating procedures which will enable all individuals to maintain their own optimum stress levels.

RESPONSIBILITIES OF SOCIETY

13.7   The responsibilities of society in the management of stress levels parallel those of the organization in part, but extend beyond. Members of society should call upon the appropriate levels of government to adopt affirmative policies for the reduction of the levels of unwanted stress and the development of eustress. The related governmental plans should include specific provision for the reduction of distress and increase of eustress; for example, the plans might include provisions for more effective control over the various types of environmental stressors mentioned in chapter 6 (noise, air and water, and other types of pollution, etc.); for provision of better facilities for the diversion of stress, such as recreational facilities and opportunities, and greater encouragement of participative sporting activities (in lieu of spectator sports); reduction of the incidence of stressful contexts by provision of more extensive training in interpersonal relations at all educational levels as well as in the vocational milieu, and encouragement of the design and development of environments which promote eustress and diminish distress.

In addition, at the national level the government might provide financial and other support for medical and psychological research on the causes, effects, costs, and management of stress. Such research should also identify the types of statistics which are necessary and desirable for both research and operating purposes, at the national and individual organizational level. Further, the national government should provide for the gathering, analysis, interpretation, and publication of the appropriate statistical data. As a means of facilitating the development of such a data base, the government might provide appropriate tax relief or other financial incentives to employing organizations which cooperate in the furnishing of the statistics.

On a broader scale, and after appropriate standards and metrics have been developed, the national government might offer similar incentives to organizations which can successfully demonstrate a reduction in the levels of distress among their members. It might also similarly encourage the development and conduct of appropriate training programs aimed at the reduction of distress and promotion of eustress.

As the above mentioned stress research continues, further opportunities for additional measures at the individual, organizational, and governmental levels may emerge. A nation devoted to the promotion of a way of life based on the reduction of distress and promotion of eustress could make such advances in technology and human relations as to make the progress of civilization to date appear as only a first small step.

Bibliography

RECOMMENDED READING

The currently available literature on stress is simply overwhelming, even the experts cannot keep up with the continuing flood. The busy executive who wants to learn something, but not everything, about the subject needs helpful and objective guidance. Unfortunately, much, if not most, of the popular literature on the subject fails to provide such impartial guidance. Many articles appearing in management journals and many popular books are either too generalized and abstract to be informative or are slanted toward promotion of a specific coping technique. The scientific literature is usually too clinical or too specific in scope to be helpful to executives.

In the foregoing we have tried to provide an objective summary of currently available information. For the reader who desires to probe more deeply into the subject, we have included references in the text with complete citations for each in the following bibliography. First, however, we mention a few of the basic books we have found to be more helpful for the general reader who is interested in securing more detailed information on the systems approach, which underlies our presentation, or on human stress in general. Full citations to these works will be found in the following bibliography.

ON SYSTEMS THINKING

The father of general systems theory was Ludwig von Bertalanffy, a biologist. During his lifetime, he published a mountain of material, most of it highly scientific in nature. For the general reader, his *Gen-*

240

eral System Theory (1968) provides the best overview of his basic ideas. A number of other writers provide other and different perspectives on the subject. Russell Ackoff and Fred Emery in *On Purposeful Systems* (1972) present a systems view of individual and social behavior. A book of readings, *Systems Thinking,* edited by Fred Emery (1969) suggests the potential of systems thinking for management practice. The Society for General Systems Research has published annually since 1956, a *Yearbook,* containing the best articles of the year on systems thinking, in a wide variety of disciplines. The executive will not likely find every article in these volumes of direct interest or immediately practical value, but he will probably find at least one or two articles of interest in each volume.

The classic presentation on the science of cybernetics is that by Norbert Wiener, *Cybernetics: or Control and Communication in the Animal and the Machine* (1961). Of equal value is Ashby, *An Introduction to Cybernetics* (1956); his *Design for a Brain* (1960) is also of interest.

ON STRESS

We have mentioned Walter B. Cannon as one of the progenitors of stress research; his *The Wisdom of the Body* (1939) is a readable and informative introduction to the basic processes and to the concept of homeostasis. Hans Selye, of course, is the prime source on the subject of human stress. For executives and other general readers we recommend *The Stress of Life* (1976), and his more philosophical *Stress without Distress* (1974). For those with more clinical interests in the medical details of stress, his basic study, *Stress* (1950), is still the classic and best source. Another detailed study of stress is that by Richard Lazarus, *Psychological Stress and the Coping Process* (1966). A more popular presentation of particular interest to executives is Harry Levinson's, *Executive Stress* (1970).

Ackoff, Russell L., and Fred E. Emery (1972). *On Purposeful Systems*. Chicago: Aldine-Atherton.
Alberti, Robert E., and Michael L. Emmons (1974a). *Assert Yourself—It's Your Perfect Right*. 2d ed. San Luis Obispo, Calif.: Impact.
——— (1974b). *Your Perfect Right: A Guide to Assertive Behavior*. San Luis Obispo, Calif.: Impact.
——— (1975). *Stand Up, Speak Out, Talk Back!: The Key to Self-Assertive Behavior*. New York: Pocket Books.
Alexander, Franz (1950). *Psychosomatic Medicine: Its Principles and Applications*. New York: Norton.

Altschule, Mark (1976). "Is It True What They Say About Cholestrol," *Executive Health*, XII;11, August.

American Psychiatric Association (1968). *Diagnostic and Statistical Manual*.

Arbib, Michael A. (1972). *The Metaphorical Brain: An Introduction to Cybernetics as Artificial Intelligence and Brain Theory*. New York: Wiley-Interscience.

Aron, Michael (1975). "The World of the Brain," "Wraparound," *Harper's Magazine*, 251:6, December, 3–10, 117–124.

Ashby, W. Ross (1956). *An Introduction to Cybernetics*. London: Chapman & Hall.

——— (1960). *Design for a Brain*. London: Chapman & Hall: Science Paperbacks.

Benson, Herbert (1975). *The Relaxation Response*. New York: Morrow.

Berger, Louis, Ian Hunter, and Ron W. Lane (1971). *The Effect of Stress on Dreams*. NewYork: International Universities.

Bernard, Claude (1865). *An Introduction To The Study of Experimental Medicine*. Henry Copley Greene, Trans. New York: Dover, 1957 (reprint).

Berne, Eric (1963). *The Structure and Dynamics of Organizations and Groups*. New York: Grove Press, 1966 (reprint).

——— (1964). *Games People Play*. New York: Grove Press.

——— (1972). *What Do You Say After You Say Hello?* New York: Bantam Books.

Bertalanffy, Ludwig von (1968). *General System Theory*. New York: George Braziller.

Blythe, Peter (1973). *Stress Disease: The Emotional Plague*. New York: St. Martin's Press.

Bois, J. Samuel (1969). *Breeds of Men: Toward the Adulthood of Humankind*. New York: Harper & Row.

Brown, Barbara B. (1974). *New Mind, New Body; Bio-Feedback: New Directions for the Mind*. New York: Harper & Row.

Cannon, Walter (1942). "Voodoo Death," *American Anthropologist*, 44.

——— (1939). *The Wisdom of the Body*. rev. ed. New York: Norton. (Norton Library paperback, 1963.)

Caplan, Edwin H., and Stephen Landekich (1974). *Human Resource Accounting: Past Present and Future*. New York: National Association of Accountants.

Carr, Rachel (1974). *The Yoga Way to Release Tension*. New York: Coward, McCann & Geoghegan.

Clymes, Manfred (1977). *Sentics: The Touch of Emotions*. Garden City, NY: Doubleday Anchor Book.

Cooper, Kenneth H. (1975). *Aerobics*. rev. New York: Bantam Books.

Davitz, Joel, and Lois Davitz (1976). *Making It From 40 to 50*. New York: Random House.

Diamond, Seymour (1977). *More Than Two Aspirin*. New York: Follett.

DiCyan, Erwin (1972). *Vitamin E and Aging*. New York: Pyramid Books.

Drucker, Peter F. (1967). *The Effective Executive*. New York: Harper & Row.

——— (1974). *Management Tasks, Responsibilities, Practices*. New York: Harper & Row.

Dudley, Donald L., and Elton Welke (1977). *How to Survive Being Alive*. Garden City, NY: Doubleday.

Dunbar, Flanders (1955). *Mind and Body: Psychosomatic Medicine.* (New Enlarged Edition.) New York: Random House.

Ellis, Albert, and Robert A. Harper (1975). *A New Guide to Rational Living.* Englewood Cliffs, NJ: Prentice-Hall.

Emery, F. E. (1969). *Systems Thinking.* Baltimore: Penguin Books.

Engel, George (1977). "Emotional Stress and Sudden Death," *Psychology Today,* 11:6, November, 114–118, 154.

Englebardt, Stanley L. (1974). *How to Avoid Your Heart Attack.* New York: Reader's Digest Press.

Engstrom, Ted W., and R. Alec Mackenzie (1967). *Managing Your Time: Practical Guidelines on the Effective Use of Time.* Grand Rapids, Mich.: Zondervan.

Fayol, Henri (1949). *General and Industrial Management.* New York: Pitman.

Feldenkrais, M. (1949). *Body and Mature Behavior.* New York: International Universities Press.

Fink, David Harold (1943). *Release From Nervous Tension.* New York: Simon & Schuster. (Revised edition 1962.)

Flach, Frederic F. (1974). *The Secret Strength of Depression.* Philadelphia: J. B. Lippincott.

Flowers, Vincent S. et al. (1975). *Managerial Values for Working.* New York: Amacom.

Freedman, Alfred M., Harold I. Kaplan, and Benjamin J. Sadock (1972). *Modern Synopsis of Comprehensive Textbook of Psychiatry.* Baltimore: Williams and Wilkins.

Friedman, Meyer and Ray H. Rosenman (1974). *Type A Behavior and Your Heart.* New York: Knopf.

Geba, Bruno Hans (1973). *Breathe Away Your Tensions.* New York: Random House.

Glass, David C., and Jerome E. Singer (1972). *Urban Stress.* New York: Academic Press.

Glasser, William (1965). *Reality Therapy: A New Approach to Psychiatry.* New York: Harper & Row.

——— (1972). *The Identity Society.* New York: Harper & Row.

Goodman, David S., and Maxie C. Maultsby (1974). *Emotional Well-Being Through Rational Behavior Training.* Springfield, Ill.: Thomas.

Gould, Roger (1974). "Adult Life Stages: Growth Toward Self Tolerance," *Psychology Today,* February, 74–78.

Graves, Clare W. (1970). "Levels of Existence: An Open System Theory," *Journal of Humanistic Psychology,* 10:2, 131–155.

——— (1974). "Human Nature Prepares for a Momentous Leap," *The Futurist,* April, 72–87.

Green, Elmer (1973). "Biofeedback for Mind-Body Self-Regulation: Healing and Creativity," *Biofeedback and Self Control 1972,* David Shapiro et al., Eds. Chicago: Aldine.

———, Alyce M. Green, and E. Dale Winters (1976). "Biofeedback Training for Anxiety Tension Reduction," *Relax: How You Can Feel Better, Reduce Stress and Overcome Tension,* John White and James Fadiman, Eds. New York: Dell.

Grinker, Roy R., and John P. Spiegel (1945). *Men Under Stress.* Philadelphia: Blakiston.

Groen, J. J., and J. Bastiaans (1975). "Psychosocial Stress, Interhuman Communication, and Psychosomatic Disease," *Stress and Anxiety*, Vol. I. Charles D. Spielberger and Irwin G. Sarason, Eds. New York: Wiley.

Gunderson, E. K. Eric, and Richard H. Rahe. Eds. (1974). *Life Stress and Illness*. Springfield, Ill.: Thomas.

Hall, Edward T. (1959). *The Silent Language*. Greenwich, Conn.: Fawcett.

—— (1966). *The Hidden Dimension*. Garden City, N.Y.: Doubleday.

—— (1976). *Beyond Culture*. Garden City, N.Y.: Doubleday Anchor.

Hamman, Kalen (1972). "What Structural Integration (Rolfing) Is and Why It Works," *The Osteopathic Physician*, March. (Reprint.)

Harris, Thomas A. (1967). *"I'm OK—You're OK: A Practical Guide to Transactional Analysis."* New York: Harper & Row.

Holmes, Thomas H., and Minoru Masuda (1972). "Psychosomatic Syndrome," *Psychology Today*, 5:11, April, 106.

——, and Richard H. Rahe (1967). "The Social Readjustment Rating Scale," *Journal of Psychosomatic Research*, 2:213–218.

Horney, Karen (1942). *Self-Analysis*. New York: Norton.

Jacobson, Edmund (1934). *You Must Relax*. New York: McGraw-Hill.

—— (1970). *Modern Treatment of Tense Patients*. Springfield, Ill.: Thomas.

—— (1976). "Who Can Be Relaxed," *Relax: How You Can Feel Better, Reduce Stress and Overcome Tension*. John White and James Fadiman, Eds. New York: Dell.

Janis, Irving L. (1958). *Psychological Stress*. New York: Wiley.

Johnson, Wendell (1946). *People in Quandaries*. New York: Harper.

Johnston, William (1974). *Silent Music: The Science of Meditation*. New York: Harper & Row.

Jonas, Gerald (1973). *Visceral Learning: Toward a Science of Self-Control*. New York: Pocket Books.

Jourard, Sidney M. (1971). *The Transparent Self*. rev. ed. New York: Van Nostrand.

Karlins, Marvin, and Lewis M. Andrews (1972). *Biofeedback: Turning on the Power of Your Mind*. Philadelphia: Lippincott.

Klir, George J. (1969). *An Approach to General Systems Theory*. New York: Van Nostrand Reinhold.

Koestler, Arthur (1967). *The Ghost in the Machine*. New York: Macmillan.

Kohler, Mariane (1973). *The Secrets of Relaxation*. New York: Warner Paperback.

Kory, Robert B. (1976). *The Transcendental Meditation Program for Business People*. New York: Amacom.

Korzybski, Alfred (1941). *Science and Sanity*. 2d ed. Lancaster, Penna.: The International Non-Aristotelian Library. (3d ed., 1948.)

Kovel, Joel (1976). *A Complete Guide to Therapy*. New York: Pantheon.

Lakein, Alan (1973). *How to Get Control Of Your Time and Your Life*. New York: Wyden.

Lazarus, Arnold, and Allen Fay (1975). *I Can If I Want To*. New York: William Morrow.

Lazarus, Richard S. (1966). *Psychological Stress and the Coping Process*. New York: McGraw-Hill.

Lee, Irving (1952). *How to Talk with People*. New York: Harper & Row.

Lesser, Philip J. (1967). "The Legal Viewpoint," *To Work Is Human*. Alan A.

McLean, Ed. New York: Macmillan.

Levi, Lennart (1967). *Stress: Sources, Management & Prevention*. New York: Liveright.

Levinson, Daniel (1978). *The Seasons of a Man's Life*. New York: Knopf:

Levinson, Harry (1970). *Executive Stress*. New York: Harper & Row.

———— (1973). *The Great Jackass Fallacy*. Boston: Division of Research, Graduate School of Business Administration, Harvard University.

Lindemann, Hannes (1973). *Relieve Tension the Autogenic Way*. Konrad Kellen, Trans. New York: Wyden.

Lindgren, Henry Clay (1953). *How To Live With Yourself and Like It*. Greenwich, Conn.: Fawcett.

Lowen, Alexander (1972). *Depression and the Body*. New York: Coward, McCann & Geoghegan.

Luce, Gay Gaer (1971a). *Biological Rhythms in Human & Animal Physiology*. New York: Dover.

———— (1971b). *Body Time: Physiological Rhythms and Social Stress*. New York: Random House.

Maisel, Edward (1972). *Tai Chi For Health*. New York: Holt, Rinehart & Winston.

Maslow, Abraham (1970). *Motivation and Personality*. 2d Ed. New York: Harper & Row.

McCay, James T. (1959). *The Management of Time*. Englewood Cliffs, N. J.: Prentice-Hall.

McCllelland, David C. (1961). *The Achieving Society*. New York: Free Press.

———— (1975). *Power: The Inner Experience*. New York: Irvington.

McLean, Alan A. (1975). "Occupational Stressors," *Man and Work in Society*. Eugene L. Cass and Frederick G. Zimmer, Eds. New York: Van Nostrand Reinhold.

Meininger, Jut (1973). *Success Through Transactional Analysis*. New York: Grosset & Dunlap.

Melzack, Ronald (1973). *The Puzzle of Pain*. New York: Basic Books.

Miller, Benjamin F., and Lawrence Galton with Daniel Brunner (1972). *Freedom From Heart Attacks*. New York: Simon & Schuster.

Mines, Samuel (1974). *The Conquest of Pain*. New York: Grosset & Dunlap.

Mok, Paul P. (1975). *Transactional Analysis Tool Kit*. Dallas, Texas: Transactional Analysis Press.

Morehouse, Lawrence E., and Leonard Gross (1975). *Total Fitness in 30 Minutes a Week*. New York: Simon & Schuster.

Mumford, Lewis (1951). *The Conduct of Life*. New York: Harcourt Brace Jovanovich.

Myers, M. Scott, and Vincent S. Flowers (1974). "A Framework for Measuring Human Assets," *California Management Review*. XV1, 4, Summer.

Nathanson, James A., and Paul Greengard (1977). " 'Second Messengers' in the Brain," *Scientific American*, 237:2, August.

Newbold, H. L. (1975). *Mega-Nutrients for Your Nerves*. New York: Wyden.

Nicholas, Ted (1975). *A.M.: How To Teach Yourself Meditation*. Wilmington, Del.: Enterprise.

Novey, Theodore B. (1973). *Making Life Work: Transactional Analysis and Management*. Sacramento, Calif.: VALMAR.

Odiorne, George S. (1974). *Management and the Activity Trap: How To Avoid It and How To Get Out Of It.* New York: Harper & Row.

Ornstein, Robert E., Ed. (1968). *The Nature of Human Consciousness: A Book of Readings.* San Francisco, Calif.: Freeman.

―――― (1972). *The Psychology of Consciousness.* San Francisco, Calif.: Freeman.

Overstreet, H. A. (1949). *The Mature mind.* New York: Norton.

Paykel, Eugene S. (1976). "Life Stress, Depression and Attempted Suicide," *Journal of Human Stress,* 2:3, September, 3–12.

Payne, Buryl (1972). *Getting There Without Drugs.* New York: Viking.

Pelletier, Kenneth R. (1977). *Mind as Healer, Mind as Slayer.* New York: Dell.

Penfield, Wilder (1975). *The Mystery of the Mind.* Princeton, N. J.: Princeton University.

Peskin, Dean (1973). *The Doomsday Job: The Behavioral Anatomy of Turnover.* New York: Amacom.

Pickens, Richard, Ed. (1965). *The NFL Guide to Physical Fitness.* New York: Random House.

Powers, William T. (1973). *Behavior: The Control of Perception.* Chicago, Ill.: Aldine.

Prinzmetal, Myron, and William Winter (1965). *Heart Attack: New Hope, New Knowledge, New Life.* rev. ed. New York: Simon & Schuster: Fireside Book.

Quick, Thomas L. (1972). *Your Role In Task Force Management: The Dynamics of Corporate Change.* Garden City, N. Y.: Doubleday.

Quinn, A. E. (1972). "Workmen's Compensation," *Encyclopedia of Occupational Health and Safety,* Vol. II. New York: McGraw-Hill.

Rice, Dorothy P. (1966). *Estimating the Cost of Illness.* Washington, D. C.: Public Health Service.

Richardson, Frank C. (1976). "Anxiety Management Training: A Multimodal Approach," *Multi-Modal Behavior Therapy,* Arnold A. Lazarus, Ed. New York: Springer.

Riesman, David, Nathan Glazer, Reuel Denney (1961). *The Lonely Crowd.* New Haven, Conn.: Yale University.

Rolf, Ida P. (1973). "Structural Integration: A Contribution to the Understanding of Stress," *Confinia Psychiatrica,* XVI.

Rosa, Karl Robert (1976). *You and AT: Autogenic Training—The Revolutionary Way To Relaxation and Inner Peace.* Helen Tuschling, Trans. New York: Dutton: Saturday Review Press.

Rubin, Theodore I., and Eleanor Rubin (1975). *Compassion and Self-Hate: An Alternative to Despair.* New York: McKay.

Schafer, R. Murray (1977). *The Tuning of the World.* New York: Knopf.

Scheimann, Eugene (1974). *Sex Can Save Your Heart . . . and Life.* New York: Bantam.

Schon, Donald A. (1967). *Technology and Change.* New York: Delacorte.

Schoonmaker, Alan N. (1969). *Anxiety and the Executive.* New York: American Management Association.

Seligman, Martin E. P. (1975). *Helplessness: On Depression, Development, and Death.* San Francisco: Freeman.

Selye, Hans (1950). *Stress.* Montreal: ACTA Medical Publishers.

―――― (1956). *The Stress of Life.* New York: McGraw-Hill. (Revised edition, 1976).

—— (1974). *Stress Without Distress*. Philadelphia: Lippincott.

Shah, Douglas (1975). *The Meditators*. Plainfield, N. J.: Logos International.

Shah, Idries (1968). *The Pleasantries of the Incredible Mulla Nasrudin*. New York: Dutton.

—— (1971). *The Sufis*. Garden City, N. J.: Doubleday Anchor.

Shiffrin, Nancy (1976). *Encounter! A Guide to New Low Cost Techniques*. Chatsworth, Calif.: Major Books.

Smith, Manuel J. (1975). *When I Say No, I Feel Guilty*. New York: Bantam.

Sobel, David S. (1973). "Gravity and Structural Integration," *The Nature of Human Consciousness*. Robert E. Ornstein, Ed. San Francisco: Freeman.

Society for General Systems Research, 1956—. General Systems I—.

Stearn, Jess (1976). *The Power of Alpha-Thinking: Miracle of the Mind*. New York: Morrow.

Steincrohn, Peter J. (1960). *MR. EXECUTIVE: Keep Well—Live Longer*. New York: Fell.

—— (1968). *How to be Lazy, Healthy and Fit*. New York: Funk & Wagnalls.

—— (1973). *Questions and Answers about Nerves, Tension, and Fatigue*. New York: Hawthorn.

Steiner, Claude M. (1974). *Scripts People Live: Transactional Analysis of Life Scripts*. New York: Bantam.

Stieglitz, Harold (1958). "Barriers to Communication," *Management Record*, 20:2–5, New York: National Industrial Conference Board.

Tart, Charles C. (1975). *States of Consciousness*. New York: Dutton.

Taylor, Frederick W. (1947). *Scientific Management*. New York: Harper. (Original 1911).

Toffler, Alvin (1970). *Future Shock*. New York: Random House.

U.S. Department of Health, Education, and Welfare (1973). *Work in America*. Report of a Special Task Force to the Secretary of Health, Education, and Welfare. Cambridge, Mass.: M.I.T. Press.

Uris, Auren (1972). *The Frustrated Titan: Emasculation of the Executive*. New York: Van Nostrand Reinhold.

The U.S. Factbook for 1975: The American Almanac (1974). New York: Grossett and Dunlap.

Veiga, John F. (1973). "The Mobile Manager at Mid-Career," *Harvard Business Review,* Jan.-Feb., 115–119.

Wallace, Robert K., and Herbert Benson (1972). "The Physiology of Meditation," *Scientific American*, 226:2, 84–90.

Webber, Ross A. (1972). *Time and Management*. New York: Van Nostrand Reinhold.

Whorf, Benjamin Lee (1956). *Language, Thought and Reality*. John B. Carroll, Ed. Cambridge, Mass.: M.I.T. Press.

Wiener, Norbert (1950). *The Human Use of Human Beings: Cybernetics and Society*. New York: Avon.

—— (1961). *Cybernetics: or Control and Communication in the Animal and Machine*. 2d Ed. Cambridge, Mass.: M.I.T. Press.

Wolf, Stewart, and Helen Goodell, Eds. Harold G. Wolff's *Stress and Disease*, 2d Ed. Springfield, Ill.: Thomas.

Index